BEYOND SURVIVAL
GOD'S HEALING GRACE

FROM BROKENNESS TO FEELING FULLY ALIVE

An exploration of my relationship with God through narrative,
journaling, and poetry

By Ardie Hamilton Sarris

ISBN10: 1534737421
ISBN-13: 978-1534737426

DEDICATION

I dedicate this book to all the men and women who are desperate and in need of help. We all carry crushing burdens from the past that weigh us down from living life to the fullest; the way God intended for us.

I pray that you may find strength, comfort, and hope within these pages.

CONTENTS

PROLOGUE

He lurks in the shadows. I can't get away. Where can I go? There's nowhere to run; no place to hide. Whatever happens, I'm on my own. No one here protects me. No one comes to my rescue. How do I fight someone who is bigger than me? I say "NO!" but he doesn't listen. I move from place to place; he follows me. I'm afraid. I feel alone and helpless. What can I do? This is my home.

"We are either in the process of resisting God's truth or in the process of being shaped and molded by His truth" (Stanley, as cited by Neal, 2012, p. 35).

Recovery is a process of change, growth, and healing to those of us who are struggling with the most difficult of life's experiences: overcoming the negative effects of our childhood. I personally believe that recovery is a spiritual process involving becoming the whole person that God created and intended me to be. It is a never-ending path of spiritual and emotional growth. I will continue to deal with painful memories, to battle my compulsive tendencies, and to release my frozen feelings throughout my life.

When I thought I should write a book of my life experiences, it was solely to leave a legacy for my children and grandchildren. I know it's traditional to leave money and personal belongings which I'm doing, but to me, I wanted to leave something of lasting value. My life story is meaningful not only because of what I experienced but it reveals the deepest parts of me that really say who I am. Even more importantly, it says who God is.

Many painful events throughout my life have continued to haunt me causing me emotional heartache. How did I arrive at this point in my life without being in the throes of addiction? The reason is God's grace. It easily could have happened to me. I had all the makings of an alcoholic and the hysterical emotions of someone ready to snap. Many are the times that I pleaded to God, "Let them come and take me away and lock me in a padded cell. I can't take any more of this painful hell." A padded cell would have been a relief, but I am a survivor.

In my forties, my son Brian's uncontrollable behavior compelled me to seek counseling for my family. This was the beginning of a long, painful, and wonderful journey of self-discovery. What started as a request for help to solve my problems with my son, became the catalyst for healing my own lifelong struggle. As I began to look at what I had experienced growing up in a rigidly religious home, I realized that the three family rules I learned well as a child *(Don't talk, don't trust, and don't feel)*, prepared the way for my impoverished relationships with dysfunctional men, as well as my own children. How I was raised by my parents became the model for parenting my own children and the result was a catastrophe... ...nothing but conflict until I found recovery where I learned a new way to relate to my adult children. Today, I have healthier, more loving, and supportive relationships with family and friends.

I use journaling, letter writing, and poetry as a way to explore and express my feelings. Through the use of these tools my walk with God has changed dramatically. As I learned to trust God and my God-given capabilities, my faith has grown stronger, and my heart is at peace. The miraculous healing that I have experienced has transformed the pain of loss and betrayal into the beauty of art in the written word. One of the incredible gifts that I received was a lost part of myself; my inner child... ...the child who celebrates life in a joyful, creative, and playful way. I now see and understand that all of my past experiences have made me who I am today; a unique, precious, and valuable child of God, who is beautiful, creative, feminine, playful, intelligent, capable, and filled with love and compassion.

My message to others reading my life account is this: There is hope. That has become my new purpose in writing this book: To inspire readers not to give up. No life, no story can be so bad that you have no option but to give up in despair. You may want to do that, as I did many times, but if you just hang on even if you do so with only what seems to be a mere glimmer of hope, something happens that cannot be denied. There is strength and courage you never thought you had that comes shining through. Things begin to change when you embrace the pain you only wanted to end.

As you allow yourself to feel the pain, the pain diminishes and eventually disappears. Let go of the resistance and surrender to the process. Complete the past and move on. Once you have done the work, you will never have to repeat it (Bloch, 1991, p. 84).

It doesn't happen overnight. It is long, slow, and tediously painful work, but so worthwhile. There is healing for your heart, and peace for your soul.

My hope is that as you read about my life, the poems expressing my feelings, and my faith in God, you will be inspired to hang on, to reach out for help, and take a proactive step in your own recovery. There is hope and healing for each and every one of us who comes from an oppressively abusive family system filled with emotional deprivation. If you can relate to my journey, may God bless you on your own journey to find the healing needed to give you hope for a fully alive future. You can do it! Even if it's only one baby step at a time you will get there!

"I gave Him my pain. I gave Him my shame. And He gave me the grace to heal" (Jakes, 2014, Dedication page).

SERENITY PRAYER

God, grant me the serenity to accept the things I cannot change, the courage to change the things I can, and the wisdom to know the difference.

Living one day at a time, enjoying one moment at a time, accepting hardship as a pathway to peace.

Taking, as Jesus did, this sinful world as it is; not as I would have it.

Trusting that You will make all things right if I surrender to Your will.

So that I may be reasonably happy in this life and
supremely happy with You forever in the next
(Niebuhr, as cited by Baker, 1998).

1

Pounding Heart

"God is our refuge and strength, an ever-present help in trouble" (Psalm 46:1).

Waiting Room

As I sat in my therapist's waiting room, I wondered whether I could go through with it. My heart was pounding. I didn't even know whether he would show up, but the thought that any minute he could walk through the door paralyzed me with fear.

After having a male therapist for many years, I spent seven more years with Barbara. Her loving, nurturing manner symbolized the mom I wanted but didn't have. Listening to my story every week, she accepted the parts of me not easy for me to tolerate. She validated my feelings, and that gave me the healing I desperately needed. Having completed extensive anger management therapy, I progressed to grieving painful losses, and for the first time I felt alive.

It was 1993, I turned forty-six, and by that time, I had labored thirteen years total in recovery. Barbara encouraged me to write a letter telling my story, which I did and had no intention of sending it. More intense a struggle than I had originally thought, the letter had taken me three years to finish. Writing my truth granted me freedom.

With the letter completed, Barbara declared with assurance, "You're ready."

"To do what?" I asked.

"To read it to him."

It was as though time had stopped. Wanting to run, I couldn't move.

"I can't. It's too scary."

"Of course it's scary. You have more courage than you know. You can do this with my help. All you have to do is read your letter to him. I will sit next to you. If you need my help, I will gently touch your arm to show my support. Together we can do this. You are ready."

I took it all in, tried to process my feelings, but felt numb. Agonizing over the choice I had to make, I thought there were so many reasons not to confront him. His anger petrified me. His sobriety did not make it any easier. He could still rage at any given moment.

But having finally made the decision, I didn't waste any time. Calling to invite him to my therapy session, I asked for his help in dealing with an issue. Shocked that he agreed to come, I called Barbara. We planned to meet him there at the next session.

* * *

Back in the room, waiting for him, my thoughts were interrupted by the opening of the front door.

"Hi there, Chicken!" That's what he always called me. I hated it. But today it fit.

"My name is Ardith. Please call me by my name."

"Sure. Are you okay?"

I nodded yes.

As we waited for Barbara, my thoughts once again took over. I chose a seat where he would not be able to sit next to me. He probably won't even remember. Drunk much of the time, his memory left patches of blank holes. When I tell him what he did, how will he react? I wondered.

Barbara came in and we walked into her office. He was all smiles to Barbara. He could be so charming to women.

After making conversation to make him more comfortable, Barbara said, "Ardie has written you a letter she would like to read to you now. Is that okay with you?"

"Sure," he nodded.

As I looked at the letter, my hands turned to ice. Trembling, I began to read. I didn't dare look into his eyes.

> It's been a very long time since we've talked or seen each other. I needed some time to sort out my feelings and collect my thoughts about what happened in our past. There are some very important things I want you to know. Our family has continued a cycle of silence. Now I choose to break it by talking about the secret no one else will. I want you to know and feel the impact of what happened to me.
>
> It occurred about the age of seven or eight. I was abused sexually and molested over a long period of time, several years that I can remember. I want you to know that this has had very definite negative consequences all my life. I tried to forget that it ever

7

happened because I felt so dirty and ashamed, but it is still affecting me today. I am recalling, re-living, and feeling some very painful memories called flashbacks.

It's devastating for a child to be violated, not once, but repeatedly over several years. Touched inappropriately, I experienced severe psychological damage. When I was molested, the violation of my boundaries and sense of control devastated me. As a child, I was blameless for the abuse inflicted on me.

"It was just wrong!" I declared.

I paused to catch my breath. Barbara requested, "Before Ardie goes on to read the rest of her letter, is there anything you want to say to her now?"

I looked at Dad for the first time since I started reading the letter.

"I had no idea that was going on with you and your older brother. My God, he was a teenager and you were just a little girl," he said while looking at the floor. As he struggled with his words, my Dad's troubled face grimaced and his body cringed. I could see that he truly was surprised by what I had just told him.

Then looking directly at me, he said, "You've been through hell!" I was surprised but relieved that he understood what it was like for me. I looked back at my letter and continued reading:

I have persistent feelings of inadequacy and emptiness, weakness and

8

helplessness. I have doubts about myself, questioning my sanity and my sense of reality. Shy and frightened of other people, especially men, I isolate because of a lack of protection and refuge.

Part of that lack of safety and security is also a result of alcoholism. Your drinking had a massive negative impact on me. And although you've been sober for many years (and I'm glad you stopped drinking), the times that you were drunk wounded me deeply. I felt fearful. Living in our house with unbearable tension made it extremely uncomfortable.

Yet, there was no way to get away from it, no place to hide. When I walked in the door, I never knew what I would find. Would you be drunk or sober, affectionate or screaming vulgar obscenities? I never knew what could happen. I wondered if it would ever end.

Sometimes you were kindhearted and loving. We did some fun things together. That was fantastic. At those times, you were attentive to me. I remember you and Mom loved to fish. We went every Saturday to different piers along the coast of CA when you taught me how to fish. I loved to fish. I wanted to feel close to my daddy. That's the only time you weren't drinking.

But sometimes when you were drinking at home, you ranted and raved, arguing with Mom. Never knowing what to expect, I always felt desperate and anxious. When you were grouchy and irritable, I didn't understand why. You were so pleasant and courteous to your friends at work and church, yet raged at us with ear-piercing profanities. I felt terrified because of all the catastrophic brawling between you and Mom.

I remember one incident that almost destroyed me. I was twelve years old, and had been cleaning the house. Mom had gone to the grocery store. You were drunk and got so angry that you smashed a box of drinking glasses and kicked the back door. I was so frightened. You turned your anger on me, chasing me, threatening to take my life. I really believed that you could. Terrified, I ran into the bedroom and held the door closed. You pushed and kicked the door trying to get a hold of me, yelling "I'm going to kill you." As I *screamed for help, our neighbors came over to stop you. Diego lured you into the backyard with a beer.*

Then Mom came home, angry and shocked that you would do such a thing to your daughter.

Hysterical, it took me a long time to calm down. I carry the pain and terror of that incident still to this day. You may not even recall any of this because of your drunkenness—but I remember. Deeply injured, I carry those wounds today.

Again I hesitated.

Barbara intervened, "Is there anything you want to say to your daughter?"

"I know I was hell to live with when I was drinking. You've certainly been through torment in our family."

If that's all he could say, I was grateful for that. At least he didn't deny or minimize in any way like my brother did when I had confronted him. Dad became an admirable man in my eyes when he took responsibility without making excuses, when he owned his part in what happened.

I continued…

I realize that this letter may come as a shock. Prior to my writing it, I didn't know how to talk to you about all this. I was frightened of your reaction.

I don't know what the future holds, but for now, I am choosing to do what's best for me. I'm taking steps toward self-respect in dealing with all the issues surrounding alcoholism and sexual molestation. I'm learning how this kind of abuse has affected me my entire life.

I did not write this letter to criticize or blame you for what happened. I just wanted you to know the truth and for you to begin to know who I am. I wanted you to know my feelings.

Recently, both my older brothers Lamar and Greg reacted with anger when I confronted Greg.

Relationships have ended because of the unwillingness to talk about such sensitive subjects. I hope that isn't true for us. I do want to have a conversation and hear how you feel about this letter. Maybe we can talk about it. I'd like to. I hope you will too.

"All I can say is you've been through hell," he gasped.

I want your support, Dad. I want to create a new connection with you, a relationship where I can be an individual, different and separate from you. I want to be treated with respect. Call me by my name; don't call me "chicken." I am no longer a child. I'm an adult woman. My body is also my own. I don't want your hands all over me, tickling me, hugging my waist, patting my buttocks, or kissing me on the mouth. I want my space and my distance.

If you can respect my wishes, we can make a new start to mend our relationship. My hope is for healing of the past. Healing is a process of coming to know, accept, forgive, enjoy, and rejoice in each other as whole and separate human beings. I want us to be individuals and equals, living lives that are appropriately close and mutually supportive. I hope that we can begin to take the steps necessary to have the kind of bond I've just described. It's one that I've always wanted with you.

After a long silence, "Alright, I can and will respect your wishes. Let's begin again, Ardith. I love you."

I hoped that my Dad would live up to his promise, but given our history together, it didn't seem likely to happen. But I've always been the optimist wanting and hoping for the best and smiling as if he had miraculously changed over time. Deep down I knew the realities of who my Dad really was—someone incapable of abiding by my boundaries. I left my therapist's office feeling hopeful but cautious and watching my Dad's every movement and listening to his every word to me.

Greg, Dad and Me 1955

No Answers for a Little Girl's Questions

How did I get to this moment in therapy with my dad? It was a long time coming. When I was a little girl, I remember praying at night for my dad to stop drinking. How I longed for my parents to stop fighting. I prayed to God imploring Him to save me from my older brother's sexual advances. I knew the Ten Commandments that I learned from Sunday school. My understanding then was that sex was a sin, but I couldn't stop my brother. I felt so guilty because I thought what I did was wrong. Why didn't God stop the abuse? Why didn't He hear me? Why didn't God stop the pain? I didn't have any answers. With no one to talk to, I grew up feeling dirty.

My childhood dream that began as a wish turned into a prayer. It echoed in my mind every day: *God, put me into another family, any family at all, not this one.* Until I turned sixteen, Dad's raging alcoholic personality dominated our home. His clingy ways caused him to hang all over my mom, other women, and me. His affectionate slobbery kisses could turn any moment into angry rage, yelling obscenities, and cursing. I never knew who would appear: kindly Dr. Jekyll or hideous Mr. Hyde?

My Alcoholic Dad

I can remember my two older brothers, Lamar, fourteen years older than me, and Greg, seven years older, having to clean the house on Saturdays. I only had to wash the day's dishes after dinner, which I hated, until my brothers moved out of the house. In 1960, I finally got my own bedroom after sleeping on a cot in my parents' bedroom for twelve years.

Sleeping in a cot was all I knew and I just accepted it. I didn't question why I didn't have a room of my own. Maybe I thought that's what people did in a small two bedroom house. I wasn't embarrassed because I never saw or heard anything my parents did. They had two double beds. Sometimes my dad had me come into his bed when I was little and he would tickle me making me laugh. I enjoyed that very much until I turned twelve when my mom shamed me for coming into his bed.

Then the ritual began of cleaning the house for an allowance of $1.00 a week. Cleaning the house entailed vacuuming the entire house which was a very small two bedroom, one bath. The house had hardwood floors throughout, with a large area rug in the living room. Two floors had to be mopped up, the tiny bathroom, and a very small hallway of a kitchen. One side of the kitchen was the sink and counter space. Three feet directly across from the counter was the pantry, stove, and refrigerator. There was only room for one person at a time there. The only room to be dusted was the living room. Not too shabby I thought, so I was eager to get my dollar allowance.

One particular Saturday will forever stand out in my mind as the horrendous day I'll never forget. I was twelve years old. Mom went to the grocery store as she often did, leaving me to my chores. She had purchased a carton of twelve drinking glasses the day before. I was to wash them and put them in the cupboard. I hated washing dishes. Having cut my hand deeply in two places while drying glasses, I hesitated washing them for fear it would happen again. They were last on my "to do" list. The carton was on the dining room table, so in order for me to clean the table, I put the carton on the floor by the kitchen sink. There was no room on the counter. I had to walk around the carton to get through the back door, which was no big deal, until Dad returned home drunk that afternoon.

Dad being drunk was a usual occurrence on the weekend, so I wasn't alarmed. He had two separate personalities when he was drunk; a very clinging, slobbery, affectionate man or an angry, cursing man. I never knew which personality would show up. Dad tried to get through the kitchen to go outside and tripped over the carton of glasses on the floor. He immediately cursed and kicked them, breaking some of the glasses. Now I was scared. He told me to get them out of his way. Crying, I tried to move them, but I was shaking.

"I can't do it, I might cut myself."

He started yelling and cursing at me and tried to grab me, but I ran away from him which made him angrier. He yelled, "Come back here you goddamned brat! I'll get you and I'm gonna kill you!" Whether he meant it or not, I took that threat literally. I was only twelve years old. I ran into the bedroom which had no lock, and I held the door shut. He tried to open it, but couldn't somehow. I don't know where I got the strength to hold that door closed, but I did. He started kicking the door in, yelling at the same time, "I'm gonna kill you!" Screaming at the top of my lungs, I shrieked hysterically, "Help! Somebody please help me!" No matter how my dad meant it, I thought: *He's drunk, he can and he will kill me if he makes it through this door.* I continued screaming for help!

I heard our next door neighbors, Diego and Mary, come through the front door trying to calm my dad. Diego lured him into the back yard with a beer, and Mary came to calm me down. I was still screaming when mom came home. She could not believe what had happened. She stayed with me until I fell asleep. I can't remember what happened after that. We never talked about the incident again.

And just as you would do with the proverbial elephant in the living room, everyone in the family skirted the subject and pretended it wasn't there. We never talked about Dad's drinking, or the arguments between my parents, or the verbal fighting and vicious names they called each other.

By the time I was an adult, I married an alcoholic just like Dad. We had four children together. Mom finally talked about the incident that occurred when I was twelve years old. She told me that after I fell asleep, she went into the backyard where dad was still drinking. Angrily grabbing a broom, she pointed the handle end, shoving it into his stomach and said, "If you ever touch our daughter or do anything like that to her again, I'll shove this broom up into your stomach until your insides are hanging outside your body." I guess she thought she was protecting me, but the thought of handling violence with more violence was not comforting to me even as an adult.

Dad

Me
age 12

Dad and
Diego
in the Back
Yard

My life as a child was traumatic. This incident, as well as all the other tormenting things that happened, drove me to food for the only enjoyment I could look forward to. Food helped me to survive and remains a comfort for me today.

Hunger Pains
February 26, 1992

I've lived
My whole life long
Looking for a man
Who would be strong

My courageous knight
On a sturdy white horse
He will be Prince
Charming
Of course

Who would sweep me
Off my feet
Living happily ever after
How sweet

Now I realize the "dream"
Isn't real
It's just a fantasy
I wanted to feel

Not what I bargained for
I feel empty and alone
For sure it's all
I've ever known

So the more I eat
To hide the pain

The more and more
Pounds I gain

I'm working real hard
I'm letting down
My guard
To love and trust
And bond with you
But I am fearful
What will you do?

Take that risk
Walk through the fear
My inner wisdom's
Message I hear

Who knows
What's best for me?
I do
You see

Only I
Walk in my shoes
Only I experienced
This abuse

I feel the feelings
The hard work is mine

18

This is my journey
And I've turned out
Just fine

Powerful
Courageous
Lovable and free
All these words
Describe me
Ardie

After all
I've been through
Now I find
I'm special

And unique
One of a kind

I do have value
Which is perfectly clear
I'm a human "being"
I deserve
To be here

Not for what I "do"
But just as I am
A child of God
His cherished
Precious lamb

Letter to Dad – never sent
August 8, 1995

I'm having difficulty saying what I want to say to you. Where do I begin to tell you how I feel? I have such sadness. I loved you so much. You said I was your little chicken. I wanted to be your special little girl, but you weren't there for me, not what I wanted -- it was what you wanted and needed. You made me your slave saying "Get me this, bring me that, do this for me." I'm tired of it and I'm not going to take care of you anymore. I wish you had been there for me in the way that I needed. You weren't there for me, and you were never there for me. I have given up all hope of you ever being there for me.

Journal Entry

August 17, 1995

There's a black cloud hanging over me. I'm grieving the loss of my marriage and the loss of the dream that we would live happily ever after, and that my husband would be the dad I never had. It is a huge loss, and I feel the pain. It is the ultimate grieving of what I didn't have and never will. Dad is not coming to take care of me. That really hurts. I still think: *"This man" (my husband) will love me in the way I need him to.* But no man can. No one can fill God's shoes. God is the only one who can love me with that deep unconditional love for me no matter what I do. Men are human and disappoint me, often hurting me. God never does and He never abandons me nor neglects me. God is always looking out for my best interest, even when I push Him away. I want to heal this wound that I have from a childhood filled with chaos and anger, fear and abandonment, criticism and judgment, neglect and abuse. Only God can walk with me on this journey. He alone has the strength to carry me through as I take one step at a time.

Dad Was Not There For Me

August 17, 1995

Love that I've
Been waiting for
There's never enough
I'm wanting more

Because I didn't get
What I needed
From Dad
The loss
Is a major one
And I feel so sad

He was never there
His alcohol came first
He drank to try to

Quench his thirst

He too
Was wounded
At an early age
And continued
To drink himself
Into a rage

He frightened me
With his loud voice
I couldn't stand
His arguing choice

I wished

And I prayed
He would change
I did what I could
To rearrange
My life for him

To win his approval
And love
Whatever I would do
It was never enough

I felt abandoned
And alone
Lost and afraid
All my playful creativity
Began to fade

My needs weren't met
Dad was not
there for me
There's grieving
To be done
If I want
To be free

The tears I shed
Will heal
My childhood pain
And I won't
Allow abuse
In my life
Ever again!

Journal Entry

January 9, 1997

Why do I feel compelled to go to bars of all places? Okay, I love to dance, but what caliber of men am I going to meet in bars? I'll probably meet alcoholics just like my dad. Is this old behavior that I keep falling into? I don't drink anymore, yet I am going to meet a man in a bar that probably does drink and may even have a drinking problem. Have I been here before? At least I have come to this awareness. Now, I want to look deeper and discover the reason why I keep doing this.

Childhood Emptiness
January 9, 1997

Unloved by Dad
Has caused
A great deal of pain
Of loneliness
And emptiness
That continues to remain

Long after childhood
I've grown up
And moved away
But I'm feeling the feelings
As if it happened yesterday

Dad was not there for me

In the way I needed him to be
A hole inside me
began to grow
Love from wrong places
my status quo

Creating more pain (ROM 2:19)
I was lost and alone
God in His mercy
Called me
To be His own (1JN 3:1)

I am God's child
In His image
He created me (GEN 1:26)
I know this
I've been blind
Now I can see (JN 9:25)

No one is hopeless
Whose hope
Is in the Lord (ISA 40:31)
If I draw closer to Him
I will not be ignored (JAS 4:8)

He wipes the slate clean
God's pardon is full and free
(ISA 55:7)
For Jesus died for me
On Calvary (JAS 19:16-18)

He is the Resurrection
And the Life (JN 11:25)
No longer do I need
To feel the strife (PROV 17:1)

Of filling that hole inside of me
God's unconditional love
And grace

Has set me free (2 THESS 2:16)

"Taste and see
That the Lord is good" (PS 34:8)
I am accepted
Loved and understood (JER 31:3)

My faith in God
Is my anchor
Keeps me steady
And calm (HEB 6:19)
When I need uplifting
I go to the Psalms (PSA 145:14)

"Your Word
Is a light
For my path
And a lamp
Unto my feet" (PSA 119:105)
In Your Word
I find the peace
And serenity I seek (ROM 5:1)

Lord God
Thank You
For loving me (PSA 119:76)
Give me the grace
To grow
To be all
You created
And intended
Me to be (1COR 15:10)

Quiet my anxious heart
By healing
The very depths of my soul (2KINGS 20:5)
Continue to fill me
With Your love
Where there was

Once a hole (PSA 17:7)

Keep me close
To You
And nurture me (ISA 40:11)
Give me eyes
To see You
More clearly (PSA 119:18)

You are compassionate
Abounding in love
And mercy (PSA 103:8)

To You alone
Belongs honor
Praise and glory (PSA 8:5)

And when the emptiness
From childhood
Again I feel
Reassure me
With Your unfailing love
So that my wounds
Can heal (JER 30:17)

2

My Controlling Mom

"Ask and you will receive; Seek and you will find; Knock and the door will be opened to you" (Matthew 7:7).

Mixed Messages

Although I had an opportunity to address my issues with my Dad in therapy, my Mom passed away long before I could address our mother-daughter issues. Actually it took my mother's passing away in 1989 before I felt free enough to pursue therapy regarding my childhood. Therapy became a healing process in which I worked toward the goal of bringing ease and order in my life where there was only chaos and pain. That's when the real work actually started. The work of going into my past, revealing what transpired, expressing how I felt about it, and finding out what I needed from my parents. Feeling the sadness came easy. I knew how to cry. The hardest part was grieving my losses. That required going deeper, reliving the emotions of the little girl who had locked everything inside. Thinking back to how it felt living with a controlling Mom angered me.

My mom controlled and dominated my life. I had no voice, no opinions, and no likes or dislikes. My wants, desires, and dreams faded into oblivion. It was her way or the highway as Mrs. Right *(my mom)* squelched my freedom. She grilled me with accusing questions and belittled my every thought, feeling, and action. Humiliating me in front of others, her abusive and cutting words hurt me deeply. When I cried, she criticized my tears asking, "Why are you so emotional?" She called me names such as *crocodile tears*. "Crocodile tears are considered a false, insincere display of emotion such as a hypocrite crying fake tears of grief" (Wikipedia, 2015, para. 1). Mom accused me of *pretending* to cry.

All my life I have been filled with fear, anxiety, sometimes terror, and sometimes panic. I was terrified of people and the world. I was frightened of my family and later of school. I dreaded going to public places where I would be required to interact with people. My life was filled with trepidation and apprehension. There was a sense of foreboding, of ominous, and threatening disaster looming everywhere.

Growing up in a "religious" home had such mixed messages for me. I believed in God with all my heart. At the same time, family members who were supposed to love me, whom I was supposed to be able to trust, abused me. Something was terribly wrong. I knew that fact even though I was a little girl. Mom zealously pursued religion. Mom used God and Bible verses to beat me up verbally, scarring me emotionally. I grew up feeling negative against religion because of my mom's legalistic religiosity. I remember thinking: *here comes the sermon...* It took me many years to get over that negativity and find the beliefs that I could value and cling to.

Journal Entry
December 20, 1989
"My mother" – I'm crying because I don't have *"my mother"* anymore. That's what I always called her in front of my teachers with the emphasis on *"my."* She's gone now. She's no longer here for me to go to if I would choose to. She has now passed from this life to the next. I'll never see her again.

Letter to Mom never sent
December 20, 1989

> I feel so sad for you. You went through so much suffering. Dad was cruel and hurt you so many times. And he got drunk just like your Pappy did. And all

you wanted was to be loved. That's all I wanted from you. We could have been close, but somewhere along the line you became bitter and resentful. I tried to pull away from you and be independent. You became critical of my emotions. You were jealous of me because I could feel my emotions. You hid yours and never understood why I wasn't strong like you. You became judgmental of me as a wife and mother.

When I was a little girl, I think you turned to me for the relationship you didn't have with Dad. When I tried to separate from you and be an adult with capabilities, you couldn't acknowledge my independence. You felt abandoned once again and took it out on me. I understand you more now because I know why you acted that way. I miss you and I miss what we could have had - a close, loving, caring, and supportive relationship. Today I can have it with my own daughters and I'm working toward that goal and achieving it!

Mother, where do you end and I begin?
We're fused together.

Fused so much that I am afraid to venture out on my own.

I still look to you for approval.

Approval that I know will never come.

I'm an adult woman, married with children of my own.

And yet, I am still the little girl.

I'm afraid of what you will say. I'm afraid of what you will think of me. I'm afraid that you will think I really am a bad little girl.

I only wanted you to acknowledge me as a woman in my own right, with feelings, with value and competence as a mother.

I am a mother with knowledge and skills that you never had.

That didn't make you a bad mother.

You just didn't know how to be any different.

I want more. I want growth. I want to learn and share what I've learned with my children.

And I want my children to be individuals, separate from me.

I want them to be able to choose their own lives, not what I want or what anyone else wants them to be.

And I want to be me and accepted just as I am.

Journal Entry

March 1, 1991

I'm tired of the struggling and I don't know what to do anymore. I'm grieving the loss of the mothering that I didn't get as a child. My therapist said to me, "I see you." She really does and I know that will heal my broken heart. My mom didn't see me, not who I really am. Mom, why didn't you let me cry like I wanted to without criticism? Why didn't you hear me? Why didn't you see that my tears were real; not "crocodile tears?" I was in pain and why couldn't you see that?

My needs and wants didn't matter to you. You weren't there for me in the way I needed you.

I'm really angry with you because you didn't give me what I needed, so I wasn't able to give my own children what they needed. I loved my children as well as I could, to the best of my ability. I still messed it up and I'm really sad about that. I loved my children and I acted inappropriately with them. That was the best *"mothering"* I could do and I can own that. I wished that I had better mothering skills, but I had no healthy role model. I am sad that my son Brian acts out my dysfunction. I'll get him all the help he needs to get out of the hole he's in. He needs to feel my real strength and know that I'm here solidly and clearly as his mother.

Letter to Mom never sent
May 11, 1991

I'm trying to get in touch with my anger toward you for the abuse that you inflicted on me. Although you died two years ago, I'm still afraid of you. I'm afraid of your anger because you had so much anger inside of you. Every time you let that anger out, I became terrified. You were violent and cruel, physically and emotionally abusive toward me. I didn't deserve the venting of your frustrations and anger. How dare you do that to me? I'm a precious child of God and He tenderly loves me and cherishes me as a person, who sees me as I am -- unique and special. You didn't know me, and you certainly didn't see me. I tried. I tried so hard to win your love and approval. You were brutal, cutting me down every chance you got. I hate you for that. I hate you for leaving this mess for me to figure out and clean up. It's so hard fighting against you. Even in your death I feel the force of your power and I struggle to fight the memory of your harshness because it was so strong. I'm afraid of my anger since I could lose all of the good memories I have of you and the love I thought I had. I feel so alone without you now that you have passed.

The things you said to me were so cruel. I could feel that hurt and cry, but I've never felt the anger. You attacked me and I have every right to feel angry. When you said, "You sure got fat." I was so frustrated that I ate my feelings to stuff them down and not feel them. That's what you taught me and modeled for me. You were always looking at my outward appearance. You were obsessed with anything having to do with my body. You always made sarcastic, ridiculing, and humiliating comments. I didn't want to be around you for fear you'd criticize me again. I was so frustrated with trying to please you. I tried so hard to please you so that you would be happy and like me. I couldn't measure up. You found fault with me no matter what I said or did. I thought there was something wrong with me because you told me that! You said, "There's something wrong with you. I never had that problem. What's wrong with you?" When you took me to the doctor to see what was wrong with me, he validated that I was normal. There was nothing wrong with me. To which you replied to me, not to him, "What does HE know?"

I needed compliments and praise from you about my accomplishments. I didn't hear positive things only negative, nit-picking criticism and judgment. You said that "in order for me to improve." What lies! You were always shaming me for wanting to do things saying, "Christian girls can't do that." My feelings were discounted. You would say, "Why do you feel like that? I was never like that. You're always afraid of everything. Just do it. Be strong. I am. I had to be. I had to prove I was just as good as anybody else."

I longed for you to see me, accept me, and love me for who I am. I tried so hard. Instead, I was rejected and

betrayed. I trusted you to take care of my
needs and to take care of me. You
weren't there for me in a positive way. I
needed reassurance but you gave me
criticism. I always thought you loved me.
You appeared as if you loved me. You
appeared caring, generous, and loving.
Inside I felt empty, rejected, and
betrayed. I hate you for that. You led me
to believe there was something wrong
with me. There wasn't and still isn't
anything wrong with me. I am a
precious and unique child of God. God
loves me for who I am and He doesn't
judge me. He forgives me when I make
mistakes. You said that you forgave me,
but you never let me forget anything I
ever did. I felt devalued and shamed in
the very core of my being with messages
like, "Can't you do anything right?
What's wrong with you? Why do you feel
that way? I don't feel that way. Why
don't you use the brains God gave you?"

I wanted you to stop judging me. You
said, "The Bible says... God tells me...
These are God's words, not mine... I must
do this... God says that I must do this."

I yearned for positive strokes from you.
I wanted you to see me, hear me, mirror

me, validate me, and love me. I wanted to find my own voice and I wanted you to accept my voice as being mine -- special and unique. I didn't get what I needed from you so I filled those needs with food. Food was there for me. You weren't there for me. You were brutal and cruel. I hate you for that.

Christian Child
September 2, 1991

Growing up a Christian
Had its ups and downs
Sometimes I could smile
And lots of times I frowned

There were so many rules
I was confused
One thing for sure
If I "sinned"
I'd be bruised

From little on
I knew I loved God (PSA 71:17)
But I thought
He couldn't love me
Because I was flawed

I hoped He could
And I wanted His love
But somehow
I thought
I couldn't do enough

To earn His forgiveness

For the things I had done
Too unspeakable
To put into words
I'd run

My emotions
Were too much for me
So food became
My way to flee

I used food like that
For years
Until I could no longer
Control the tears

I was a Christian
But I was in pain
If something didn't change
I would go insane

Then began
My journey of recovery
To my surprise
What a discovery

I could have my faith
And be sane too
Today I have
A brand new view

Of God
Walking with me
Flaws and all (MIC 7:18)

I'm not afraid
If I stumble and fall

It's a process
And God's love
Is real (ISA 43:4)
Today I can talk
I can trust
I can feel

Journal Entry

May 3, 1992

I'm sitting in the backyard early in the morning. I've already taken my walk. I feel grounded and alive. I'm listening to the sounds of God's creation. There are different kinds of birds, crows, sparrows, and at least two other kinds. I can hear cars in the distance. Occasionally I can hear a plane or a train. I watch a leaf fall to the ground. The sun is shining, but I'm in the shade. It is cool here. It is so quiet and calm. I feel content. I listen. I am relaxed. I'm not rushing anywhere. I look at my little fig tree that my mom gave me. I planted it in her honor. I've watched it grow, then lose its leaves, almost dying from lack of rain. I've watered it and watched it come back to life again. It's been three years since my mom died. I've come back to life. I'm struggling with letting go of the old me -- what she molded me into, what she wanted me to be and how she controlled me. I'm letting the old die and letting the new be born -- to live! It was a struggle for me to look at Mom. Today as I dream, I feel her warmth, her love, in my mind, as she puts her arms around my shoulders. How I wish she was here now. I did love her so very much. I want to remember only the good. I don't want to look at the evil, the cruelty, the sharpness of her tongue, and the hurtful words. Mom, you hurt me so much. Why did you do that? You said you loved me. I was so confused. I was so afraid of you. You shouldn't be afraid of someone you love and who says she loves you. All Mom knew was rules and regulations. All I heard was "You can't do that!" I wanted to rebel, "Why not? What's wrong with being ME?"

I gave the little girl inside me a voice. I only wish Mom could have listened to the feelings I had throughout my childhood. She was oblivious.

Journal Entry

May 19, 1993

Terror -- the word is scary to write because I can feel that feeling as if it happened yesterday... I've spent years stuffing that feeling down... I don't want to feel it. It's so scary to see the look on my mother's face. I'm going to die. I don't want her to be angry with me. I must stop doing what she doesn't like me to do. I must give up being me. She doesn't like the real me. My feelings anger her. I've got to stop those feelings. I loved her so much that I couldn't lose her, so I lost me.

The pain hurts my body. Why does my mother hurt my body? This is my body. I want her to stop. I cry and I scream. But she hits harder. Why isn't she gentle with me? She can be. Why can't she be gentle all the time? It's not fair. She's rough and loud. I want her to be soft and gentle, to hold me and rock me, not just when she wants to, but when I need her to.

Rock Me

May 19, 1993

Rock me
Sing to me sweetly

Hold me tight
Love me with all your
might
Never let me go

The dreams of a child
Are not at all wild
I wanted love
I prayed to God above

But I got abused

Rather than soothed
And the pain deep inside
Cannot be denied

My pain is real
Now I can feel
I couldn't then
Didn't know when
I'd be hit again

Strapped to a potty
Tied to a post
These things I hated most

I screamed
She ignored me   *And I wished*
My feelings didn't matter   *That I could*
Just made me sadder   *Run away*

Journal Entry

July 14, 1994

As a child, I didn't feel loved. I tried to tell my mother, but she couldn't hear me. I took care of myself the only way I knew how by eating. Love was missing, so I filled up with food to fill up the emptiness. Food was my love. Eating was my way of being loved. Food was available when my parents weren't. Food didn't get drunk like my dad did. Food didn't hit me like my mom did. Food didn't molest me like my brother did. Food didn't belittle, humiliate, or criticize me like my family in which I grew up in did… Food was always there and tasted good. Food was my comfort and my friend. Food became the closest thing to love that I knew.

But it is only a substitute for love. Food is not, nor was it ever love.

Journal Entry

January 29, 1997

I'm wanting "Mom" again. Does that longing ever go away? As a matter of fact, God longs for a relationship with me. No one person can fulfill that need for me.

I'm jealous that my girlfriend is going to meet another woman for dinner and a movie. She's not meeting me. I want her to have other friends, so what is this? I'm wanting her to be "Mom" to me. I want all of her attention because I want to feel special. I'm crying now because I'm feeling the loss of my childhood. I didn't feel special to my mom. She didn't love me in the way that I needed. Why can't I realize that I don't need Mother's love anymore? God loves me and wants a relationship with me.

There is so much pain surrounding "mother's love." That's why I look for "mother" substitutes – usually my addictions. I'm not willing to go there anymore. With God's help, to the best of my ability, and one day at a time, I will face my pain and not deny it.

Mother's Love
January 29, 1997

Mother's love
She gave me
What she could
I'm glad
But I really miss
The "nurturing mom"
I never had

She wasn't there
For me
In the way
I needed her to be

I cried a lot
Something was wrong
A hole inside of me
Began to grow
And I would long

For her to come
And fill me up
I would cry some more
Her anger would erupt

I became
Frightened and confused
I wanted comfort
But was called a "brat"
I was ridiculed
For having needs
No child
Deserves that

I was left alone
When I needed
Her most
As a toddler
To keep me in line
She tied me
To a post

I cried all the more
She wasn't aware
Of what I needed
She couldn't
Give me
Nurturing care

This hole is deep
I feel it today
I look for
"Mother" substitutes
This longing
Doesn't go away

Food has always
Been a source
Of comfort for me
And an escape
A way
For me to flee

From this deep pain
Of the loss
Of mother's love
Here is

Another opportunity
For healing
A gift from above

God has a plan
He's answering
My prayer (JER 29:11, 1JN 5:14, 15)
He wants to heal
My childhood hurts
Layer by layer

And even
When I think
I have had enough
If I can just
Hang in there
When the going
Gets tough

The pain
Will subside
The tears will
Be wiped away (REV 7:17)
What started out
As stormy
Becomes
A bright new day

I see clearer
I can laugh
And I can cope
Every cloud
Has a silver lining

There is hope

God doesn't
Abandon me
As my mother did (DEUT 31:6)
He's walking
With me
Step by step
Helping me to rid

My life
of painful issues (LEV 26:12)
From the past
Although my mom
Was inconsistent
God is always steadfast (HEB 13:8)

When there is
Nowhere else
To turn
And my heart
Begins to yearn

For "mother"
Who wasn't there
For me
I can grieve the loss
And know
I am a child
Of God
Precious
And free (1JN 3:1)

Two incidents my mother always talked about, possibly to shame me, I don't have a conscious memory of. Both occurred around the age of three. As a child I loved candy. When Mom walked me to the grocery store, she would give me a penny to put in the gum ball machine or candy machine and let me turn the crank. I loved to do that.

One day as I was playing in the backyard, I climbed the chain link fence *(I was very adventurous)* and walked myself to the store. I don't know how I crossed the busy streets, but I got there. Only thing was I didn't have any money. I was trying to get the candy out anyway, and a strange man walked up to me.

"Where's your mother?" he questioned me.

"At home." I cheerfully volunteered as I continued to try for the candy.

"Where do you live?" he asked nicely.

"I don't know." I said truthfully *(I didn't know my address)*.

If I get your candy for you, could you show me where you live?"

"Yes!" Now I was excited about getting the candy.

He held my hand while we walked together and I ate the candy. I showed him exactly where I lived.

He knocked on the front door, and my Mom was surprised to see me with a strange man. He reamed her out for not watching me and told her where he found me! She apologized to him and he sternly said, "Don't let her out of your sight again!"

After he left, I got a whipping for running away. She never let me forget that story implying there was something wrong with me. As a young child, I thought what's wrong with wanting candy?

So every day after that, she tied me with a rope to the clothes line post, so I couldn't run away again. I would cry for hours. Finally a neighbor would knock on the front door and yell at my Mom for not taking care of her child. I think I got another whipping for that. She told me I was always embarrassing her! I didn't even know what that word meant, but I knew by her tone that she was displeased with me again.

Today I'm sure she would have been reported for child abuse but not back then. That was 1950.

Another time I loved to play in the back yard. I was potty trained and was supposed to come in to go to the bathroom on my little chair with a metal potty. It seems I neglected to come in most of the time and she got tired of having to change my wet clothes. So to teach me a lesson, she tied that metal potty to my bottom. I had to walk around with it on. I didn't care. Matter of fact, I even tried climbing the chain link fence again. My Mom came out and caught me because she could hear the clanging of the potty against the fence. I got another whipping for that. Seems as if I got many, many whippings.

Another letter to Mom never sent
February 22, 1998

> How could you shut me up with candy? You had no right to do that. I needed my tears to express my pain. God gave me those tears, and he saves every single tear of mine in a bottle. "You have seen me tossing and turning through the night. You have collected all my tears and preserved them in Your bottle! You have recorded every-one in Your book" (Psalm 56:8, Life Recovery Bible, NLT).

> He knows how valuable my tears are. You didn't know or see my value. You hated that I cried and you would do anything to shut me up rather than find out what was wrong and what I needed.

Now I am fifty years old still giving candy to the little girl inside who is crying out for love and comfort, wanting to be cherished and adored. I'm afraid, afraid of getting too close to people, especially men. I'm afraid of being hurt again. I'm afraid of being judged and criticized rather than be accepted and loved for who I am. My body, I hate my body. My body got me into trouble. Guess I've never forgiven my body because I still abuse it.

The pain of carrying this burden is overwhelming. I'm alone with my struggle and it is such a struggle. I have no Mom to tell me I'm okay just the way I am. I have no Mom who will love me no matter how much I weigh. I have no Mom to tell me I'm acceptable, capable, lovable, forgivable, and valuable.

I Don't Want to Go to School Today!

Sound asleep, I barely heard Mom's voice in the distance, "Time to get up for school, Ardy!" That's what Mom has called me ever since I can remember, Ardith is my real name. Mom picked it from a book she read. She liked the name because it was different. Linda, Nancy, or Barbara didn't suit her. There were lots of little girls with those names; she wanted a name unlike any others because of my specialness. I liked that she considered me special. I sure wanted to be, but I didn't know that at school I might get more attention for being different than I really wanted.

Starting to drift back to sleep, I abruptly awoke to... "Ardy, it's time to get out of bed. You don't want to be late for school. The bus will be here soon to pick you up."

She had no idea what today would be like for me. I thought: *"I don't want to go to school today! Today is Measurement Day."* Every year in September and June, the teacher would weigh us and measure our height to see how much we had grown. *"I don't care how much I've grown, and I don't want to know how much I weigh."*

Being in the fourth grade this year was no different than any other. Attending Selby Grove Elementary School in Rivera, California, in 1956, I had no say about it. Being nine years old, I had to be measured and weighed. I tried to think of a way I could stay home from school. Figuring if I was sick, Mom would not make me go to school. I had forgotten her rule: Unless I was dying, there's no excuse to stay home. Mom wouldn't allow it, and she always got her way.

Dressing quickly, grabbing something to eat, I ran just in time to catch the bus. The bus ride took a long time, and I dreaded every part of the trip. Arriving at school, we were told to wait in line for the teacher to take us into our classroom. The other kids were looking at me and snickering. Hanging my head in silence was all I could do.

I doubted my teacher, Mrs. Mendoza, realized what I was going through today. I knew she liked me; she even invited me to her home last month to have lunch with her. Mom said I couldn't go. She insisted I embarrassed her because I'm such a picky eater. Mom thought Mrs. Mendoza probably would've made homemade Mexican food, so I didn't go to lunch. I was very disappointed that once again Mom got her way. I wondered if Mom told Mrs. Mendoza the truth about how I eat. How embarrassing!

Soon Mrs. Mendoza came to take us to our classroom. Once indoors, we sat down at our desks. She announced that we were going to the cafeteria to be weighed and measured. Inside I groaned, but outwardly I acted as if I didn't care.

We lined up alphabetically, and I was last as usual. With a last name like Wilfinger, where else would I be but at the end of the line? Since both my names are hard to pronounce, teachers usually couldn't figure out how to say my name. Reason enough for the other kids to make fun of me. But this time, Mrs. Mendoza pronounced it right. I heaved a sigh of relief, but not for long.

Nervously waiting, I knew what to expect next. When I stepped on the scale, Mrs. Mendoza called my name out loud to her teacher's aide who wrote down the results. The class got quiet for the big announcement. They couldn't wait to hear how much I weighed.

I have to tell you that I've gained weight every year since I can remember. That's okay because I'm growing, but I always was the fattest kid in the class. Last year, I went from eighty four pounds in September to ninety-five pounds in June. I only grew an inch and a half. Most of the other kids were sixty-five to eighty pounds and about the same height as me. Clearly I was getting fatter. So from June to September I probably gained a whole lot over the summer. I had no idea what the number on the scale would be, but waiting for the inevitable announcement was grueling.

As my name was called out loud every muscle in my body stiffened. Closing my eyes really tight making a frown on my face, she yelled out loud and clear, "Four feet seven inches tall and one hundred and a half pounds!" I was the only kid who broke into three digits. Gasps echoed throughout the whole cafeteria and I felt humiliated. Oh, Mrs. Mendoza told the class to quiet down, but that didn't stop them from calling me names. As I walked past them, I heard "Fatty, fatty, two by four, can't get through the cafeteria door." If only I could run away and hide. Nowhere for me to go I blinked away the tears. Finding an empty table, I sat down by myself.

I thought: *"Will this ever be any different? Why do the kids make fun of me because I weigh more than they do? Is there something wrong with me? I don't like being different if it means that kids laugh at me. It hurts to be different because I don't fit in, and I sure don't belong."*

The next day, I woke up to Mom's voice again. I wondered what today would be like. Would it be a quiet day at school when no one would laugh and make fun of me? Some days the kids would ignore me and laugh at another kid. After yesterday's embarrassment at the scale, I hoped the kids would choose someone else to laugh at today.

Once inside the class, I looked around at my classmates. I could see all the popular kids. Jackie Ferguson is the most beautiful girl in my class, probably in the whole school. Her hair is long. She wears it in a ponytail shaped in one long swirl. Having a very thin body, she can wear all the prettiest dresses she wants. I can hardly find clothes that fit me because I'm so big. Mom takes me shopping for school clothes at the Chubby Department at Sears. How embarrassing is that?! That's not Jackie's problem at all. She's so lucky.

Bobby Ross is so cute. All the girls like him. I've had a secret crush on him since the second grade. He doesn't even look at me, except when making fun of me. Being the class clown, he laughs at how big I am.

Poor Linda Achiolas. I can't even pronounce her last name. It sounds strange to me. She's a little chunky but not as big as I am. Her clothes are wrinkled and ripped. She doesn't smell very good. I wonder why she doesn't take a bath. The kids make fun of her and call her "Cooties." I don't know what "cooties" are, but know I don't want them. At least when making fun of her, they don't make fun of me.

All the rest of my classmates are either smart or funny. Some can paint or play the piano. Others are good at sports or take vacations that are fun and interesting to share with the class. They do fun things as a family. They have important fathers and sweet mothers. My dad drinks too much and my mom is very bossy. I don't have much to say on Share Day.

Hey, wait a minute. There's someone I don't know. Who is she? It must be a new girl. I've never seen her before. She sure is skinny. Wearing glasses draws attention to her big nose. Her dark colored skin stands out since all of us are so light. And straight shiny black hair is very different compared to blonds like me. She's alone. No one is talking to her. I think I will go over and ask her name. Maybe she will talk to me. I would like that. I know she is different, but so am I. I finally can have a friend.

***

Three years later, I was old enough to be in my Mom's Sunday school class. I remember my mother being active in church organizations. She was a Sunday school teacher for many years. I had mixed feelings about being in her class because I knew she would be harder on me. I didn't think that was fair, but couldn't ask to be transferred to another class.

Journal Entry

1959 Age 12

Question from my Sunday school teacher-my mother

What are we to do as Christians?

"We are to obey the Ten Commandments, to tell other people about Jesus and how He died on the cross to save us from our sins. We should say our prayers every day; for other people, for spiritual things and then for earthly things and say, 'If it be Thy Will.' If He thinks we should have it, we will. When we are tempted to do something bad, we should say a prayer to help us from doing it. We should obey our parents, teachers, Sunday school teachers, and Pastors. And we shouldn't fight with anyone."

"We should be kind to our friends and our enemies too. We should read the Bible and learn the Word of God. We should do things for our parents without having them ask us. We should help others, just like the Good Samaritan did."

Mom was program director at the church I grew up in. For fellowship and fun, she would write silly rhymes. Back then, I thought her "poems" were really goofy, but I realize now she had a talent for writing. She wrote those rhymes coming from her sense of humor. My writing talent comes from her and is a gift from God. That talent and my love for God are the two most important positive gifts she gave me for which I am very grateful. She never knew she passed on that writing talent to me. She died only knowing the negative impact. Someday when we meet again in Heaven, I will tell her.

Through my years in therapy I began to see Mom for the flawed individual she was with good and bad qualities. I learned to integrate all of who she was, enjoy the good she gave me, forgive her for how she hurt me, and let go of the past. What a good feeling to be able to do that. I delight in my fond memories of the board games we played, our laughter, our singing, and our love of fishing. I loved her cooking and baking and the favorites she made me by hand, and all the love she put into those dishes.

Journal Entry
May 10, 1998
It's Mother's Day. I'm sitting at my mother's grave. It's been nine years since she passed away. I think about her and miss her.

Mom liked to take a nap in our back yard under a tree on a blanket on the grass.

I'm lying here by her grave on a blanket. I feel the sun on my legs. It feels warm. I feel warm, relaxed, and safe.

Mom loved to laugh. Her laugh was infectious. My daughters called her "Nonny." We all loved to laugh with her. My girls are with me now reminiscing about their Nonny.

And she loved the Lord. She loved to sing praises to the Lord. I love the Lord, too, and love to sing praises to Him.

Mom is no longer with me physically, but I carry her memory inside. Thank You, Lord, for a "Mom" who taught me that Jesus is my Savior and showed me that loving You is more precious than anything!

Mom Age 49

3

Two Older Brothers

"Hear my cry, O God; listen to my prayer: From the end of the earth I call to You, when my heart is faint. Lead me to the rock that is higher than I" (Psalm 61:1-2, NRSV).

Early Happy Memories

At one time, growing up with two older brothers made me proud. I looked up to them with admiration and love. Being their sister made me happy. I can remember Greg making a puppet theater and painting the title on the screen *(sheet)* "Greg & Ardith's Puppet Theater." How delighted I was to be included!

Greg at Greg and Ardith's Puppet Theatre

Every Saturday my Dad would take the whole family fishing. That's where I learned how to fish and loved it right from the start. We had contests to see who could catch the first fish *(usually me!)* and the biggest fish of the day. It was just a fun family day!

Lamar, Mom, Dad, Greg
and Me 5yrs Old

My oldest brother, Lamar, who always protected me, left the family to get married when I turned seven. I was so sad to see him leave. My brother, Greg, who stayed, was seven years older than I. Soon after Lamar left, I became very afraid of Greg. I grew to hate him because of the abuse he inflicted on me.

When we watched television, I was watching cartoons. Greg would change the channels, laughing, and holding down the channel, so I couldn't change it back. He would also ride me on the handle bars of his bicycle and pretend to steer toward the cars parked on the street as if to hit them. I was so frightened I never did that again. He just laughed at me.

Abuse

Then the abuse turned ugly. When my brother started molesting me, the words he said sickened me. I hated the sounds of those words. He said he wanted to kiss me and lick me between my legs. Afraid of him I felt too terrified to tell anyone. So I lived with sexual abuse for several years. Greg would walk around nude masturbating, lurking in the shadows, then would come to me sitting beside me touching and rubbing my vagina. I would ignore him, then get up and go to another room. My parents had already gone to work, so there was no one to protect me and no locks on any doors. I didn't feel safe.

At first Greg would ask if he could do these things and I said no. But then, Disneyland opened and I wanted to go so badly that I came up with a plan. I went to Greg. "If you take me to Disneyland I'll let you do those things to me." Of course he said yes. He told me to lie face down on his bed. He took my panties off and got on top of me. I could smell the Vaseline as he rubbed it on himself. He attempted to penetrate me anally. It hurt so I screamed. He stopped. He tried again. I screamed even louder. He stopped, got up and walked into the bathroom leaving me to get up and put my panties back on. I went into shock and don't remember anything that happened the rest of that day. All I know was that I felt violated, shameful, and dirty. After that day, he continued to ask me to do it again and I said no. He never gave up asking. It took me two years to get up the courage to finally tell Mom. I was so scared and confused about what she would do to me and to Greg. I was crying and I don't remember the words I used, but I remember her answer, "You mean he stuck that thing in you?" I nodded my head yes. In my mind that's what he did.

When Greg came home, my Mom brutally beat him until he fell on the floor. Even though at seventeen, he was bigger than my Mom, he did not fight back but begged her to stop. She kicked him over and over. All this right in front of me. I was petrified. Was she going to turn on me next? She didn't. But Greg packed up and moved out. I don't know whether it's because Mom kicked him out or he left voluntarily. I was relieved on the one hand but I was left feeling lost and alone. Mom never said another word about it. She never hugged me or told me it wasn't my fault. And of course she never took me to a doctor to see if I was okay physically or to a counselor to help me emotionally. I felt abandoned and unloved. I had no answers for that little girl.

Greg Age 14
And
Me Age 8

Some families can be loving and supportive, full of laughter and joy. My family filled with conflict, chaos, and heartbreaking abuse, drove me to feeling lost and abandoned. Feeling stuck with this family, my situation felt hopeless. Therefore, I turned to food for comfort as a little girl, gradually turning to alcohol and prescription pills in my adult years. I lived a promiscuous life having numerous sexual partners for many years. It's amazing how hard I tried to run away from the pain of my abusive past.

I Know That It Happened
November 13, 1989

I know	*So long ago*
That it happened	*And yet*
It seems	*I re-live the woe*

As if
It happened now
I told him "NO!"
It didn't
Mean a thing
All I felt
Was the sting

Of pain
Humiliation and shame

How could he
Do this to me?
All I wanted
Was for him to see

I was just a little girl
Who looked up
To him
With eyes of wonder
He crashed my hopes
With resounding thunder

Things were different now
A secret between us
Kept us apart
Deep down inside
I knew in my heart

Someday
I'd have the courage
To tell my story
To those
Who understand

No longer silent
The little girl can cry
Now she doesn't
Have to understand why

I know that it happened
I can feel the pain
I survived!
I'm not
Going to be
A victim
Ever again!

Journal Entry

May 2, 1991

My stomach hurts and I breathe. With each breath I want to cry. I'm hurting inside for what was done to me as a child. All I wanted was to be loved for who I am—just for being me. Me—Ardie. I'm special and unique. There's no one else in the world like me. It hurts to feel that pain deep down inside that black hole that is endless. I keep trying to fill it up with food, especially sugar to take that pain away. It hurts so much. I feel totally alone, abandoned, unloved, and unwanted. I loved them and trusted them, and I was betrayed and wounded.

The Little Girl's Secret
March 25, 1991

There's a secret
Locked inside of me
To open up
I need the key

Trust and safety
Are what I need
Take my hand
And I will lead

You to that place
I often go
Where you can learn
To trust and know

The little girl
Who's been
Waiting for you
Lost and afraid
Hidden from view

She's precious
Creative and bright
Her face is aglow
With the light

Of the truth
She's always known
The secret
That belongs
To her alone

Messages from the past
Are nothing new
Just listen
And she'll

Speak to you

Too painful
To let anyone see
What was so brutally
Done to me

Because I did
Something bad
And Mom's going
To be real mad
At me

For doing
Something wrong
It's not going
To take very long

To figure out
This secret's safer inside
All I have to do is hide

But I'm alone
And I don't like it
Don't like it
One little bit

Need to belong
Need to feel love
I need to know
I am enough

Just as I am
Just to be me
I want to
Finally feel free

Of the chains
I've felt all my life
Awful pain
As if a knife

Was stabbed
In my heart
To feel that pain
Is the start

Of my journey
To heal
And to grow

At last
The truths I know

Are no longer secrets
Kept locked inside
My little girl feelings
No longer denied

I am enough!
I am okay!
Today
Is the beginning
Of a bright new day!

Journal Entry

February 21, 1993

Out of the depths of darkness comes a groaning and moaning so deep and painful. I could not feel it as a child. It would have killed me. I feel it now and I think I'm going to die. It hurts so badly. Hold my hand – tight – tighter – until it subsides. I don't want to be alone. I'll die if I'm alone. This pain – I want it out. Get out! I'm so little, so little. Why do my parents want to hurt me?

Is Anyone Near? Does Anyone Hear?
February 21, 1993

Den of thieves
Code of silence
Live the lie
Of pretense

We're a happy family
There's nothing wrong
They just fight and scream
While I live in a dream

Someone

Come and rescue me
Before I'm drowned
In this sea

Devoured by these alligators
Who live in my house
I try to be quiet
As a mouse

To no avail
I cannot hide

They find me
And I'm never
Left alone

They keep bothering me
Such torture
I don't deserve
But don't know
How to stop

I'm so little
If I pretend
Not to notice
Maybe he'll go away

No
He stays
He's so ugly
A monster

I don't like monsters
They frighten me
Just let me be
It's not fair
STOP!

NO!

Hear my cry
It feels as if
I'm going to die

Is anyone near?
Does anyone hear?

I need a safe place
Where I know
I can trust
And not be afraid
A place to rest
And sit in the sun

Terror and pain
No more
There is none

Warmth and comfort
Peace at last
Laid to rest
Is the past

Journal Entry

October 26, 1994

I know not where my journey takes me, but I am compelled to
continue it, one step at a time. Each day that goes by, I am aware of
this driving force, a strength, and a courage that I never knew I had
within me. Sometimes I feel that I am a warrior gearing up for battle
against the enemy – ignorance, prejudice, betrayal, and abuse.
Although the abuse should never have happened, I didn't deserve it.
Nothing I did caused it to happen to me. My parents didn't know any
better. They did the best that they could. It wasn't what I wanted or
needed. They were brutally abusive to me causing me much pain.
Each day that I work hard to heal from the past brings me to

acceptance of what happened to me.

I have joy today that I feel to the fullest, feeling totally alive. I have joy knowing who I am. I am grateful for the past experiences that have contributed to who I am today—a precious, valuable, child of God, beautiful, creative, playful, feminine, intelligent, and powerful. I am enjoying life, delighting in the place where I am today.

Journal Entry
July 1, 1997

All I did was ask a question about fear to John Jollife at Saddleback's Single Parents Meeting. I was given a choice to walk through my fear to reach an insight. I was willing to take that risk. My heart was pounding so intensely. I was embarrassed. It was difficult to get up in front of such a large group *(about two hundred),* then get up on stage, not to read a poem, but to... Well, I didn't know what I was going to do or even what this Christian psychologist was going to ask me. He said that I knew the answers. Was I willing to explore, become aware, and then share it with the group? I was.

Even though I was willing and committed to following through, it still was difficult. I've learned, though, that nothing happens by accident. There was a reason for me to be up on that stage dealing with "Mom" issues again. Fear. What am I afraid of? People. Why? What are they going to do? Judge and criticize me. Why? Because I'm not good enough. Why am I not good enough? Because Mom said so. I'm not like her at all. I think differently, so is there something wrong with me just because I have feelings?

Mom said, "What's wrong with you? Why do you feel that way? I never felt that way. I was always strong, never afraid. What is there to be afraid of? What can they do to me? I'm just as good as anyone else."

Fear. I'm afraid to try anything. I'm afraid to say anything. I'm afraid to do anything. I'm afraid of people. I'm afraid of new things. I'm afraid of going to new places. I'm so afraid. I keep risking. I keep changing. I keep growing.

Journal Entry
July 2, 1997

I want to write another poem. I've been feeling feelings. Now I have a headache. How can I write a poem now? Nothing inspiring is coming up. Maybe I've lost it. Maybe I can't do it. I wanted to write about fear. Something is holding me back. It's as if I'm choked up -- no words are coming. Maybe I should just give up and go to bed. I am tired. Lord, please use me for Your purpose, Your tool, to do Your Will. If I can help somebody, please let me.

Walking Through Fear
July 2, 1997

Fear
It churns
Inside my chest (EX 2:14)
My heart is pounding
I'm feeling stressed

I panic
I feel terrified
Something is wrong
I've felt this way
My whole lifelong

It's not easy
Walking through fear
It's as if I'm
Walking in the dark
The path is not clear (JN 12:35)

I'm afraid of falling
I might get hurt
Feeling pain
Most of my life
Has made me
An expert (JER 15:18)

I try to run
But God
Has other plans (ISA 10:3)
He reaches out
To take my hand (PS 37:24)

"Know I am with you"
Says the Lord (MT 28:20)
My faith
And reassurance
Are once again restored (HEB 10:23)

I have confidence
Because there is hope (2COR 7:16, PS 130:5)
What God did
For me
Is beyond any scope (2COR 3:18)

Of human understanding
His love for me
Is evident in all His planning (PS 40:5)

He sent
His Son Jesus
To be my Savior (1JN 4:14)

Our relationship
He wanted to restore (PS 80:3)

How gracious
How merciful is my Lord

What a gift
He gave to me (NEH 9:17)
I'm no longer
Imprisoned
At last I am free (PS 61:1)

Freedom is precious
Jesus shed His blood (1JN 1:7)
To show me
How much
I'm cherished and loved (PS 86:15)

Just as I am
Exactly where I'm at
He's made my heart
His habitat

Now there is nothing
That can hold me back
When I choose to stay
Directed on God's track (PROV 3:5)

When something
Unexpected
Happens to me (PS 10:1)
And fear
Causes me
To want to flee (PS 139:7)

I stay
With the feeling
Today I have a choice
Not to run

But to listen
For God's voice (DEUT 30:20)

His wisdom
Guidance
Strength and power (REV 5:12)
Will see me
Through the darkest hour (PS 18:28)

My trust
And my courage
Is divinely renewed (JOSH 1:9)
My heart is filled
With unquenchable
Joy and gratitude (PS 42:1, 2, 4)

God is great!
God is good! (DEUT 10:17)
The fears I have
He's always understood (DEUT 1:29, 30, 31)

I need Him
Right here beside me (JOSH 1:9)
His light
Shines brightly
So I can see (PS 19:8)

I can climb that mountain
I can go the distance (HEB 12:1)
I can walk
Through the fear
In any circumstance (PS 56:4)

I am secure
I have peace
I can rest (ISA 26:3)
God's love is boundless
I am abundantly blessed (PS 86:15)

Journal Entry

2015

He lurks in the shadows. I can't get away. Where can I go? There's nowhere to run; no place to hide. Whatever happens, I'm on my own. No one here protects me. No one comes to my rescue. How do I fight someone who is bigger than me? I say "NO!" but he doesn't listen. I move from place to place, he follows me. I'm afraid. I feel alone and helpless. What can I do? This is my home.

Journal Entry

December 6, 2001

When I least expect it, another trigger can occur today that sends me to flashbacks of my childhood. I experience the same feelings as if they were happening to the little girl inside me right now. I'm frightened again. My home is not safe. I know this person who scares me is not my brother, but my reaction is the same—terror. There's no way out and I feel trapped.

This event occurred just after I met and married my husband. My daughter and I settled in his home with his son which immediately felt like my home. I relaxed, breathed a sigh of relief and I was very happy. I had always gotten along with his son. He was nice and a gentleman. In college he was gone to classes most of the time, but came in and out as he chose. We lived in a big house and because I was not aware of his schedule, I wasn't concerned. He was a grown man and could take care of himself. On more than one occasion he would come home so quietly that I didn't know he was even in the house. This was not the problem. It was only that he did not let me know he was home, but just quietly snuck up behind me scaring me out of my wits.

"Don't do that! It scares me when I don't know you're home." He laughingly said, "I didn't mean to scare you."

"Please don't do that again!" I sternly said.

"Okay."

But it kept happening. He would just laugh at me mockingly. I immediately flashed back to my childhood. Pictures of my brother and all the things he did to me came to my mind haunting me. I no longer felt safe in my own home. My husband's son was triggering feelings from my childhood.

Looking For a Place to Rest
December 6, 2001

Lord I lay my heart
Before Your throne (HEB 4:16)
I'm feeling broken
Lost and alone (PS 73:2)

I live in agony
Every day (LK 16:24)
I don't feel safe
In any way (2COR 7:5)

In my own home
It's like a catacomb
I roam

Looking for
A place to rest (JER 6:16)
I find none
I'm so oppressed (ISA 53:7)

I live in anxiety
Not knowing when (LK 21:34)
He will frighten
Me again (PROV 29:25)

Every waking moment
I'm focused on him
Makes my life miserable
I feel condemned (ROM 3:16)

No way out
I'm trapped
This is torture
I don't think
I can endure
Any more (2COR 1:8)

Lord where are you?
I'm in so much pain (JER 15:18)
Just like when
I was a little girl
This is insane

To live through
That terror again (JOB 9:34)
Under this stress
And strain
All my energy is drained

Please help me Lord
I need Your power (EPH 3:20)
In this
Very painful hour (HEB 12:11)

You've promised
To hear me
When I

Cry out to you (PS 18:6)
You've promised
To see me
All the way through (PS 145:13)
The darkest tunnel
Ever imagined (2SAM 22:29)

I'm counting on You
To rescue me (PS 31:2)
I want to feel safe
I want to feel free (PS 118:5)

I lift my hands
Toward Your
Most Holy Place (PS 63:4)
Protect me
With Your everlasting arms
As I seek Your face (DEUT 33:27)

"The Lord is my light
And my salvation
Whom shall I fear?" (PS 27:1)
As I rely
On Your strength Lord
I can persevere (JAS 1:3, 4)

Thank you Lord
For loving me (PS 13:5)
Because of Christ

This is my guarantee (ROM 5:8)

Jesus died
For my sins
To completely
Set me free (PS 146:7)

I'm no longer
Imprisoned
By my fears (PS 34:4)
Jesus Himself
Wipes away
All my tears (REV 7:17)

My heart is comforted
I'm filled
With Your peace (ISA 26:3)
Your everlasting love
For me
Will never cease (JER 31:3)

I am in awe
Of Your mercy
And Your grace (1PET 1:3)
To You
Belongs
All the glory
Honor and praise (PS 8:5)

4

Pennsylvania Dutch Heritage

"And now these three remain: Faith, Hope, and Love. But the greatest of these is Love" (1 Corinthians 13:13, NIV).

Relatives from Pennsylvania

My Mom would tell me stories of our Pennsylvania Dutch relatives. I found a plaque that is part of my heritage. It is a beautiful hex design that says, *"Dear Lord, Thank you for letting me live and laugh again, but please don't let me forget that I cried."* This has been hanging in my kitchen since I got married in 1970 as a reminder of the tradition and culture of my ancestors but also reflects my personal recovery journey through life.

I wanted to know more about my heritage so she gave me the assignment to research the Pennsylvania Dutch at the library.

Legendary Pennsylvania Dutch Hex Signs

"We grow too soon oldt and too late schmardt." "Outen the lights onct." "Throw Papa down the stairs his hat." "Fill the pitcher, the milk is all." "Let's walk the street down." "The hurrier I go, the behinder I get."

> This is the language of the Pennsylvania Dutch, a quaint sing-song combination of German and English. The Pennsylvania Dutch people are actually not Dutch at all, but German. Hex Signs were first

seen painted on the sides of barns, stables, and houses of the Pennsylvania Dutch and used to decorate homes and barns as a religious symbol and "good luck" for the farm. Today the signs are used merely to brighten their homes since the colors are so brilliant and flamboyant (Wikipedia, Pennsylvania Dutch, 2015).

I'm glad I have something in my home that reminds me of the legacy of my ancestors.

Love and
Romance

Sun, Rain
and Fertility

Welcome

Goodwill and
Abundance

Pineapple
Welcome

Home Blessing

Marriage

Friendship

Child Blessing

Birthplace

Although I was raised in Southern California, my birthplace is Allentown, Pennsylvania, made famous by the singer, Billy Joel, in 1982. Although I only lived there as a baby, the stories passed down to me by my mother told me all about where I come from.

"Allentown is a town in Northeast Pennsylvania about forty five minutes away from the Pocono Mountains" (Songfacts.com, 2015, para. 1). Allentown's economy wasn't doing very well once the steel factories began closing down. This didn't affect my parents because they worked in a cotton mill, but it affected my grandparents greatly.

Both my parents were born and raised in a smaller town near Allentown called Emmaus, Pennsylvania. They came from large families, both having eight siblings each. I have many aunts, uncles, and cousins still living in the surrounding towns.

Summer Vacation to My Hometown

My first contact with my Pennsylvania Dutch family occurred during a summer vacation when I was thirteen. My mother had gone back to work in a factory specifically to save enough for her and me to go to Pennsylvania. It took her two years to save enough money for the four day long train ride across ten states, 2,687 miles to Chicago, then another train to Pennsylvania. Flying was not an option because it was too costly for our middle income family. Dad drove us to the Union Pacific train leaving Union Station in downtown Los Angeles. It was my first trip outside California and my first train ride. We could only afford a regular rail fare with coach class seats which reclined for sleeping. They supplied pillows and blankets for our comfort, but I was too excited to sleep, so Mom and I played Gin Rummy to pass the time. We ate our meals in the dining car. I thought it odd that nothing ever spilled while we ate when the train boasted going fifty mph. When we reached Harrisburg, the capitol of Pennsylvania, the train rides were over. We then boarded the Greyhound Bus for the eighty one miles left to go to reach Allentown.

Mom hadn't seen her parents since she left Pennsylvania twelve years ago. Now it was 1960 and I would be meeting my grandparents for the first time. All their children and grandchildren called them Memmy and Pappy. At the ages of sixty four and seventy four, they spoke English most of the time, but when they got into a hot argument, they spoke Pennsylvania Dutch. They were trying to spare me the angry words they were saying, but I could tell they were quarreling. At thirteen I understood more than they thought I did.

Pappy was always the instigator but Memmy gave it right back to him. I guess that's where my mom learned to bicker with my dad when he started arguing. That's all she knew and what was modeled for her.

My grandparents lived in the State's first public housing project called Hanover Acres located in Allentown.

> It opened in 1939 the fifth public housing project in the U.S. and the first in Pennsylvania. The 322 brick-veneer homes were heralded as an example of what the country needed during the Great Depression: public housing for low-income workers. However, the barracks-style homes are considered outdated and small by today's standards. Demolition began in 2006 with families being relocated and a new development took its place (Soper, 2006, para. 4).

While my grandparents were alive, this was their home. They had struggled so long waiting to become eligible for Hanover Acres. At last they moved into the projects in the early 1950's. In 1953, Memmy wrote my mom a letter where she described her new home:

I have a two story four room house with a lovely bathroom and bedroom upstairs, a back and front lawn, no cellar, and no attic. It has a small apartment size gas stove with four *burners and a small Westinghouse refrigerator. The house is lovely and cozy. We pay $36 a month for rent with heat, lights, and gas furnished. Now that Pappy is working as a janitor and making $50 a month, we may have to pay $44 rent, but that is cheap. He works three hours a day five days a week.*

I saw where they lived and spent a month during the summer of my thirteenth birthday with them in that four room house. They were married for almost fifty years by then and had been through so many rough and painful times. Having nine children presented many challenges including housing and feeding all of them. But now their children were grown and gone leaving Memmy and Pappy living alone.

Being cantankerous and crotchety in their old age was understandable as Pappy became bitter after having been laid off and only able to get odd jobs here and there for short times. He worked the longest at Lock Ridge Iron Furnace in neighboring Alburtis.

The fires of the furnace were extinguished forever in 1920. Parts were dismantled and sold for scrap and the place fell into ruin. Restored in 1974 covering some eleven acres, Lock Ridge Park is open for visitors to tour and as many as three thousand come to enjoy the tour, craft shows, and square dancing. Slide shows and a motion picture of the history of Lock Ridge are also presented. Lock Ridge Furnace still stands as a silent reminder of immigrant determinism to build an industry and leave a legacy (Wikipedia, Lock Ridge Furnace 2015, para. 2).

Lock Ridge Furnace

Lock Ridge Iron Furnace in the 1870's

Lock Ridge Furnace
(Wikipedia, 2015)

Pappy's Drinking

Although I don't know exactly what Pappy did, I know he was a laborer. Pappy was lost without his job. Memmy wrote my mother a letter:

> *It is a lot of suffering for the person who is around a mixed up person. I hope your son Lamar understands his wife needs help. No one knows it better than I. Today Pappy is moping around. He is getting so thin. I can't have no conversation with him at all. It's pathetic but I still pray.*

Drinking beer every day was all Pappy could do to cope. Memmy wrote to my mother complaining about her troubles with Pappy:

> *Pappy drinks so many beers. He's polluted almost every day. I guess you know what that is like (referring to my dad's drinking). Pappy's getting old and as cranky*

as heck, which he always was. He hates children, mostly his grandchildren. When he's polluted he plays with the neighbor's kids, which I don't understand.

I know he was an angry, bitter man who took out his troubles on Memmy. And although they would get on each other's nerves, they were still quite lovable to me. In spite of her troubles Memmy had a good sense of humor and loved to laugh. I watched her laugh until she couldn't catch her breath and no sound came out of her mouth. I remember one day at lunch we were making our own sandwiches while seated at the kitchen table. Memmy looked around for something and couldn't find it, so she asked, "Where does my lettuce live?" Mom and I immediately looked at each other then looked at Memmy. She burst into laughter and we all joined in. We laughed all the more just watching her silent laugh.

Another time that summer all the relatives gathered for a family reunion. It was so odd to hear them talking and saying things such as, "Do you want to go to the store, say?" What the heck does that mean? I finally figured out that was just a word added on to the end of their sentences to emphasize what they were saying. Pennsylvania Dutch; strange language indeed!

My newly found family loved music and used "homemade" instruments such as a jug, a washboard, ukulele, and guitar. It was so much fun for me, who had never seen anything like it before. They were such a fun-loving group as well, laughing and joking about the weirdest stuff, like the women taking their purses and putting them on top of their heads imitating Carmen Miranda dancing to the music. Mom and I had watched old black and white movies on television and knew exactly who Carmen Miranda was.

She was a Portuguese-born Brazilian samba singer, dancer, Broadway actress, and film star who was popular from the 1930's to the 1950's. Nicknamed "The Brazilian Bombshell" Miranda was noted for her signature fruit hat outfit she wore in her American films. By 1945, she was the highest paid woman in the United States (Wikipedia, Carmen Miranda, 2015).

Memmy and Mom

Relatives, Mom and Memmy

It was so much fun getting to know these quirky Pennsylvania Dutch people who became my beloved family. I enjoyed being with them. Three years later in 1963 when I was sixteen, I eagerly looked forward to my next and last visit to Allentown. A month long vacation just didn't seem enough time so I took advantage of every moment. For the three years in between my visits, I had continued to write my cousins getting to know them better. It truly was a reunion for me. Of course Memmy and Pappy were just as eager as I to see each other again, especially after Memmy and I wrote letters getting to know each other better. Secretly, I know Pappy liked me, even though he was gruff to everyone else. I just hugged him and loved him just the way he was.

Memmy's Letters

1963

Ever since I was born, Memmy had written me letters and postcards which Mom had saved to give me. Preparing for our visit, Mom gave me those letters to read. I still have them today and re-read them from time to time to remember the essence of who Memmy was and her experiences with Pappy. In one letter from 1957, Memmy revealed her character to me through a letter when she wrote to my mom:

Mom and Me Age 16

I was glad when you told me of your troubles with your oldest son, Lamar. I was so speechless and helpless after I read your letter that I started to eat and eat until I realized what I was doing. When I get anxious I eat. I wish I could do something to help. I can and will pray for you. I know how you feel about Lamar. You can't turn him out. I hope he realizes that his innocent little children need him.

I feel so sorry for children. If I had the

money, I would open up a home for children. I would have all my employees treat the children like they were their parents. Children need the parents' love, not their money. I was sorry many times that I whipped my children. I think back about different times and whippings I gave them, but I always loved them. Maybe I didn't show it much but, I surely did all I could and still would. But I was crying and praying for forgiveness for punishing them. Then I thought I heard in my thoughts, but I only whipped them when they were naughty. I guess you did the same with your children.

I hope and pray Lamar gets a job and goes back to his family. Maybe Lamar could go in the service. That way his wife would have support. Maybe he would appreciate home life again. But who am I to give advice? It was only my opinion.

So I will close with love and a prayer. I pray for all my children and grandchildren almost every night. I also ask God for a better life in my house. I am asking God for an awful lot. Bye now, pleasant dreams. God bless you *and best of luck.*

Write soon,

Mom

My Memmy's heart came shining through her handwritten words in these letters. I am very grateful for the amazing gifts she has passed down to me including insight into my mother's world, the abuse my Mother endured and hence my own. It seems history repeated itself. My grandparents were abused, and they in turn abused their children. My parents knew no other way and so they repeated the dysfunctional family system. Nothing was ever talked about or new skills taught or modeled for them to be any different with me. And even for half my life, I did the same thing until I found recovery and therapy. I learned a new way of being with my family. It's never too late to go back and do the repair work. Broken relationships can be healed and forgiven.

These letters from my Memmy really helped me to understand my heritage which has always been important to me. The Hex Signs which I've always thought were interesting are now a reminder of where I came from. I'm passing the letters as well as the plaque with the Hex Sign and prayer on it to my children to share with their children.

Pappy passed away first in 1965 when I was eighteen. He died of cirrhosis of the liver and although that was sad, I did not have the same emotional connection for him that I had for Memmy. I think I am like my grandmother in many ways that I never understood until now. I loved her dearly and grieved her loss deeply two years later in 1967 when she passed of complications from diabetes after having both her legs amputated.

I'm so grateful that I got to meet them both and spend some time with them getting to know them better before they passed. These are times I won't ever forget. I'll always remember my Memmy and Pappy with loving affection, and my quirky Pennsylvania Dutch family.

Memmy and Pappy

Relatives, Mom, Memmy and Pappy

5
My Childhood Religion

"The choice to heal through connections starts with our connection with God. Changing our behavior, doing the next right thing, and choosing to do what is right are ways we can strengthen our connection to God" (Arterburn, 2005, p. 25).

As I look back on my life, it was my Mom who took me to church and Sunday school every week in the Lutheran church. I fell in love with Jesus at the age of three. *"Jesus loves me this I know…"* …how I loved that song. I thought as a child, He was the only one who truly did love me.

Lutherans only baptize babies, and my Mom had already baptized me as a baby while we still lived in Pennsylvania. I actually was baptized in St. John's Church in Emmaus, PA, on August 2, 1947, when I was one and a half months old. My parents and my two older brothers, ages seven and fourteen witnessed the baptism. St. John's is still there.

There was no nursery back then, so as a three year old, I sat between Mom and Dad in church. She gave me a pen and a bulletin to write on to keep me occupied. After church I went to my Sunday school class while my parents went to adult Bible study. My teacher taught the Bible with the help of a flannel board and felt cutouts. The fabric props were used to recreate some of the greatest stories in the Bible which made the stories even more interactive and memorable than reading a book. I loved those Bible stories. I truly am a visual learner. This was my life every week.

As I grew older, I guess I got tired of going to church every Sunday. When I balked about going, my Mom would say, "You're going to church no ifs, ands, or buts! And that's final!"

Eventually my Mom became my Sunday school teacher. She was harder on me than she was on the other kids. I had to memorize Bible verses perfectly and of course I did. I was always good in school... ...getting mostly A's and some B's.

When I turned twelve, it was a given that I would go to Catechism class for two years memorizing Martin Luther's Small Catechism, all 206 pages. It is a book of instruction in the form of questions and answers containing the chief parts of Christian doctrine, the Ten Commandments, the Apostles' Creed, the Lord's Prayer, Sacrament of Holy Baptism, Office of the Keys and Confession, and Sacrament of the Altar (Holy Communion). I memorized every question and answer verbatim.

This was all in preparation for Confirmation. Confirmation is the rite by which a baptized person renews her/his baptismal vow, publicly confesses her/his faith, and is received into communicant membership by the congregation. This was a really big deal in the Lutheran Church. My Confirmation Pledge -- I pledge this day:

To make diligent use of the Bible in private and public worship. To attend the Lord's Supper (Holy Communion) frequently for the strengthening of my faith in the forgiveness of my sins. To witness for Christ in all I do or say, because He has called me out of darkness into His marvelous light. To seek the company and companionship of my fellow Christians and work with them in the holy task of spreading the Gospel. To pray regularly for myself, for my fellow Christians, and for all mankind. To live every day as though Jesus died yesterday, rose today, and is coming back tomorrow. To lay my sins on Jesus the spotless Lamb of God, and daily repent of the evil I have done and the good I have failed to do. To look forward in faith to my Lord's return, when He shall take me and all believers to Himself in Heaven.

But first, I had to go to a public examination in front of the congregation to see if I understood the Lutheran teaching and knew the Bible and catechism well enough to be confirmed. The examination was a cinch for me... ...I knew that book backwards and forwards perfectly... ...but I was still nervous only because my Mom was sitting there watching and listening for just one mistake. The pressure was on. I think back to what a heavy load I was carrying and that coupled with all the pain of past abuse I thought was my fault. It was just too much to bear for a young person.

I came through with flying colors and easily passed the exam. Then on Palm Sunday, which was the traditional day of Confirmation, I stood up in front of the whole congregation and dedicated my life to Jesus, renounced the devil and all his works and ways. My life verse given to me on that day was 1 Thessalonians 5:23-24: "And the very God of peace sanctify you wholly; and I pray God your whole spirit and soul and body be preserved blameless unto the coming of our Lord Jesus Christ. Faithful is He that called you, who also will do it."

My Confirmation Certificate states: This certifies that Ardith Wilfinger having received a thorough instruction in the sacred teachings of the Christian religion as found in the Holy Scriptures and confessed by the Lutheran Church and having vowed before God and this Christian congregation to be faithful unto our Lord Jesus Christ and His saving Gospel was received into communicant membership in Peace Lutheran Church at Pico Rivera, CA, by the solemn rite of confirmation on the 26th day of March, A.D. 1961, Paul L. Lemke, Pastor.

That day I became a Christian and it was a vow I made to God and everyone that I was new; a changed person. I was fourteen and really did not fully understand what I was doing. It was an obligation that I had to follow my Mom's religion, but you know I actually wanted to at that point because I loved Jesus and wanted to put a smile on His face. I really wanted to hear Him say, "Well done, my child!" On Confirmation Day, I know I was different from the other kids because they were joking and laughing in church, but I was serious.

This was important to me so I told them, "Be quiet! We're in God's house and this is an important day." Wow, I was in awe of God and the bigness of who He is compared to little me.

So I really am grateful to my Mom for my religious beginnings. It was such a firm foundation of my beliefs today. What has changed for me over the years that I have matured and grown in my faith *(from nudgings from the Lord)* is that I have given up a "religion" and gained a close and personal relationship with Jesus Christ, my Savior and Lord. There is a huge difference between the two. I know because I lived through them both. This book is going to be a reflection of the life experiences that allowed me to move in the direction that God had planned and purposed for my life. I'm so grateful to God for that.

When I was fourteen, my brother Greg came back to live at home. He began to be active in church activities again. He had learned how to play the guitar and was writing songs. He was much different toward me now, more loving and supportive. I liked this side of Greg and I certainly didn't ask questions why this was now happening.

That summer there was a talent show at church. He asked me if I would sing a folk song with him while he played the guitar. I was ecstatic. My mom even made us matching vests. He wore black slacks, and I wore a black skirt, white shirts and these plaid vests. He sang the melody and I harmonized. We practiced so many times until we both knew the song perfectly. On the performance night, we had three verses to sing. The first two went perfectly. But on the third, he forgot the words. He looked to me who knew the words perfectly and I carried the song until he remembered and picked it back up. We didn't skip a beat and nobody knew the difference. I felt proud that he looked to me for help. It was a wonderful night and a wonderful memory for me.

Here is the song we sang.

"A well-known American folk and gospel song likely originating in the early 19th century about a plaintive soul on the journey through life" (Wikipedia, Tillman, 2015, para. 1).

The Wayfaring Stranger
by Charles Davis Tillman, 1891

I'm just a poor wayfaring stranger
While traveling in this world of woe
Yet there's no sickness, toil, nor danger
In that bright land to which I go
I'm going there to see my Father
I'm going there no more to roam
I'm only going over Jordan
I'm only going over home

I know dark clouds will gather 'round me
I know my way is rough and steep
But golden fields lie out before me
Where God's redeemed shall ever sleep

I'm going home to see my mother
She said she'd meet me when I come
I'm only going over Jordan
I'm only going over home

I'll soon be free from every trial
This body asleep in that churchyard
I'll drop the cross of self-denial
And enter on my great reward
I'm going there to see my Savior
To sing His praise forevermore
I'm only going over Jordan
I'm only going over home

6

Looking for Love

"God's plan and His ways of working out His plans are frequently beyond our ability to fathom and understand. We must learn to trust when we don't understand" (Bridges, as cited by Neal, 2012, p. 147).

As I look back on my life, it's important for me to tell the stories of my marriages and my children.

My First Love

The first time I experienced love occurred when I was a very naïve twenty-one year old. Living away from home for the first time, I was single and living the party life. Every weekend my co-workers and I went nightclubbing.

Our favorite was a dance club in Long Beach, CA, called "The Clubhouse." My girlfriends and I patronized this particular club because it was the local hangout for sailors since we loved guys in uniform and loved to dance. This place was perfect. Sawdust on the floor, picnic tables with benches and popcorn to munch on, not quite what was expected at a "nightclub," but it was casual and we loved the atmosphere. A live band, strobe lights, and a disco ball changed the ambience and we were transported to Cinderella's ball. No hard liquor was allowed, but the beer and wine that was offered sure enhanced our dancing. Of course, all the guys had chug-a-lug drinking contests to vie for beer champion, but I could out-drink most of the sailors there.

Songs popular on the radio that year were "I Heard It Through the Grapevine" by Marvin Gaye, "Proud Mary" by Ike and Tina Turner, "YMCA" by The Village People, and my personal favorite, "Celebration" by Kool and the Gang. The band was pretty good sounding just like the original artists. Being there consistently every Friday and Saturday night, we had gotten to know the band personally and they often played our requests. We were always the first ones on the dance floor. It was 1969 and we were there to party with the U.S. Navy.

Bill was a handsome man with a slight moustache. Being just a little taller than I, he was a good dance partner for me and I liked that. His physique was average. Light brown curly hair cut short completed the package. Nothing I could put my finger on, yet there was this connection between us. Even though he was dressed casually in civilian clothes, I knew he was a sailor. After all, this was *their* "hangout."

I remember the first time Bill asked me to dance. It was a slow dance and he held me close and whispered in my ear, "Don't I know you from the class of '65?" I laughed because it was such a corny line, but there was something about his voice, deep, yet he almost spoke in a whisper which gave me goose bumps. Later on, I was shocked to find out he was from Mississippi since he had no audible southern accent. I was raised in California, so no way were we in the same high school graduating class even though we were the same age. Nevertheless, I still loved that line and it became our conversation opener whenever he asked me to slow dance.

Bill and I soon became a twosome. People at "The Clubhouse" recognized us as a couple. We had five glorious months together dancing every weekend until 2:00am, then going to Denny's to eat breakfast. As is the custom of sailors assigned to a ship, the ship must go out for cruises. It was time for Bill's ship, the *U.S.S. Long Beach (CGN-9)*, to leave for a six month Westpac overseas tour of duty. I would laugh when Bill explained to me all about his significant ship.

> *The Long Beach* is the only American cruiser since the end of the Second World War that is entirely new from the keel to the top of her mast. She is the only cruiser to be propelled by nuclear power with the box-like superstructure which houses her sophisticated electronic equipment. *The Long Beach* was a nuclear-powered guided missile cruiser. She was the only ship of her class and the third Navy ship named after the city of Long Beach, California (Wikipedia, The Long Beach, 2015).

I remember going on the ship many times to visit Bill and even to take a family cruise to Catalina and back. It was a thrill for me to be a part of his Navy life. It was interesting to me to follow what happened to his ship once he left it. Ships don't last forever and it was sad to hear what eventually happened.

> The Long Beach was commissioned September 9, 1961. The ship deployed to Vietnam during the war and served numerous times in the Western Pacific, Indian Ocean, and Persian Gulf. She was celebrated as the first nuclear-powered surface warship in 1961, but just over thirty years later, nuclear power was deemed too expensive to use on surface ships smaller than an aircraft carrier. Instead of refueling her, *The Long Beach* was decommissioned May 1, 1995. What remained of the hull after the superstructure had been removed was sold for scrap in 2012 at Puget Sound Naval Shipyard, Bremerton, Washington (Wikipedia, The Long Beach, 2015).

Bill's Ship, "The Long Beach"
(Wikipedia, 2015, p. 1)

As the day approached for the ship to leave, I was not laughing. His wonderful ship was taking him far, far away from me to the war in Vietnam. I became very antsy. We loved each other and had talked about wanting a baby together, but nothing was ever said about marriage. Now he was leaving. Would he come back to me? We vowed we would be loyal and wait for each other. I knew I could do it, but could he? I wasn't sure. This might be his final departure. My heart stopped. I hoped this would not be goodbye because I loved him so. I hadn't dated in high school, so he was my very first love.

I gave Bill my high school graduation picture. On the front I wrote:

Darling, my love is yours forever!

I signed it *Ardith Gail,* as he affectionately called me. On the back I wrote:

The sweetness of your love will remain with me long after this picture fades. Although we both graduated in '65, it took us four years to meet. But it only took one month to cultivate a love that will keep our stream of life "rippling" 'til the sands of time run out.

Ripple was the name of our favorite wine. I continued:

I love you, honey bear, and I can never tell you enough or how much you mean to me.

Yours (literally), Ardie 6-8-69

The day arrived for us to say our last farewells. We hugged and kissed so many times I lost count. I was crying hysterically and he said, "Sweetheart, six months will be over before we know it and I'll write as often as I can. Together, we'll get through this time we'll be apart. I love you very much."

Then the last call came for him to board the ship. I couldn't stop crying. The ship pulled out slowly while he stood at the rail waving to me. I stayed on that pier crying relentlessly while watching the ship. Gradually the ship became smaller and smaller until I could barely see it in the distance. Then in an instant it disappeared and had vanished. I was devastated. I could not believe that the love of my life was gone. I became so hysterical that I couldn't drive my car home for over an hour. "What if he doesn't come back to me?" I couldn't imagine living without him.

Normally my bodily cycle is like clockwork. One week after the ship pulled out, my period was overdue. What's wrong with me I thought? I was still crying over missing the man I had fallen deeply in love with. Maybe my daily emotional outbreaks were causing my body to overreact physically. Three months went by and still no period. I couldn't figure it out. I had no morning sickness at all, so I could not be pregnant. Then one hot summer day I was with my mother in downtown Los Angeles. A crowded room on the fourth floor of a building with no air conditioning was stifling. I hadn't eaten breakfast that morning. When I stood up, my knees buckled and I began to faint. My mother caught me and sat me down. Quickly grabbing her hankie and dipping it in the cold water she was drinking, she put it on the back of my head as I bent over. She said, "Next time, eat breakfast! You could have fallen and hit your head!"

Now I thought I better go to the doctor. He confirmed that I was pregnant. *"Oh my God, what am I going to do now? I can't tell my mother. I'll never hear the end of it."* What is she going to say? Being a staunch Christian, she will certainly judge me. I could hear her words "You know the Ten Commandments. Sex is wrong outside of marriage. What were you thinking? How could you do this evil in God's sight?" I knew all of that was true. I didn't want to hear it from her. Actually I really wanted Mom to understand what this was like for me and why this happened, but we never really talked on that level. Everything that ever happened to me got swept under the carpet never to be talked about again. She knew Greg had sexually molested me because I told her when I was a little girl. That abuse was the driving force in my life, affecting every decision I made about the world, who was not safe, and what I could expect from men. Somehow I felt guilt and shame over what I allowed to happen when I knew it was wrong. I grew up feeling flawed, stained with sin, and unworthy of anything but abuse.

When I was nineteen, my life became a series of sexual encounters. I didn't care at that point. I certainly wasn't following God. I felt too ashamed to match up to my mom's expectation of dating and marrying a Christian.

Now I am in love with an alcoholic just like my dad, and I'm pregnant. In my mind I wasn't aware of the fact that I really wanted Mom's acceptance and approval and chose this behavior unconsciously because she was pregnant before she married my dad. Surely she'll understand *I thought*. Besides, Bill was an alcoholic like Dad, and she'll realize what this was like for me. Had I told her I want to marry him only because I love him, she would have advised against it because he drinks too much and isn't a Christian. Now that I'm pregnant, the right thing to do is marry him.

So actually the first person I told in the family was my oldest brother Lamar. I knew he would understand. He hugged me, but did ask "What are you going to do?" When I told him I was waiting to hear from Bill, he said, "You're going to have to tell Mom." I knew he was right. I left feeling doomed that I would have to face the music with Mom, but not today.

It was torture keeping the secret. I didn't dare tell my girlfriends because I worked with them. If they unintentionally let it leak out at work, I would be humiliated and ashamed from the gossip it would create at my workplace. This was still a time when having a baby out of wedlock was a scandalous thing. I wanted to get married first, then have a baby. I didn't even know if Bill was coming back to California, how he felt about this baby, or if he wanted to marry me. What was I to do? While he was with me, we openly talked about how excited we were about the possibility of having a baby. I was never concerned about marriage and we didn't talk about that at all. I guess I was afraid to bring it up for fear of driving him away. I just knew he would marry me had I found out I was pregnant before he left.

We had stopped using protection, when we were serious about having a baby. He had professed his love to me, but maybe that was for me to continue having sex with him. I was so mixed up and didn't know what to do. I really didn't know how Bill truly felt about me. I was so insecure since he had sex with many other girls before me and was used to playing the field.

I had heard horror stories of sailors having a girl in every port and now that I was pregnant with his child, I didn't know how he would react to the news he was going to be a father.

I decided to write him a letter. This was 1969 before the age of computers, emails, cell phones, and texting. Good old snail mail was all we had to communicate to each other. So a handwritten letter telling the love of my life we were having a baby together was all I could do. Oh, how I struggled to write the exact words that I hoped would excite him. I would write something, crumple it up, throw it away, and then start another letter. I did that repeatedly as I wrestled with what to say. It took me many agonizing days to write that letter, but finally I finished it. The only true test now was to send the letter telling Bill the news and wait for his reaction.

Sometimes letters took weeks to get to his ship, then more weeks until a letter was sent back to me. I had already received several letters from Bill saying how much he missed me, so I was eager to hear his reaction to this particular letter.

Every day I would check the mailbox for a letter in his familiar handwriting. Every day I was disappointed. Tormented, I wondered, "When will I receive the letter where I will know how he feels? What if he doesn't want to marry me? What will I do if I don't hear from him at all?" I couldn't even comprehend the possibility that I would be forced to have this baby on my own. It was too much to bear. I had to hope for the best and wait.

Waiting caused me such anguish like sitting on pins and needles every single day. My head was swimming with all these questions I had no answers for. At work I couldn't concentrate. At home I couldn't relax.

Then one day Bill's letter actually arrived one month after I had sent him mine. At first I couldn't open the letter. There was no way to tell what his answer would be. I will just die if it's not the answer I so desperately needed to hear. My hand was shaking as I opened and read what he had written:

> *Oh my darling, how exciting that I'm going to be a father. I went to the Chaplain right away to ask for emergency leave to come home to marry you. I can hardly wait, sweetheart, to hold you in my arms.*

This was music to my ears!

What I had hoped for, longed for, was going to come true. We were going to be a family, Bill, myself, and sweet little baby Carla Ann.

Me and Bill Haley

Now that I was sure of Bill's love for me and that he wanted our baby, I could finally face the music and tell my mom. I was still fearful and knew what she would say, things I didn't want to hear, but I had to tell her.

I went home to see her and Dad, and waited for the right moment when she and I were alone.

"Mom, I have something to tell you. Bill is on his way home to marry me because I'm pregnant."

She was silent, then said sadly, "Ohhhhhh."

I hung my head in shame. She continued, "This is so wrong. How could you sin against God? You know the Ten Commandments. Your marriage is starting on the wrong foot and your sin will follow you. You'll have so many problems to overcome. I don't know what you were thinking!"

In boldness I said, "You should know, you were pregnant with Lamar when you married Dad!"

"And I've been sorry for it ever since."

"Mom, it's going to be different with me and Bill. We love each other very much and really want this baby. We're going to be very happy!"

Mom was silent and let it go.

"I've got to go. I'll talk to you later."

Bill wasn't able to get off the ship until I was six months pregnant. We planned to go to a Justice of the Peace to get married. Mom had become supportive and tailored a white dress I had already, so it fit me. Then we drove to Long Beach to be married. We stayed in a honeymoon suite, while he enjoyed his cocktails. I didn't realize then how his drinking would be the downfall of our marriage.

What started as a sweet love story turned sour over the years. Bill and I have four children together over a span of fifteen years. Those were rocky years for me of course mixed with short times of happiness because of Bill's escalating drinking and affairs. Drinking and other women were #1 for him. My size has always been a struggle for me and I thought that if I lost weight, then my husband would give up other women and drinking. So I got thin. He got worse and I felt abandoned and alone. Bill went overseas and I thought he would divorce me for sure because he was so distant.

Feeling so lonely my girlfriend talked me into going dancing at the club in San Diego. I met a guy and I just wanted someone to love me, so an affair began. When he also left for overseas I couldn't stand being alone. I quickly went looking for someone else to love me. It's not easy for me to admit that I had two affairs back to back in 1974. We had only been married four years. I felt so guilty. I don't even know how I could turn my back on God but I did. I was very immature in my walk with Him and so easily fell into sin. I see now that the mistakes I made contributed to the deterioration of our marriage. It wasn't all one-sided.

One night in 1984 I came home from a TOPS (Take Off Pounds Sensibly) meeting, Bill was drunk and had broken vodka bottles on the kitchen floor and my typewriter also on the floor. He was passed out. I immediately took pictures of the damage and left the mess.

The next day Bill woke me up, "Clean up this mess!"

"No!" I said. So he grabbed my arm and pushed me to make me clean it.

Again I said "No! I'm calling Security" *(we were living in Navy housing on the base)*. He followed me to the wall phone in the kitchen and ripped it right off the wall!

"Okay, I'll go next door and use *their* phone." He immediately left the house to go to the ship. I didn't call Security, but I wish I had just to put his violence on record. But I was naïve and didn't know about these things. What surprised me was that I stood up to him for the first time. I had always been so compliant, not wanting to rock the boat.

Of course he said he didn't "remember" any of this and promised never to do it again. I believed him... ...because I loved him.

All of the evidence I had found previously, including letters from girlfriends, I completely ignored. I could no longer deny the truth.

It was 1984, I woke up one night to talking downstairs. Bill was on the phone. I listened.

"Oh honey I miss you too and can hardly wait to hold you in my arms again" Bill said.

What went through my mind was how could he say that to *her?* Didn't he mean it when he told *me* the very same thing? He was my first love and we had four children together. Don't *I* matter to him more than this *fling* he's having? I couldn't stop to dwell on my pain but knew I had to take action and stop this from continuing to happen.

That was the last straw. An anger so deep welled up inside of me. "Get out! And take the old car, leave the new one for me and the children. I'm getting a divorce!"

He complied without a word.

Later he tried to wiggle back in, but I wouldn't have it. It was the most painful decision I had ever made and I was crying every night, until I met Jeff. Bill was dragging his feet on the divorce because of his retirement. California is a 50/50 split in divorces. So I was entitled to 50%. He said, "Take 30% or else no divorce."

By this time, Jeff and I were in love. I cannot stand feeling any more pain, so I'd rather be in love. Then we found out we were pregnant. Of course I wanted the divorce over and done with or I would have fought for 50%. I just didn't want it to drag on any longer.

My Second Love

Jeff and I didn't start out with ideal circumstances. I was six months pregnant with Jenny and we were members of my family's church. This was the second time I had to tell my mother the news without being married first, not easy to do with a very religious mother. Besides, Jeff and I had to tell the Pastor and Elders of the church. We had to confess our sin, ask for forgiveness, and of course get married... ...which had to be done privately. We could not have showers, either wedding or baby. We had to write a letter to the congregation and it was to be read on Sunday after the church service. We chose not to be in attendance that Sunday. How humiliating to walk through this experience, but I did not want to be excommunicated from the church. We felt we had no choice.

Needless to say, our marriage was just as rocky as my first. After ten years and two more children, Jeff said he wanted out, it was mutual, and we divorced.

Me and Jeff Hamilton

The Divorce is Final

Divorce is gut-wrenching to anyone who's been through that wringer. How could anything good come out of such anguish, heartache, and pain? After experiencing two divorces I learned valuable lessons. When I overcome obstacles that are thrown in my path, my character grows.

When husband number two came to me about divorcing, he did so with a plan that, since he knew I had no biblical grounds to get a divorce, he would file and I could be innocent. I admit that was generous of him. He filed divorce papers in 1995, I had no clue how I would handle it all. How would I survive emotionally, let alone manage financially on my own? Terrified to be alone I had no one to rely on. For the first time in fifty years, I had no parents, no brothers, and no husband to help me.

With my bags packed, I moved out of the house and rented my own apartment. What a relief. Moss Creek Apartments appealed to me, becoming my unique *"Shangri-La,"* for its peaceful, soothing, and calm environment. The flowing creek with small waterfalls trickled throughout the complex. As I listened to the serene sound walking from the gate to my front door, I relaxed. During the day, living there delighted me but when night fell, my apartment became a menacing place.

Nightmares of someone breaking into my apartment haunted me and I felt powerless and vulnerable. Signing up for a self-defense class, I wanted to learn as much as I could to stand up for myself. The class called *"Model Mugging,"* is designed to empower women while teaching personal safety and self-protection.

Taking my turn that first night to face my *"male assailant,"* my heart pounded in my throat. My hands began to sweat. Not hearing the instructions given to me, I panicked. Sobbing uncontrollably, I froze. The group of women in my class rallied around to cheer and support me. The female instructor lovingly validated my feelings as she encouraged me to believe in myself, "You can do this, take back your power. Let your anger be your strength to fight off this attacker," she said. What seemed to come out of nowhere, rage welled up inside me and a loud "NO!" came from deep without my soul. I couldn't believe I was screaming

Model Mugging Self-Defense developed the original protective body armor described as the "padded assailant".

(Model Mugging, 2015, p. 1)

at the top of my lungs! My anger gave me the energy I needed to fight back and I won! Feelings of excitement and exhilaration flooded my body because I did it! Each week my self-confidence grew stronger. I discovered the ability to take care of myself in any situation that could possibly arise.

My support system grew as well as my confidence. Venturing out of my comfort zone, I learned to risk opening up to safe people. Learning to trust again in spite of past hurts, I made new friends. What a gratifying feeling to know that I can take care of myself. God will be with me.

Why Model Mugging?

What Makes The Model Mugging Program Different?

Model Mugging Self-Defense provides students the greatest impact in personal safety and overcoming personal fears of being assaulted through role model mastery. Many self-defense courses are simply comprised of a group of techniques without continuity between techniques, strategy, and the reality of effectiveness for women.

Other programs have copied our innovative teaching methods and padded assailant concept. A copy of a any program loses critical details where realism is diluted, safety suffers, and content is distorted. Model Mugging is the original Adrenaline Stress Training course, established from crime analysis, and organized upon Five Principles of Self-Defense©.

Rape defense eye strike applied full force during Model Mugging self-defense course.

There are many choices in self-defense and personal safety measures. Briefly, the Model Mugging curriculum is founded on researching thousands crimes, review of academic literature, martial arts, and decades of experience conducting reality based self-defense scenarios.

It is important that you assess your goals for personal protection when considering your options in personal protection and self-defense training.

(Model Mugging, 2015, p. 1)

After living alone and waiting almost a year for the final divorce papers to be signed, an all too familiar voice recorded a message on my answer machine. Jeff, my ex-husband stated, "The judge signed the papers. You're a free woman. Good Luck!" With those words came the finality of another failed marriage and another loss to be grieved.

The Divorce is Final
August 24, 1996

I feel alienated
Discarded
Now we have parted

The divorce is final
It's the end
Of the struggle
And conflict
Of where I've been

He said, "Good Luck"
As if I didn't
Have a chance
For a moment
I slipped into a trance

Then the shock
Of what's real
Happens
As the pain hits
I feel the sadness

I grieve the loss
And move to a place
Where God
Gives me the grace

To carry on
In spite of the loss
I take time
To reflect
And to pause

When the pain lifts
And reality sets in
I realize now
I can begin

To build a life
That's meaningful
For me
To be all
God created
And intended me
To be (EPH 2:10)

I don't know
What God
Has in store
Although one is closed
He'll open another door

And it will be better
Than I ever hoped
Far beyond the scope

Of my imagination (EPH 3:20)
Now I feel
The anticipation

Of exciting opportunities
Whatever they may be

Yes I have fears
To walk through
Whenever I experience
Something new

But today I have faith
God gives me peace

I can feel my feelings
And release

Them to God
He knows my pain
In His everlasting arms
I remain (DEUT 33:27)

Loved and supported
Cherished
Just for being me
I am His child
Precious
And free (1JN 3:1)

I'll Never Be The Same
December 10, 1996

I have no partner
I am alone
But my
Faith in God
Is all my own

Now I have
The opportunity
To have
A greater awareness
Of my spirituality

I can renew
My commitment
To walk closer
With God (HEB 10:22)
To walk the straight
And narrow path
Rather than the broad (MT 7:14)

Road that
Leads to destruction (MT 7:13)
My hunger
For material things
Doesn't satisfy (ISA 55:2)
When on someone else
I try to rely

I am hungering
To know and feel
God's presence and power (MT 5:6)

God
You are my hope
My soul opens
Like a flower (PS 42:5)

Fill me

With Your joy
And peace (PS 4:7)
Unconditional love
That will never cease (JER 31:3)

You alone
Created me
Sustaining my life
With breath and energy (PS 139:13)

The Spirit of God
Enlivens and restores me (PS 23:3)
You oh Lord
Are at the core
Of my being

You've given me
This talent
My poetry
I now bring (1COR 7:7)
Before You
To use me

As Your instrument (2TIM 2:21)
To help others
And give them
Encouragement (1COR 12:28)

In this stage
Of my life
I have no partner
The single life
Is not
What I prefer

But I am on a journey
And I know God
Walks with me (LEV 26:12)
His Grace

Transforms the impossible
Into reality (1COR 15:9, 10)

Faith serves
As a ladder
A tool I use
Every day (MK 11:22, 23)
I am part
Of God's
Glorious plan
He'll reveal it
As I pray (JER 29:11)

Thanks and adoration
Praise His Holy name (PS 30:4)
Yes I am alone
And I'll never
Be the same

God is the source
Of all I need (HEB 5:9)
If I keep
My eyes on Jesus
I will succeed (HEB 12:2)

He came to earth
As a baby
On that first
Christmas Day (MT 1:23)
To be my Savior
And His Father's Will
I obey (MT 1:21)

He laid down
His life for me (ISA 53:12)
And rose again
To set me free (ROM 4:25)

My heart sings

With joy
And happiness (PS 89:1)
Love and peace
Are what God
Created me
To express (1PET 1:22)

With God
All things are possible
If only I believe (MT 19:26)
And if I believe
Miraculous blessings
I will receive (MT 17:20, 21)

So I await
With eager anticipation
And look to God
With awe
And appreciation (JOB 25:2)

Wherever I go
Whatever I do
I am in God's
Tender loving care (PS 25:10)
And to be more
Like Jesus
Will be my
Daily prayer! (PHIL 2:5)

Re-discovering the God of my childhood in a new and different way, I realized I would be all right. After feeling so much heartache and pain when my marriage ended, my faith in God provided serenity. Accepted and loved just as I am, God loves me in a way that no *"man"* can. Yes I am alone, but I am at peace.

Life after divorce sucks! In my case the issues were pretty intense. This was my second divorce and I had given birth to six children. Two girls, Carla and Lori, were grown and on their own. Two boys, Brian and Matt, were now living with their father (my first ex, Bill) in Mississippi. And two girls, Jenny and Becca, ages nine and seven were left shuffling between two houses here in California. After ten years of marriage, my recent ex, Jeff, had moved in with his girlfriend when our house was repossessed. He married her the day our divorce was final. Now a step-mother for my girls was added to the mix. It was a great deal for me to handle as well as many losses to grieve.

Abandoned and Abused

June 14, 1997

He closed the door
And I was stunned
Once again
I felt abandoned
What a feeling
Of being disconnected
He turned away
From me
I felt rejected

I once was bonded
To this man
To meet my needs
That no man can (PHIL 4:19)

As a child
Mom and Dad
Weren't there
Nurturing comfort and love?
They had none to share

The loss that I experienced
Created a black hole
Of emptiness and pain
Grieving that loss
Is now my goal (JN 16:20)

For that wound
To be healed (PS 147:3)
For that hole
To be filled (ROM 15:13)

With God's
Never ending love
And grace (EPH 1:7)

Tender mercies
Shown
In wondrous ways (MIC 7:18)

How awesome
Is the gift
Of His Son (GAL 4:4)
Jesus Christ
There's no equal
Not one (PHIL 2:10)

He is The Way
The Truth
And The Life (JN 14:6)
He has ended
All my conflict
Chaos and strife (PS 7:9)

God's unmerited pardon
Is full and free (ISA 55:7)
Because of
What Jesus
Did for me

He gave
His precious life
On the cross (JN 19:17, 18)
So I could be saved
I'm no longer lost (LK 19:10)

His love is unfailing
He won't abandon me (PS 36:7)
The door
Is never closed
Jesus is the key (JN 10:9)

I have hope
I have love
And I have joy
In my heart (PS 28:7)
Because of
My Savior's promise
To never depart (MT 28:20)

The only security
I have is
His promises
Are sure (HEB 10:23)
It's the thing
That keeps me going
The only way
I can endure (PS 145:14)

People in my past
Have hurt me
Abandoned
And abused me
Brutally

My pain eases
As I grieve
Those hurts (JN 16:20)
God comforts me
With His tender
Loving words

"Your wounds
I will heal" (JER 30:17)
He knows exactly
How I feel (PS 34:15)

Today I am affected
By what happened
In my past

But God's
Pure unfailing love
Is continually steadfast (PS 57:8)

Gratitude
For what He's done
Envelops me (1JN 4:9, 10)
Daily
I give Him all the praise
Honor and
Glory (ISA 25:1)

My heart is overflowing
With love
To my Savior
And King (1 TIM 6:15, 16)
To Him alone
I forever will cling (PS 63:8)

I am uplifted
God's grace
Sees me through (HEB 4:16)
The hurts
Of my past
He always knew

Even before
They happened
That I would
Need His love (PS 17:7)
Which He continues
To shower upon me
From above (PS 26:3)

Through His people
We build
Each other up
Not destroy (EPH 4:12)
I'm grateful

I love God
My heart

Is full of joy (PS 28:7)

7

Single Again

"Whether you turn to the right or to the left, your ears will hear a voice behind you, saying, 'This is the way; Walk in it" (Isaiah 30:21).

I had joined the Single Parents support group at church to have a family of Christian brothers and sisters sharing in raising our children without a partner. We had fun outings with and without the children, which made it easier for me to deal with the challenges of parenting.

I was single for four long, painful years of waiting on my own terms, which really wasn't waiting at all, but doing, doing, doing. I was determined to find a *"man"* on my own without God's help. I tried all kinds of singles'

Me 1996

activities, personal ads, computer chat rooms, and dating all kinds of frogs to find my prince. It just wasn't happening. I even lowered myself to promiscuity once again, trying to fill the loneliness with sex. I was leading a secret double life and I don't know how God did not give up on me. But that's why His unconditional love, mercy, and grace are so valuable to me. He never gives up on us, no matter how far from God we've gone. No sin is unforgiveable. Believe me, I know.

My brokenness from childhood has been a major factor in the choosing of my partners over the years. Since my second divorce four years ago, there have been a number of ways that I have again tried to meet men: Christian dances, personal ads, coed recovery meetings, and most recently online... ...love at AOL.com!

I met a man. Everything clicked between us and we started to get to know each other on the telephone. Feelings inside me propelled me to continue even when I knew he wasn't a Christian. He said he was spiritual, so I justified to myself it was okay. He said the most wonderful things to me and the size of my body didn't matter to him. He saw me as I am on the inside and adored me. He was very seductive and I began to fall. We arranged to meet, and I was caught up in the excitement of what he was offering me; a romantic, sexual relationship. But God, in His grace, continued to send me messages from His Word, and from His people, my Christian friends who loved and accepted me, who also held me accountable. God convicted me to stop what I was doing.

Journal Entry

October 5, 1996

I am committed to living a purpose driven life for Christ. God has a plan and a purpose for me.

God Has a Plan

October 5, 1996

God what do You　　　　　　*You want me to be? (LEV 11:45)*
Have planned for me? (PS 40:5)
What is it　　　　　　　　　*I'm looking for answers*

I don't know
What to do (1SAM 14:41)
I've always
Looked to others
Now I'm looking
Directly to You (PS 105:4)

You alone
Know my heart
And how I feel (PS 26:2, 3)
Your will
I'm wanting You
To reveal (MT 16:17)

Give me
The power
To carry that out (EPH 3:20)
Strengthen my faith
Remove all my doubts (MK 9:24)

I love You Lord
I'm grateful for
What You've done (COL 3:16)
Especially
The precious gift
Of Your Son (ROM 5:17)

I'm here
Because
You created me (GEN 1:27)
Open my eyes
So I can see (PS 119:18)

Your plan
What You
Want me to know (JER 29:11)
Lead me
In the direction

You want me to go (PS 5:8)

I'm willing
I surrender
I accept Your Will (PS 40:8)
Your purpose
For my life
I want to fulfill (PS 138:8)

Today I have peace
Serenity and joy (PHIL 4:7)
That no problem
Or circumstance
Could ever destroy (2COR 7:4b)

God chose me
To be His own (2THES 2:13)
He's always
With me
I'm never alone (MT 28:20)

So whatever
He chooses
For me to do (PS 37:3a)
He'll be right here
Beside me
To see me through (ISA 43:20b)

God has a plan
I know and believe (ISA 14:24)
He's putting it
In place
It will be achieved (ISA 14:24)

Thank You Lord
Your Will
Not mine (1THES 4:3a)
Your love for me
Continues to shine (PS 13:5)

Me to be *(EPH 2:10)*
I am Your child
Precious
And free *(EPH 5:1)*

I will grow
To be all
You created

Journal Entry
November 19, 1996
My struggles with addictions continue. This is so painful for me. I wish I had an answer. It is a fight between good and evil, between flesh and spirit.

Flesh and Spirit
November 19, 1996

The good
That I would
I do not

The evil which
I would not
That I do *(ROM 7:19)*
How am I
Ever going
To get through

The temptations
Of the flesh
It's like a web of sin
I feel enmeshed

Struggling
Fighting
This is a war
Between flesh and Spirit
God I implore

You

To strengthen me
During this time
It feels
Like a mountain
I must climb

I have no skills
My flesh is weak
Lord Your strength
And power I seek

You alone enable
And empower me
When temptations come
You help me flee

When I want
To give in
To the moment
And when I do
I am so penitent

I am so sorry

In my weakness
My walk with You
I regress

The forces of evil
The powers
Of the dark (EPH 6:12)
Are trying hard
To make their mark

I need
The full armor of God
For me to stand (EPH 6:11)
I need You Lord
Please hold my hand

Walk with me
During this dark hour
God's Word
The sword of the Spirit
Gives me the power (EPH 6:17)

The shield of faith
Extinguishes

The flaming arrows
Of the evil one
God has promised this
It will be done

In His mercy
And His grace
He loves me
No matter what
In His heart
He has a spot

For me
I am
The apple of His eye (PS 17:8)
To God alone
I will praise
And glorify

His holy name
And sovereign majesty
His love for me
Has set me free (1JN 3:1)

Journal Entry

November 21, 1996

I hate this! I said NO! I set a boundary! I ended a relationship, a very
unhealthy relationship which is not an easy thing to do! I am giving up
something I liked and wanted. Do You know how difficult and how
painful that is, Lord? Why do You require so much of me? It's so
difficult to be abstinent from unhealthy relationships especially when it
feels so good in the moment. Instant gratification feels good.
Discipline and self-control are so very difficult for me. I can't do it
alone. I need You, Lord. I need Your strength and power. I'm
trusting Your promises. I'm trusting You will be with me. I'm trusting
You will help me in my struggles. I'm trusting You will give me the

patience I need to wait for Your timing. I'm trusting You will give me the patience I need to wait for *"the one"* You have planned for me. Please give me the strength that I need.

I Have a Need in Me
November 21, 1996

My cry
For You Lord
Is real
Your perfect love
For me
You continue
To reveal

I'm stubborn
Impatient
And I disagree
Your love
Understands
Accepting
The worst
In me

I have
A need in me
Only You can fill
When I take time
To be still

I know You
Are the great
"I AM" (EX 3:14)
You are
My Shepherd
I am Your
Precious lamb (ISA 23:1)

The gratitude I feel
Just isn't adequate
Your Mercy
And Your Grace
Are infinite

You are
The Alpha and Omega
The rock
Of my salvation (REV 22:13)
You've given me
Freedom
From the curse of sin

You've provided
A Savior
Jesus Christ
The Lord
Because He died
On the cross
And rose again
Heaven
Is my reward (ROM 4:5)

To You
I give all
My thanks
And praise
I am in awe
Of Your wondrous
Mysterious ways

You make
Your presence
Known to me
Father
Son
And Spirit
The Trinity

My faith
Grows stronger
Every day
And even
When I'm weak
And turn
And walk away

You gently nudge
And remind me
Your way is best
You give me
Peace and solace
I can rest

To You
Belongs the glory

Holy is Your name
You never change
You're always
The same (HEB 13:8)

King of kings
Lord of lords
Prince of Peace (1TIM 6:15)
Someday
At the
Wedding Feast

You will come
For Your bride
In You alone
I find
My true delight

Because I have
A need in me
Only You can fill
I will follow You
And just as the
Angels in Heaven
Gladly do Your Will

Journal Entry

May 5, 1998

So much has happened today. In this moment of time, I am at peace even though I am experiencing loss. Loss of a fantasy and loss of a dream. Loss of the desires I wanted to fulfill my own way, rather than wait on God's choice in God's time. I came close, so very close to being seduced down a path that in the moment would have satisfied the desires of my flesh but would have been hurtful to me. And in the end, I would still have felt unfulfilled and longing for more.

Ardie Hamilton Sarris

He Wasn't a Christian

May 5, 1998

I'm hurting Lord
In the deepest part
Of my soul *(PS 39:12)*
I was trying
Once again
To fill up that hole *(PS 42:2)*

The one inside me
That feels so empty *(1PET 1:18)*
I just wanted
To feel his arms
Around me gently

He sounded so good
And kind
And caring
It didn't matter
How my body looked
Or what
I was wearing

He was sincere
And wanted
A relationship
With me
But because
He wasn't a Christian
It was never
Meant to be *(2COR 6:14)*

And I struggled
Because
I wanted it so much
And I wanted to feel
His tender touch

A desire welled up
Inside me
I almost satisfied
I was willing
To turn from God
Go my own way
Then hide *(JON 1:3)*

But God
Convicted me
To run from sin *(1COR 6:18)*
And definitely
Not to indulge
Or give in

I stopped
Before the deed
Was done
Not by my strength
But only through
God's Son *(1COR 1:25)*

"I can do
All things through Christ
Who strengthens me" *(PHIL 4:13)*
And I will
Continue to grow
To be all
He wants me to be *(2PET 3:18)*

God loved me
So much
Not to let me
Go my own way *(JON 2:1-9)*

I praise Him
Honor Him
And thank Him
As I pray (PS 96:1, 3)
I surrender
My will to His
And humbly obey (1THES 4:3)

My life is Yours Lord
Use me in Your plan (JER 29:11)
My heart
My soul
My voice
My hands

I dedicate to You (MT 22:37)
Jesus has changed
My life

From old to new (2COR 5:17)

I feel joy
I feel strength
God's love
Is very real (ROM 5:5)
I'm on the straight
And narrow path
I'm beginning to heal (PS 41:4)

I hear my
Father God
Calling to me (1THES 5:24)
I am loved
And cherished
Precious
And free (ISA 43:4)

Journal Entry

June 2, 1998

I had stopped talking to this man who wasn't a Christian, only to pick up the phone and start up again. I knew I was playing with fire, but Satan is so provocative and alluring and hits me at my weakest, most vulnerable spots; when I'm lonely and hurting. It's not easy dealing with such power, but God is more powerful. I don't need strength. God provides that. I just need to be obedient. It took a second effort after meeting this good-looking man who desired me even at my weight and age. It would have been so easy to give in to the desires of my flesh, but God kept sending messages to me convicting me that what I was doing was wrong and not His plan for my life. I thank and praise Him for not giving up on me even when I wanted to go astray.

After many months of living with this secret, God convicted my heart to stop this uncontrollably compulsive sexual behavior on the computer, on the phone, and finally in person on a date. I ended my AOL membership on the computer and stopped putting personal ads in the newspaper, and stopped calling these men. I was so relieved to stop this double life. I asked for God's forgiveness and knew He was working in my life.

God, You are so kind and good to me and so very awesome, Lord. You shower me with unconditional loving kindness filled to overflowing with grace and mercy. Thank You, Lord, I give You praise and honor and glory. *"Holy, holy, holy is the Lord God Almighty who was, and is, and is to come. With all creation I sing. Praise to the King of kings! You are my everything. And I will adore You" (Riddle, 1999, p. 1)!*

I wish I could say that I've been stronger since then and avoided temptations with men. It's been a constant struggle, and sometimes I've fallen flat on my face and given in to sin. I've had to pick myself up each time, ask for God's forgiveness, which He freely gives because of His Son, Jesus Christ. I've had to be willing to learn another valuable lesson God is still trying to teach me, such as, don't wait until I am in the heat of the moment to come up with a plan for how to say no to sex. It takes planning, effort, and a willingness to remove myself from tempting situations or better yet, not to put myself in them in the first place. A valuable key is to stay close to my brothers and sisters in Christ for their supportive friendships, be real with them about what I'm struggling with, and stay accountable to them.

I have come to know a deeper relationship with God as I've drawn closer to Him through everything I've experienced. I have a Savior, Jesus Christ, who was willing to die on the cross for me so I could be forgiven and have life everlasting. That fills me with so much gratitude and love. Because of that love, when I long for a man, I listen to Jesus when He asks me, "Do you desire him more than you desire Me?" "Is the sexual pleasure of the body worth more to you than the pleasure I give to you in intimate communion with Me?" "Did I not show you how much I love you by giving My life for you?" "Will you surrender your heart, mind, soul, and body to Me, until I bring the mate I have planned for you when the timing is right?" These are the questions Jesus wants me to answer before I make my choices to live a godly single life.

I am compelled to continue this journey starving the flesh and feeding the Spirit.

Journal Entry
June 2, 1998

This is the message that my Single Parent's friend gave to me to uplift me during this time:

Be Satisfied With Me
by St. Anthony of Padua

Everyone longs to give themselves completely to someone,
To have a deep soul relationship with another,
To be loved thoroughly and exclusively.

But to a Christian, God says,
"No, not until you are satisfied, fulfilled, and content
With being loved by Me alone,
With giving yourself totally and unreservedly to Me,
With having an intensely personal and unique relationship with
Me alone.

Discovering that only in Me is your satisfaction to be found,
Will you be capable of the perfect human relationship
That I have planned for you?
You will never be united to another until you are united with Me,
Exclusive of anyone or anything else.
Exclusive of any other desires or longings.
I want you to stop planning, to stop wishing,
And allow Me to give you
The most thrilling plan existing...one you cannot imagine.
I want you to have the best.
Please allow Me to bring it to you.

You just keep watching Me, expecting the greatest things.
Keep experiencing the satisfaction that I am.
Keep listening and learning the things that I tell you.
You just wait.
That's all.

Don't be anxious.
Don't worry.
Don't look at the things others have gotten or that I've given them.
Don't look around at the things you think you want,
You just keep looking off and up to Me,
Or you will miss what I want to show you.

And then, when you're ready,
I'll surprise you with a love far more wonderful than you would dream of.
You see, until you are ready and until the one I have for you is ready,
I am working even at this moment to have both of you ready at the same time.
Until you are both satisfied exclusively with Me and the life I prepared for
you, you won't be able to experience the love that exemplifies your relationship
with Me.

And this is the perfect love.
And dear one, I want you to have this most wonderful love,
I want you to see in the flesh a picture of your relationship with Me,
And to enjoy materially and concretely the everlasting union of beauty,
perfection, and love
That I offer you with Myself.
Know that I love you utterly.
I am God.
Believe it and be satisfied!

Journal Entry

May 23, 1998

What does anything matter if I have no one to share it with? I'm so lonely, Lord. I'm hurting. You know how much I'm hurting. How long must I wait, Lord, how long? If two people, a man and a woman are connected to You and growing in Your Word, they can certainly grow together in love for each other and in their love for You and serve You together. I want that so much, Lord. I want a godly man whom I can respect, who will respect me and respect my choices to walk in Your Will. I want a godly man who loves You as much as I do and thirsts for a deeper relationship with You. I want a godly man who gets excited when he sings praises to You because he feels in his heart how awesome You are.

Come Walk With Me
May 23, 1998

Lord come walk
With me a while
And hold me
Until once again
I can smile

I'm hurting right now
And feel so lonely
The pain is deep
I think
No one loves me

This is old stuff
From my past
My heart is heavy
My eyes are downcast

My tears are flowing
I need Your arms
Around me
Compassionately
Loving me
Unconditionally (PS 103:8)

Let me feel
Your love for me
Right now
As I walk
Through this desert
Show me how

To take each step

To get through
Each day
You alone
Have the answers
And know the way

I love You Lord
I trust what You say
Your Word is sure
Your promises come true (HEB 10:23)
No matter
What happens to me
You always come through

With glorious things
I can't even imagine
Especially
The gift of forgiving me
All my sins

Sending Your Son
Jesus to be my Savior
My relationship to You
To restore

So that today
I can walk with You
Feel Your love
And healing
And have
My hope renewed

Lord You are so awesome
I give You
Praise and glory

I am Your child
I feel precious
And free (1JN 3:1)

I'm Rebelling Again
February 17, 1999

I'm
In this place again
When will I learn Lord?
When?

I'm running away
Instead of
Coming to You
I'm rebelling again
I know this is true

Why do I think
That I can
Run and hide?
Is it my selfish
Rebellious
Stubborn pride?

That I think
I can do this
On my own?
I continue to reap
What I have sown

Discontent
Dissatisfaction and grief
I'm tired of struggling
I need relief

I don't want
To rebel

But that's exactly
What I do
Cleanse my heart Lord
I want to be renewed (PS 51:2)

I need Your strength
My flesh is so weak
Humble me
And give me a spirit
That is meek

I want to follow You
Your way certainly
Is best
You alone
Have the peace
That will give
Me rest (PHIL 4:7)

You hold me
Securely in Your gentle
Loving hands (JN 10:27,28)
You are the only one
Who truly understands

How I feel
And what I
Really need
Is reliance
On a Savior
Who has

Already guaranteed *(ROM 5:8)*

My freedom
From eternal death
And the curse of sin *(1JN 4:9-11)*
I continually
Find my sinful flesh
Falling in *(ROM 7:18,19)*

I know I'm forgiven
Jesus Christ
Has set me free *(PS 146:7)*
I'm a new creation
In Christ
He now resides
Inside of me *(2COR 5:17)*

Empower me Lord
To live a
Christ-like life *(2COR 5:20)*
To be filled
With Your
Holy Spirit

And not fall
Into strife *(EPH 5:18)*

Mold me
And make me
Break me
If You must *(ISA 64:8)*
So in You alone
I will completely trust *(PS 13:5)*

In all things
And in all ways
God lovingly
Holds the key
I'm His child
I'm His treasure
He'll not
Let go of me *(DEUT 26:18, JN 10:27,28)*

I can relax
I am loved
I feel precious
And free *(1PET 2:4)*

Journal Entry

June 6, 1999
"Be still and know that I am God" (Psalm 46:10).

You are my God. I love You, Lord, and I worship You!

Lord, You say to be specific in my prayers. I desire a godly man who puts You first, who will respect me because he loves You, and wants to walk a Christ-filled, Christ-centered holy single life, giving God the glory for self-control. I want a spiritually mature godly man who prays about anything and everything even our dating, wanting to do all things right in Your sight even when his flesh says something else. I want a man who is learning and growing, who is on a path of processing his feelings, patterns, and behaviors. He doesn't have to be perfect, Lord.

You know I'm flexible. Give me patience, Lord, to wait on Your perfect timing. Strengthen my resolve to do this Your way. Thank You for Your grace to convict my heart when I keep going astray. I'm sorry, Lord, I am so weak and foolish, wanting my own way, my own will and giving in to my sinful flesh. I am sorry, Lord, please forgive me. I know You do, but I just need to say it. Change my heart, Lord. Cleanse me from all unrighteousness. Heal my brokenness that keeps driving me to old coping behaviors. Fill me with Your Holy Spirit, with Your love that never ends. Keep me on Your path. Give me a desire to do Your Will and surrender my life to Your hands and Your timing. I want to obey. I want to be fully Yours, Lord, in a way I've not known before or even wanted before today. I want to be in close communion with You, truly intimate with You. Be my friend, my Best Friend, my lover, my husband, my all in all who gives me life, hope, freedom, and eternal life with You in heaven. I love You Lord with all my heart!

Since having a change of heart and attitude, I put my energy into finding a small group through Saddleback's Singles Ministry.

8

Looking for Belonging

Jesus said, "I am leaving you with a gift—peace of mind and heart. And the peace I give is a gift the world cannot give. So don't be troubled or afraid" (John 14:27, NLT).

Needing Connection

Healing from childhood abuse has been a painful journey yet a rewarding one. I didn't know I needed healing because I didn't know I had been abused. I felt I had sinned. Abuse was not a word I knew but sin I understood from Sunday school. Sex without marriage was a sin. What Greg did to me was sex. And I went to him and said yes. I had a secret that I didn't dare talk about. The family didn't like airing out our dirty laundry in public. We certainly didn't talk about any of it within the family. My dad was an alcoholic *"but"* he just drank too much. My parents raged *"but"* they just argued a lot and every family argues.

My dad and two older brothers were into pornography. One of my brothers molested me *"but"* that's because men only want one thing... They're *just men,* or so my mother would say.

I wasn't happy and I cried a lot. I knew something was wrong, but I didn't know what it was. I thought there was something wrong with *me.* My childhood wasn't healthy or happy. Nobody loved me.

I'm suffering with loneliness. I am alone. I have many friends but I'm not connecting with them most of the time. I do this on my own, daily living life not connecting with people. People in the past hurt me and rejected me. That's why I don't reach out, or when I do they are critical and judgmental like my family when they gave me advice, or else my friends have got major problems stuck in their own pity party victimhood. I don't feel accepted or loved because of my size and weight, so I keep at a distance. Loneliness and emptiness the two feelings I have are the two main ingredients that propel me to my addictions of food obsession and overeating. Then shame and guilt set in. I'm living for the flesh, wanting the adrenaline rush of excitement that makes me feel alive, avoiding or escaping my unpleasant current reality of feeling rejected and alone.

I have a need to belong, to feel connected to others. I don't know how to attach to another person in a healthy way. I never dated as a teenager, I was fat—so food became my escape from the pain of rejection and loneliness. What was I trying to escape? My reality—an alcoholic father, and a domineering, controlling mother, both full of rage. They were loving and affectionate to each other and to me one minute—fighting, arguing, and yelling ugly, hurtful remarks to each other the next. My dad was always calling my mother names. He never directed name calling towards me, but the names he called my mother hurt me, as if he had said those words to me. I loved my mother very much. Their fighting and arguing scared me so much. I was terrified when my father got drunk. I didn't know what that meant either, but it terrified me.

Lord, I'm tired of carrying this burden of shame and guilt around. I want to be free of my past. I want to be ready for a healthy relationship, the one You want to bless me with. I don't want to take this garbage into a new relationship. I want to be fully available to love and trust the godly man You have in mind for me. I want to give of myself freely without reservation, without triggers from the past getting in the way.

I lived with the family secret for forty years. I married an alcoholic/sex addict just like the men in my family. I had four children with my first husband. I still wasn't happy. It took my son's repeated acting out to get my attention that something was wrong with this family too. His therapist began to work with me to uncover the family secret from my childhood.

Through these trials and struggles, I reached out for help. After so many unhealthy human relationships, I finally made a healthy choice in a personal relationship with Jesus Christ. Although it's been a long and painful process, God has been with me every step of the way.

> *"Consider it pure joy, my brothers, whenever you face trials of many kinds, because you know that the testing of your faith develops perseverance. Perseverance must finish its work so that you may be mature and complete, not lacking anything. Blessed is the man who perseveres under trial, because when he has stood the test, he will receive the crown of life that God has promised to those who love Him" (James 1:2-4, & 12, NIV).*

Although I've struggled with these verses for many years, I've come to a deeper realization of just what they mean. The joy I consider is not because of the pain of the trial or test, but in the fruits I reap. When my faith is tested, I do develop perseverance so that I can grow to be mature and complete. That is my goal to finally have stood the test so that I may receive the crown of life *(Heaven)* that God has promised me.

I heard it said best by Charles Stanley:

> We need to understand that these verses are not telling us to be happy in our pain, but rather to rejoice in the blessings that accompany suffering. The word consider is an accounting term that means "to evaluate." When we look at hardships from God's perspective and place the proper value on them, we can rejoice in the beneficial outcome, even while experiencing pain. Regardless of the difficulty's source, we can know that the Lord wants to use it to test our faith and thereby produce endurance and spiritual maturity. In every trial, He has hidden a beautiful and precious character gem, but whether we receive it depends upon our response. Those who really want to

be transformed into the image of Christ can rejoice in the many benefits that accompany suffering. None of us want to experience pain, but since it's an unavoidable reality in this fallen world, why not respond in a way that produces eternal benefit? Let's not waste our suffering (Stanley, 2011, p. 42).

Codependent's Anonymous (CoDA)

I was already active in Twelve Step groups to further my recovery from abuse. Codependent's Anonymous (CoDA) was an enormous source of support during my failing marriage and subsequent divorce. My group even helped me move my furniture and belongings, while listening and being with me in my painful time of grieving my losses.

While exploring what it was like to be single again, I met a guy in CoDA. We immediately became friends and enjoyed spending time together. We talked openly about everything and loved to go dancing at the CoDA dances with all our friends. It was a wonderful time for me.

Our friendship developed into an affair which lasted six months. I fell in love with this man and couldn't be happier. The only problem was that he didn't love me in the same way. He ended the relationship and I was devastated.

After feeling the heartbreak of the healthiest relationship I had ever experienced, I began feeling the need to find a new church home. I needed God in such a real way but didn't know where to find Him. I had outgrown what I call secular recovery, Twelve Step groups who understood God in such general terms as the *"God of my understanding."* *Higher Power* could be anything in your imagination. I needed the solid base of Christian recovery, if there was such a place.

Saddleback Church was that place. My prayer was answered.

Gifts From My Higher Power
November 25, 1995

My Higher Power
Jesus Christ
Has blessed me
Beyond compare

It's easy to see
His gifts of love
Comfort and care
Never giving me more
Than I can bear (1COR 10:13)

I'm never alone
He's always
By my side
Ever directing me
As my guide

My relationship
With Him has grown
It's changed
From what I've known

That too is a gift
I've received
So much more
Than I believed
Could've been possible

In recovery
My life continues
To be a discovery

Of how awesome
My Higher Power Jesus is
I strive to submit
My will to His

Joy is mine today
I talk with God
And I pray

For healing
From a painful past
All I can do
Is just hold fast

To His
Never-ending care
And love
He's all I need
And He's enough

To see me through
Whatever will be
Will be His
Precious gift to me

Journal Entry
August 26, 1996

Okay God, I'm coming to You again about this. I need help because I don't know how to let go of this desire that I have. I don't want to be alone. I will make due because I have to right now. It's not what I want. You say come to You with the desires of my heart. I'm doing the footwork. I'm going out to meet new people, especially Christians. I'm trying to get to know these people at Saddleback Church. I want a relationship. You know the kind I want: A healthy, nurturing one with someone who knows the value of recovery and therapy. Someone who is autonomous, not depressed or codependent to the best of his ability, and in touch with his feelings. Is that a tall order, Lord? My recent partner had those characteristics but was not a Christian. I do want a Christian, Lord, so where else can I find one but at church? I don't want a rigidly, religious guy, but a *godly* man... ...one who knows You intimately, and desires to grow more like Christ each day. This church could possibly be the place to find someone open to a healthy, growing relationship. Help me find the answer, Lord!

Journal Entry
August 27, 1996

Even though I am enjoying this new church, I still don't fit in. I'm like an outsider pressed against the window looking in. I want to fit in, to belong. This is really scary. I'm risking to enter into this area again, where I was wounded by other Christians and by a Pastor from my past. I'm willing to try because I want connection with other Christians so much. I'm trusting God. I trust the process. And I know the process takes time.

The Process Takes Time
August 27, 1996

I still don't fit in
It's not a race
For me to win

The process takes time
Feels as if
There's a mountain
To climb

To let people know me
As real as I can be

It's a risk
For me to trust
Safety
And support
Is a must

I'm willing
To pay my dues
I have nothing
To lose

And everything to gain

We've all been hurt
We've all felt pain

Sharing our sorrows
Healing begins
And in the process
We can become friends

God's gifts of love

Mercy and grace
Abound in this place

He gives me strength
To walk through my fear (PS 46:1, 2)
And I'm happy
And grateful
He led me here

Journal Entry

August 27, 1996

I've joined Saddleback's Celebrate Recovery on Friday nights. What a joy!

> The purpose of this program is to allow us to become free from life's hurts, hang-ups, and habits. By working through the eight recovery principles found in the Beatitudes with Jesus Christ as your Higher Power, you can and will change! You will begin to experience the true peace and serenity you have been seeking, and you will no longer have to rely on your dysfunctional, compulsive, and addictive behaviors as a temporary "fix" for your pain.
>
> By applying the biblical principles of conviction, conversion, surrender, confession, restitution, prayer, quiet time, witnessing, and helping one another, which are found within the eight principles and the Christ-centered 12 Steps, you will restore and develop stronger relationships with others and with God (Baker, 1998, p. 8).

A requirement of fulfilling my step study group and becoming a co-leader, I was to give my testimony. This personal testimony of faith was to include my life before surrendering to Christ and how I became a Christian. The final point was how the Lord has been working to change me into a mature child of God. The process included my own personal editing to cut the testimony down to twenty minutes. Then another leader cut out more of what wasn't needed. The final approval was from Pastor John Baker, pastor of Celebrate Recovery. When he was satisfied, the date was set, and I began to practice reading what I had written. I was so nervous, but I knew this was a milestone for me to reveal to the world what was done to me in the past and all my hurts, habits, and hang-ups. In the 90's the turnout on a Friday night was usually fifty. This night was special including people from other churches here for a conference. I would be sharing to over five hundred! I certainly was nervous! I had to share my feelings in my journal and then in a poem.

Journal Entry
November 7, 1996

I have come a long way. From feeling like an outsider looking in, to someone who now feels accepted and loved by my two small groups at Saddleback Church. My Single Parent "Boundaries" group and my Celebrate Recovery ACA *(Adult Children of Alcoholics)* group have impacted my life in such a very special way. I have bonded with the friends that God has brought into my life. They are precious to me and are "The Treasures of My Heart."

The Treasures of My Heart
November 7, 1996

I am in awe
Of how God works
In my life *(PHIL 1:6)*
Bringing me healing
Overcoming the strife *(PS 147:3)*

I've been through
So much
But I'm never alone *(MT 28:20)*
And with each struggle
And experience
I've grown *(1THES 1:3)*

God gives me
Wonderful gifts *(ROM 6:23)*
His Word
Continues to uplift *(COL 3:16)*

My heart
And my soul
Moving me to tears *(PS 62:5)*
Taking away
All my doubts
And all my fears *(PS 34:4)*

Bringing special people

Who touch me
In a special way
When I can't put what
I'm feeling into words
They can pray (JAS 5:16)

How uplifting
And reassuring to me
That we can minister
To each other
Is the key (1THES 5:11)

To loving
Compassionate
Nurturing care (COL 3:12)
The joy of fellowship
Not found elsewhere (1JN 1:7)

We are united
God's love
Through Christ
Keeps us close (COL 3:14)
And to each of us
Many gifts He bestows (1COR 12:8-10)

God
Is the source
Of my love
Joy and peace (JN 14:27)
As I draw closer
To Him
They will only increase (HEB 10:22)

He alone
Unites us
One friend with another (PROV 17:17)
As I open up
To being vulnerable
I discover

Connection
And a closeness
I've not known before (GAL 6:2)
And all
Because I was willing
To explore

Take a risk
Open up
Share and reach out (ROM 1:12)
The joy I feel
I just want to shout (PS 47:1)

I'm glad I'm here
God brought me
To this place (PS 66:5)
I feel love
There's a smile
On my face (ROM 12:10)

In this group
We each have a part (1COR 12:25, 26)
All of you
My friends are
The treasures of my heart

Journal Entry
March 5, 1997

God, I know You're here actively participating in my life. I know and believe that. I do thank You for not only what You've done for me in the past and what You're doing for me now, but also for what You are going to do for me in the future. I know it will be wonderful. I ask that You be with me now as I contemplate some major changes in my life. Seems like everything I've been going through is major change. I am learning, growing, risking, and changing. These things don't come easy for me. So much of the time I carry the wounds of my childhood and I feel so inadequate, as if I just can't do it. I'm almost fifty years old and I feel like a child sometimes, as if I'm learning things for the first time. Give me strength and give me courage. Give me the willingness to try new things, even when I'm that scared little girl inside. Help me to move through the difficult times.

The Promise of Recovery
March 12, 1997

Recovery
Right now
I don't feel it
And one more time
I'm willing to admit

I'm powerless
And my life
Is unmanageable
It feels
As if my whole life
Needs an overhaul

My addictions
Are flaring
Out of control
Because of past abuse
There's a hole
In my soul

I'm trying
To fill
That hole again

It's deep
Overwhelming
And feels as if
There's no end

In sight
No light
At the end
Of the tunnel

All I want to do
Is scream and yell

This is too hard
I can't do this
If only
There was an easier
Softer way
I wish

I cry out in pain
I need help
I'm alone

This is more difficult
Than anything
I've ever known

Reaching out
To tell the truth
I feel guilt
And shame
But the hope
And promise of recovery
I want to claim

So I trust the process
And take
One step at a time
I don't look
At the mountain
I must climb

But focus on taking
That first step
Which means
Having to accept
God has a plan
For me (JER 29:11)

He wants to rid
My life of the debris
From past abuse
Hurts and habits
He wants me

To have the benefits
Of healing

Wholeness and peace
And unconditional love
That will never cease

I'm not alone
God walks with me
He gives me
The strength
To be all
He created me
To be

I give thanks to God
For guiding me
When I seemed lost
And every
Line of defense
Was crossed

I give thanks to God
For loving me
When I thought
I was unlovable
And felt like
An empty shell

I give thanks to God
For filling me
With peace

When I felt
There was none
To be found
For showing me
When I'm lying flat
On the ground

I can look up
To God
For the help I need
To withstand
The storms of life
I can succeed

Of recovery come true
I can be me

Being willing
Surrendering
My will to His
Is the key

A child of God
Precious
And free (1JN 3:1)

To having the promise

Journal Entry

March 8, 1998

Lord, what a blessing tonight, for me to be a participant in an incredible evening of worship and praise and the awesome power of prayer at Saddleback's Maturity Conference, *"Praying on Purpose."* You continue to touch my heart in a profound way. Thank You for Your mercy and grace. I cannot find the words to express the love in my heart for You. Lord, I love You so much. I give You honor and praise and glory. You are God Almighty! You are holy! How awesome it is to know You and have a relationship with You. What a gift! It is a precious gift that You chose me to be Your child. You created me. You know me, every part of me. You know my thoughts even before I think them. I'm so unworthy of Your love. Maybe that's why it means so much more to have Your love. You love me anyway, not because of me, who I am, or what I've done, but because of who You are, my sovereign, majestic Creator, Redeemer, Lord, and Savior. You call me by my name. You have prepared a mansion for me in Heaven. You are waiting for me to join You and spend eternity with You. You sent Your Son Jesus, who died and shed His blood to save me from my sins and make Heaven my home. You have a plan and a purpose for me. Prepare me for Your Will and lead me where You want me to go. Where You lead, I will follow. Give me the strength and the courage to lay down anything that stands in the way of my fulfilling Your Will, whatever it may be, be it laziness, fear, a man, a relationship, fun, thrills, things, or food. I don't want anything to get in the way of a closer relationship with You. I love You, Lord. I want to be close to You every day for the rest of my life. I've wasted so much time, Lord. I've foolishly wasted my time. I'm sorry, Lord, and I know You forgive me. Praise, honor, and glory to You, Lord. You are an awesome God. "I see the Lord seated on the throne, exalted. And the train of His robe fills the temple with glory. And the whole world is filled with His glory. Holy, holy, holy is the Lord" (Falson, 1993, p. 1)!

Journal Entry
September 5, 1998

Pastor Rick continues to ask us *(his members)* pertinent questions to help us grow in our faith. What's important to me in my life? What are the essentials I need for my well-being? What are my priorities *(what are my personal needs such as people, pets, places, things, activities, conditions, etc.)?*

I need to be safe in order to explore, learn, grow, and be creative. That safety includes structure and security. Things I can count on like a job I enjoy, productivity, support group, and friends I can trust and count on. I need to feel productive, accomplish something worthwhile and meaningful. I need nurturing people in my life that I can connect with emotionally. I need to take time to be in God's beautiful creation of nature which connects me to God and soothes me. I need to be close to God, to have a spiritual connection with Him to nourish my soul. I need to be me and to have a voice. I need freedom to live my own life.

The Road to Recovery – Eight Recovery Principles, based on the Beatitudes, by Pastor Rick Warren, Saddleback Church as taught in Weekend Messages (1998).

Realize I'm not God; I admit that I am powerless to control my tendency to do the wrong thing and my life is unmanageable.

Earnestly believe that God exists, that I matter to Him, and that He has the power to help me recover.

Consciously choose to commit all my life and will to Christ's care and control.

Openly examine and confess my faults to myself, to God, and to someone I trust.

Voluntarily submit to every change God wants to make in my life and humbly ask Him to remove my character defects.

Evaluate all my relationships. Offer forgiveness to those who have hurt me and make amends for harm I've done to others except when to do so would harm them or others.

Reserve a daily time with God for self-examination, Bible reading, and prayer in order to know God and His will for my life and gain the power to follow His will.

Yield myself to God to be used to bring this Good News to others, both by my example and by my words.

Celebrate Recovery
September 5, 1998

"Celebrate Recovery"
Has been
An incredible journey
For me (COL 3:16)
My Higher Power
Jesus Christ
Has absolutely
Set me free (PS 146:7, 8)

From life's
Tormenting hurts
Hang-ups and habits (PS 6:2, 3)
Being on
The road to recovery
Has given me

Many benefits (JN 8:32)

Through these
Christ-centered
Twelve Steps
I have found
A place
Where I can step
Out of denial
And into
God's amazing grace (ROM 3:23, 24)

My addictions
Were out of control
I was powerless to stop (ROM 7:18)

When at last
I hit my bottom
I am ready to drop

To my knees
And ask God
For the help I need (PS 32:3-5)
Isolated and empty
In excruciating pain
I now concede (JER 4:19)

I can't do it
On my own
I need
A power greater than I (PS 107:13, 14)
When I let go
Of pride
I am ready
To comply (JAS 4:10)

God has the power
To heal my wounds
From the past (JER 30:17)
Only He can
Make the changes
In my character
That will last (2COR 5:17)

God loved me
So much
He sent
His only Son (2COR 5:19)
Jesus Christ
My Savior
There's no equal
No not one (JN 8:12)

He died for my sins
I'm completely forgiven

Set free (ROM 8:38, 39)
To be all
God created
And intended
Me to be (PHIL 2:13)

I'm no longer
In chaos
Or separated
From my Higher Power (ISA 59:2)
He's always
Walking by my side
He's with me
Every hour (MT 28:20)

I made a decision
My life is
In God's hands (ROM 12:1)
I'm learning
To trust in Him
I know He understands (PROV 29:25)

All my doubts
Anxious thoughts or fears
That are taboo (PS 46:1)
Here He gives me tools
To use that continue
To carry me through (JAS 5:16)

Every problem
Every circumstance
There's nothing
He can't do (MT 19:26)
What He has done
For me
He will do for you (COL 2:13-15)

Peace and serenity
Are gifts

God gives to me (PHIL 4:7)
Through working
This Christ-centered
Program of recovery (1JN 3:9)

I am calm
I have joy

I've been restored to sanity (PHIL 2:13)
God loves me
I'm His cherished child
I feel precious
And free (1JN 3:1)

Journal Entry
November 7, 1998

Lord, help me find the fulfillment I seek, to achieve more than I ever dreamed. I am a capable and creative person. I thank God for the abilities I have. I let God be God in my life. With that trust I have peace of mind. God is the source of my life; the source for living a rich and fulfilling life. God's message of assurance is the soothing rhythm of the morning tide, letting the peace of God wash over me. He whispers a message of love and peace. He's the Author and Finisher of my faith. He who began a good work in me will complete it. God has given me grace. God is my Provider. God is all I need. God satisfies the longing of my soul. When I thought I could find no peace, He filled me with serenity. When I thought I did not matter, He showed me how precious I truly am.

The Story of my Life
November 7, 1998

The story of my life
Is beginning
To unfold
As I prepare
For my testimony
To be told

It's scary
Yet exciting
To share
My experiences
With you

I am stepping out
In faith
To let God
Work it through (PHIL 1:6)

Trusting His plan
Not mine
Is the key (HEB 11:40)
I can do
All things
Through Christ
Who gives me

The strength I need (PHIL 4:13)
And His peace
That passes understanding
Is guaranteed (PHIL 4:7)

I am breaking
The silence
Allowing no excuse
I am telling the truth
Of my childhood abuse

Negative messages
Continue to break through
That could
Hold me back
If I allow them to

But God
Has a plan
And purpose for me (JER 29:11)
And I'm willing
To be His tool
Gratefully (2TIM 2:21)

He's given me
So much

He's provided
All I need (MT 6:8)
Only His power
And strength
Allows me to proceed (PHIL 4:13)

With this next step
I can stretch
And grow
His Grace to me
Will freely flow (HEB 4:16)

I am calm
I have peace
My mind is at ease (PHIL 4:7)
All those negative messages
I can now release

And rest in His arms
As He loves
And cares for me (DEUT 33:27)
Giving God
The glory
As I give
My testimony (ROM 4:20)

Journal Entry

November 9, 1998

Wow! It's the day after giving my testimony at "Celebrate Recovery." What an incredible experience! I did something that was impossible to do on my own. I told the story of my life, from my childhood abuse, to my own acting out behavior, and then to what God has done in my life. That was not easy to do. It was exciting, and scary too. I broke all the rules that my "family" instilled in me. All the shame and guilt that I ever felt about my actions immediately came out. Anxiety churned inside me. But you know what; left on my own I couldn't have done it. God took over. He gave me the courage and the strength I needed. He filled me with His peace and a calm came over me that is without explanation. It was a God-thing! And God used the body of Christ to build my confidence and keep me connected spiritually and emotionally. Each time I would reach out, be honest about what I was feeling, someone would pray for me. Every time I asked for support, someone was there holding me up. These are not accidental coincidences. God has a purpose for each and every one of us in the body of Christ, to build us up as believers and draw us closer to God and to each other. What an awesome process! What a privilege to be part of God's glorious plan. I thank and praise Him for who He is, an awesome God! I was lost without Him, and I am His own cherished child, purchased and won by the shedding of blood by Jesus Christ, God's only begotten Son, for **ME**. Thank You, Lord Jesus for loving me so much that You would give Your life to save me from eternal death. My sins are completely paid for; erased. I'm washed clean; white as snow. What a precious gift and so undeserved. That's why it is a *gift*. That's grace. I give You praise, honor, and glory. You are King of kings, and Lord of lords. You are my God, holy and worthy of my praise. There are no other gods before You. You are the one and only Almighty God whom I love and serve. Glory to God in the highest!

My process continues as I cry out to God with my feelings and rely on what I know to be true of God. He's gracious and merciful beyond compare!

9
My Spiritual Journey

"The best and most beautiful things in this world cannot be seen or even heard, but must be felt with the heart" - Helen Keller (Keller, as cited by Neal, 2012, p. xv).

My recovery journey has taken me twenty years so far, but the seven years of this chapter has become my spiritual journey. It is a meaningful discovery of things about myself I wasn't even aware of yet. I appreciate everything I continue to learn about myself because it opens up new worlds to me. I'm learning to risk more, and take proactive steps for my betterment.

I've taken classes to learn about myself, went to therapy groups and of course counseling and therapy of all kinds. Twelve Step groups were very important on this journey as well. All these things brought my attention to issues I needed to deal with.

Issues are inevitable. I believe we all have them since we've all been wounded in some way. What I have learned is that issues present opportunities to step out of denial and to grow if I choose to. I always have a choice. What I want is healing from the negative effects of my childhood. If I didn't believe that healing is possible, I would be lost, drowning in a sea of emotions too overwhelming to cope with. God promises *"He heals the brokenhearted and binds up their wounds"* (Psalm 147:3).

Journal Entry
February 29, 1992

God's love for me is not based on what I do *(performance)*. God doesn't dump me when I'm not on speaking terms with Him. He doesn't leave or abandon me, even when I'm angry with Him and tell Him so. Because of my woundedness, it's hard for me to grasp this idea. He suffered for me. He experienced everything that I go through. He cried over Jerusalem, longing for relationship.

God, what can you share with me through the Spirit? The words of this song came flooding into my mind that my Mom and I used to sing together.

> I come to the garden alone.
> While the dew is still on the roses.
> And the voice I hear
> falling on my ear,
> the Son of God discloses.
>
> And He walks with me.
> And He talks with me.
> And He tells me I am His own.
> And the joy we share
> As we tarry there,
> None other has ever known
> (Hymnal/Miles, 1989, Hymn #314).

Probing Questions

Journal Entry
June 15, 1995

From time to time my Pastor, Rick Warren, at Saddleback Church, has asked pertinent questions to consider growing deeper. Here is one of those questions:

What difficulties do you have in revealing yourself to others?

136

I am afraid of being judged, criticized, or ridiculed. Even when in my head I know this is a safe place and these people understand, I still carry the fear and anxiety. Letting you know who I am is to let my guard down and be vulnerable. I might get hurt again. I've always been afraid of getting hurt again, since it happened so many times while growing up. I put up defenses in order to protect myself, but they can also be walls to keep people out. I no longer want to be isolated like that. I like people, and I like connecting on a feeling level. I want to be known and accepted for who I am. I'm discovering how unique and special I am, and I like me.

Recovery: My Inward Journey
June 15, 1995

My inward journey
Is mine
Recovery
Is not a straight line

Whether climbing a mountain
Or sinking down low
There are benefits
On the path
That I go

I'm learning about me
And who I am
Sometimes a lion
Sometimes a lamb

I'm strong and courageous
Precious and free
And I can choose
Whatever I want to be

The journey's not easy

There's sadness to grieve
But that's where the healing is
I believe

I keep looking back
To my childhood days
And find abuse
In so many ways

In a family
Filled with anger and chaos
Hurt and abandoned
Grieving the loss

Is now my focus
Rather than blame
Striving for peace
And healing the shame

I keep on my path
Of recovery
So I can continue

Discovering

How my past
Affects me today

Feeling
My unexpressed feelings
Is the way

Journal Entry

July 23, 1995

I feel the emptiness inside that I keep filling with food. Oh God, heal the pain, so I won't try to fill the hole with food. I don't want food to be my god anymore. I want You close to me and I want to feel Your love. I know You love me. You've brought me to where I am today. I've come so far, and I thank You for leading me and guiding me but most of all for loving me just the way I am. I've been looking for someone who would love me in that way only You can do. When others can forget my name, disappoint, and hurt me, You never do. You have always known me and called me by my name before I was even formed. You even know the very number of hairs on my head. No one knows me or can know me the way that You do. I am awesomely and wonderfully made. You created me in Your image.

I have a hunger for healing and a hunger for God. Both are what I've been trying to fill with food.

I am experiencing the pain of what feels like an incurable spiritual and emotional illness, a food addiction that is destroying my mind, my body, and my ability to make a contribution to society. My disease has driven God out of my life. My compulsion has replaced God as the center of my motivation and relationships. I need help. I feel like I am powerless to stop overeating, and my life is unmanageable. Only through God is there hope and help for the guilt and the shame of this eating disorder.

Journal Entry
January 25, 1996

God,

I don't think I can take one more thing. I know I've said that before, but I'm going through so much right now. I'm dealing with my childhood issues in therapy. The feelings coming up are overwhelming. I'm hurting and feeling rejected and abandoned. I'm scared. There's so much that I have to do. My inner child has all these feelings. I'm having difficulty functioning and letting the loving adult in me *parent* my wounded inner child.

Is Anybody Listening? Does Anybody Hear?
January 25, 1996

It's hard to be little
In a grown up body
There's grown up things
To be done

Little Ardie is fighting
To be heard
Inside her voice
Has all the words

She needs
To tell her truth
All she wants
Is to be soothed

From all the anger
Hurt and fear
Is anybody listening?
Does anybody hear?

This pain

Has been buried
For so long
To keep it inside
She's had to be strong

In order to survive
Her feelings
Were buried alive

At last it's time
She feels safe enough
She feels secure
Supported and loved

The feelings come up
One by one
Unraveling the layers
Is how it's done

The wounds will heal
But scars remain

And little Ardie	*Ever again*
Will not be silent	

Journal Entry
February 25, 1996

Dear God,

I'm practicing acceptance. Accepting that I'm in this place of loneliness wanting a companion. Where is he? Okay, I'm not loving myself the way that I need to first before I can truly have a companion in my life. You know how I hate that. I'm angry that I have to take responsibility to take care of my needs and my feelings. I don't like being in this place at all. Discontent and dissatisfied I've been feeling that way for several days. Then I reach the pain of feeling lonely not much I can do to remedy that situation. I keep spending time with people, and it's not working. Okay, back to loving myself before I'm ready for a companion. I do loving, nurturing things for myself. Where do I go from here? I know where it is: acceptance of the things I cannot change!

Serenity Prayer

God, grant me the serenity to accept the things I cannot change, the courage to change the things I can, and the wisdom to know the difference.

Living one day at a time, enjoying one moment at a time, accepting hardship as a pathway to peace.

Taking, as Jesus did, this sinful world as it is; not as I would have it.

Trusting that You will make all things right if I surrender to Your will.

So that I may be reasonably happy in this life and

supremely happy with You forever in the next
(Niebuhr, as cited by Baker, 1998).

Journal Entry
September 18, 1996

Lord, I don't know what You have planned for me, but I believe it will
be wonderful. I know You're working out that plan as I am talking to
You. I believe You have been guiding me all along the way of my
journey. I need Your guidance now and I need patience. I have
relaxed. I don't feel anxious, but the longing is still here. I do feel
lonely. When I'm with men in a social situation getting to know them
better, I long for the companionship that's missing in my life. I know
You know my needs before I even speak them. I do believe You are
working this out for me already. I know the timing isn't right yet or it
would be happening. So, I need to focus elsewhere which means back
to my purpose. Help me to find out what that purpose is! Is it writing
my book? Is it speaking engagements reading my poetry and giving
workshops? Help me to find my way in what You want me to do for
Your glory. You are the Giver of gifts. I am grateful for the gifts
You've given me. Thank You for the healing those gifts continue to
bring to me.

Purpose-Driven Life Worksheet #1
Deciding What's Important - Pastor Rick Warren
October 5, 1996

1. What do I value most? What matters most?
   a.) I value my relationship with God, and what His Will is
   for me.

2. What type of person do I want to BE in life?
   a.) I want to be open to growth, honest with my feelings,
   and willing to change my character defects.

3. What adjectives would I like to describe me?
   a.) Loving, joyful, peaceful *(serene)*, patient, kind, faithful,
   gentle, moderate *(moderation; self-control)* which are the
   fruits of the Spirit (Galatians 5:22 & 23, NIV).

4. Am I doing what I really care about doing?
   a.) Yes I am writing poetry, and writing my book about my life experiences.

5. What is VITALLY important to me?
   a.) Doing what God has planned for me is VITALLY important to me.

   b.) What has SOME importance to me?
      1.) Doing what I enjoy doing is somewhat important to me. I enjoy helping people work through their psychological problems, writing poetry, going to the movies with my family, and going on day trips with my family enjoying God's creation.

   c.) What has NO importance to me?
      1.) Constantly worrying that I might behave in a way that the people I'm with may not approve of.

6. What would I like people to remember about me?
   a.) I would like people to remember my walk with God. God gave me peace and serenity through His mercy and grace in spite of the pain from past abuse.

7. If I were to write a letter to my children on what is MOST important in life, what would I tell them?
   a.) Walking with God is most important in life. To have a "spiritual" life versus a "religious" life by surrendering to God's Will, and following His plan.

8. What in my life is trivial and what is essential?
   a.) Earthly things are trivial. They fade away, break, get lost, are stolen, or are destroyed. "Things" don't last. "Things" don't bring real or lasting satisfaction. Faith in God is essential and lasts. Faith cannot be taken away. Faith truly satisfies the need and the longing for connection with my Creator.

9. What should I hold onto and what should I let go of?
   a.) Hold fast to God, His Will, and His Word. He keeps His promises. His promises are sure. Let go of people, places, and things. Earthly things fade away and don't give satisfaction. Doing God's Will satisfies the soul.

10. Where do I get my values? Where do I want to get them?
    a.) I get my values from a mixture of the world and from God's Word.

    b.) I want to get them from God. He will reveal the values that are important through His Word.

11. How much of what I'm doing will count twenty years from today?
    a.) What I do for God, out of gratitude for the love He has shown me will last. My writings and my poetry reflect my faith in God and will be my contribution to all those who read them including people today and in the future.

12. What are the ten most important values in my life? What is the meaning of the word values: What to build my life on, to hold in high esteem, to prize, to honor above riches, to appreciate, quality being excellent, useful or desirable, and worth significance. The ten most important values in my life are:

    1) God -- my relationship with Him and following His Will
    2) To love myself as God's child *(made in His image) (self-worth)*
    3) To love others *(build them up, not tear them down)*
    4) Faith, goodness, knowledge, self-control, perseverance, godliness, brotherly kindness, and love
    5) Learning, growing, and healing
    6) Truth *(honest about my feelings, thoughts, and opinions)*
    7) Helping hurting people *(compassion)*

8) Raising my children to be autonomous, not codependent, yet having a healthy need for connection with healthy people
9) Leaving a legacy for my children/grandchildren
10) Being remembered as a woman after God's heart

"Success is the feeling I get when I live out my values."
(Pastor Rick Warren, Weekend Message)

Journal Entry
March 31, 1997
Oh, God, You know where I'm at. I'm in a mess again. This is so difficult not having a job. I'm down to one prospect that I'm eligible for. I only have one month left of unemployment benefits. I need a job to pay the rent. I'm scared. I'm so scared. Is not having a job to teach me patience? Is this a test of my faith? Is this a step of growth to push me to the limit, to the very edge of the cliff? What do You want from me? What lesson are You trying to teach me? Why am I not getting it? Show me, Lord. Give me clarity.

Journal Entry
April 3, 1997
Lord, You know my heart is with You even when I put our relationship up on the shelf. I am reminded again and again when I put my trust in others, I really am not happy, fulfilled, or satisfied. I am filled with anxiety rather than peace and serenity. When I look to others to meet my needs, I lose sight of the true source of all that I need -- God. You alone can give me what I'm looking for: solace, the peace that passes all understanding, healing from my childhood wounds, forgiveness that truly forgets as if what I did never happened, and unconditional love, a love that's based not on what I do or don't do, but based on who I am in Christ, Your precious child.

Vulnerable and Fragile
April 3, 1997

Vulnerable -- capable of being wounded

Fragile -- easily broken

I've been running away Lord
But You already know that
And because I'm
Disconnected from You
My ambition falls flat

Nothing I do
Brings satisfaction
I don't seem
To finish anything I've begun
My joy for living
Is gone

Discontentment
Is in its place
There are things
I continue to do
I can't erase

Lord You know
My heart
I love You so (1SAM 16:7b)
These destructive habits
I want to outgrow

I know
I'm on a journey
You're with me
All the way (EX 3:12a)
Even when I'm stubborn

And persist
In going astray

Your unconditional love
You continue to express (DEUT 7:13a)
And give me more
Instead of less
When I'm
At my neediest

I'm amazed Lord
I deserved nothing
You gave me life (JOB 33:4)
Instead of being grateful
I create strife

Conflict and discord
Within myself
By putting our relationship
Up on a shelf

I'm sorry Lord
That's not my intent
I come before You
Feeling penitent (2COR 7:10)

I'm asking for Your help
In my daily struggle
I know my broken parts
Need healing

Please be gentle

Right now
I feel so vulnerable
And fragile
I am in that boat
In the raging storm
At sea (MT 14:24)
I'm drowning "Save me!"
Is my plea (MT 14:30 NKJV)

"Peace! Be still!"
Jesus calms the sea
With His words (MK 4:39 N KJV)
His compassionate mercy
And grace to me
Is outpoured (PS 116:5)

And even in those moments
When He can say
"O ye of little faith" (MT 8:26)
I feel His arms
Around me
And I feel safe (DEUT 33:27)

God is in control
And has a plan
For my good (JER 29:11)
If I keep my eyes
On Jesus

The raging storm
Will be overruled (HEB 12:2)

Lord I need encouragement
Wisdom
And continual guidance
You know what
I'm going through
Every circumstance (PS 139:1-3)

Help me to trust
You more (PS 13:5a)
To lead me safely
To the shore

I know You
Are the answer
To every longing
Of my mind
The more You
Are in my life
The greater satisfaction
I find

Your power and wisdom
Is stronger than anything
I could face (ROM 11:33)
And Your everlasting arms
Will be my resting-place

Part of my spiritual journey means answering more of Pastor Rick's questions. I have to decide what's important in my life and what do I value.

Gratitude List
April 7, 1997

I am grateful to God for:

I'm grateful for where I live in the beautiful apartment complex that soothes me.

I'm grateful to be alive. I can breathe.

I'm grateful for time off from work.

I'm grateful for warmth of the sun and coolness of a breeze.

I'm grateful for sounds that I hear and for my hearing.

I'm grateful for my health.

I'm grateful that I can walk and move my muscles.

I'm grateful for my body. It's a miracle.

I'm grateful for my eyes that I can see.

I'm grateful for my touch that I can feel textures with my fingers.

I'm grateful for my emotions and the healing that comes from them.

God, you are the source of all that is good, wholesome, and pure. You are the giver of gifts and of unconditional love for me.

I'm grateful for Saddleback Church.

I'm grateful for the Single Parents Group at Saddleback.

I'm grateful for my small groups at Saddleback.

I'm grateful for recovery.

I'm grateful for intelligence.

I'm grateful for knowledge.

I'm grateful for family.

I'm grateful for friends.

I'm grateful for Pastor Rick Warren.

I'm grateful for a God who loves me just as I am.

I'm grateful for a Savior who died and rose again for me.

I'm grateful for God's wisdom, power, and strength.

I'm grateful for God's mercy and grace.

Touched by the Love of God
April 7, 1997

"This is the day
The Lord has made
I will rejoice
And be glad in it" (PS 118:24)

That I have
An attitude of gratitude
Is definitely
A recovery benefit

God has blessed me
He's kind and good
I feel loved
Accepted and understood

I have so much

To be grateful for
I have a Savior
Who is my
King and my Lord

Honor and praise
I give God
All the glory
Wherever I can
I love
To tell the story

Of how He died
And rose again
For me
To save my soul

And set
My heart free

The warmth
I feel inside
Makes my face glow
My thankfulness to God
Continues to grow

He loves me
I feel it in my heart
I depend on Him
I know
He'll not depart

He's with me
Each and every day
He's guiding me
Showing me the way

"O Lord, our Lord
How majestic
Is Your name
In all the earth" *(PS 8:1)*
You knew me
Even before
My birth

"May the words
Of my mouth
And the meditation
Of my heart
Be pleasing
In Your sight" *(PS 19:14)*

You are
The light
Of my life
That ever

Shines bright

"In Your presence
There is
Fullness of joy" *(PS 16:11)*
Peace and serenity
That no one
Can destroy

"I can do
All things
Through Christ
Who strengthens me" *(PHIL 4:13 NKJV)*
Make me
More like You
So I can be
All that You
Want me to be

"By the grace
Of God
I am what I am
And His grace
Toward me
Has not been in vain" *(1COR 15:10)*

I will sing His praise
And give God
The glory
Again and again
Unconditional love
Everlasting life
And peace of mind
Just some
Of God's gifts
He's compassionate
And kind

A smile on my face

149

Is evident
And can be seen
Touched

By the love of God
I am peaceful
And serene

Journal Entry

May 8, 1997

I'm sitting here feeling amazed as I contemplate how God works out His plan in my life and how He answers my prayers. I may have to go through some trying times, but He's with me every step of the way, working it all out for my good. What seemed like an eternity *(it was only six months)* now seems like the blink of an eye. The time went by so quickly. I remember struggling and wrestling with God in prayer. I remember the painful feelings of not knowing. Fear and panic would only begin to rise when my focus became attached to the problem or circumstance I found myself in. As long as I looked to Jesus, I was peaceful and calm. As long as I stayed connected to my small support group and brought my needs to them *(as well as to God)* I felt an inner strength. God has been so kind and loving toward me. He's given me gifts of loving people in my life, and restoring the broken parts of me. I am filled with gratitude as I look at my compassionate Creator who loves me no matter what. He lets me make my choices and I make so many mistakes. But He works it all out for my good. Truly a magnificent and exciting thing to be a part of and watch unfold.

I want to write a poem to express my gratitude and the fullness of joy that I feel. It's as if there are no words to describe the love in my heart for my Lord. He truly is awesome.

God Loves Me

May 8, 1997

I'm no longer
Wandering
Lost or alone
Through the midst
Of my problems
God has shown

Compassion
Direction
Wisdom and love
As long
As I keep looking
To God above

I'm steady and calm
My course is set
If I can be patient
All my needs
Are met

God has a plan
God's Will
Not mine
Will be done (JER 29:11)
If I cling
To His promise
Then "worries?"
I have none

I am in the ultimate
Of "capable" hands
And even if I wonder
Where He is
God understands

He shows me
Time and time again
Just how much
He loves me

And wants me
To be the best
I can be

He sees me through
Each problem
There is nothing
Too small
For His consideration
He wants them all

He and I
Walk hand in hand

I feel His strength
And power
Even during
The darkest
Most painful hour

The darkness
Turns to light
I feel relieved
Through Jesus Christ
My freedom
Has been guaranteed

My heart is filled
With gratitude
Contentment
Love and joy
That Satan
With all his obstacles
Can never destroy

I am at peace
I am in God's tender
Loving care (ISA 26:3)
He answers
Each and every one
Of all my prayers

In ways I can't easily
See at the time
Together
There isn't a hill
Or mountain
We can't climb

He brought me
This far
He'll see me
To the end

151

An eternity
Of ecstatic bliss
I will joyfully spend

Glorifying and praising
My Creator
Redeemer and Lord
That God
Will touch hearts
As He's touched mine
Will be my reward

For the gift
Of poetry

He's given me
I'm extremely blessed
My feelings of gratitude
I continue to express

My time alone
With God
Is valuable to me
And even though
I make mistakes
God loves me
I feel precious
And free (ISA 43:4)

Journal Entry

October 2, 1997

Pastor Rick is so good at pointing out things to us as a church that I need to journal about.

What is important to me at this stage of my life?

The following things are important to me:

1.) A closer relationship with Jesus Christ.
2.) Healing of the broken parts inside me.
3.) More intimate friendships on a deeper level.
4.) That God would use my talents and abilities for His purpose.
5.) A permanent job that will fulfill my heart's desires.
6.) A godly man to share my spiritual walk with Christ.

Journal Entry

October 13, 1997

I found a beautiful park setting in a forest by a stream. It's almost a mountain atmosphere. How blessed I am. God is good. I feel very relaxed today. I know God will provide. God has a plan. I'm eager to see what God has in store for me.

Delaying Gratification

What do you want most in life and what are you prepared to sacrifice to attain it?

I want to share my story with others including sharing my poetry. I love to speak. I love to connect with people. I want to help others who are hurting. I want to help others grow spiritually. I want to leave a legacy. I want to be remembered for what God did in my life.

What does it take to have what I want? Is there a sacrifice involved? Am I willing? Sounds like surrender to me. Am I willing to surrender to God's Will for my life? Can I, will I, be creative in my productivity? Can I, will I, be responsible in nurturing life? I am responsible for what I have done *(accountability)*. I have responsibility for what I have created *(care)*. I can make a difference.

You Know My Heart Lord
November 24, 1997

There is
No one else
I can turn to
No one else
I can rely on
Except You

Lord You meet me
Right where I'm at
And accept me
Flaws and all
I like that

It's hard
To find people
Who love
The real me
I'm too loud
I laugh too much
Less emotional

I should be

These were
Negative messages
I have believed
But none of them
Are true about me
And I'm relieved

You know my heart
Lord
I want to trust
People who are safe
And are growing
That's a must

So I will take
That risk
To open up
And be real

And show others
How I truly
Think and feel

I want to learn
Grow
And heal
From my past
And be free
Of my family's
Dysfunction at last

It's not their fault
This is not about blame
They didn't know
Any other way
And even I
As a parent
Did the same

Today I have choices
God gives me
Unconditional love and grace
It's been long
Difficult
And painful too
I'm in a different place

Healing comes
From grieving
There is no other way
From my own experience
I have learned to say

God has been good
And kind to me
He's given me blessings
Beyond what I
Hoped could be

I have a church family
That understands
And cares
God certainly answers
All of my prayers

In His time
Not mine
I have learned
To wait
He's definitely building
My character traits

I have so much
To be thankful for
I'm excited
I don't know
What God
Has in store

For me
But it will
Be glorious
Anything He gives me
Is a definite plus

Today I'm grateful
I'm His treasure
I know He cherishes me (DEUT 26:18)
He's given me
Grace to be all
He created
And intended me to be

I am
Your beloved child
I praise
Your Holy name (PS 113:2)

I give You honor Lord　　　　　*And mercy*
Your grace　　　　　　　　　　*I proclaim*

Journal Entry
February 7, 1998

In our small group study we are following the book *Experiencing God*. We are learning about knowing and doing the will of God. From the book I learned the following:

- I will look to see what God says and how He works in the Scriptures.
- I will make my decisions and evaluate my experiences based on biblical principles.
- The Bible is my guide for faith and practice.
- The right question is, what is God's will?
- Watch to see where God is working and join Him.
- God is always at work around me (Blackaby & King, 1990, p. 15).

Although I don't hear an audible voice from God, I do know when he is speaking to me. I struggle repeatedly experiencing either listening to God's promptings or fighting Him and what He wants me to do. In the end I surrender and enjoy the benefits of following God's will.

Journal Entry
February 7, 1998

I am reading *Silent Hunger* by Arthur and Judy Halliday. It is touching my heart and soul.

Our silent hunger is our longing for intimacy where our deepest needs for security and significance can be substantially met. Intimacy includes our need to love and be loved, to be valued and be cherished, to be treated with dignity and respect, and to relate to one another at the deepest, most authentic level of our being. Unsatisfied and unfulfilled, we ache with a silent hunger. To appease it we often develop compulsive behavior that results in food, eating, and weight becoming the focus of our lives (Halliday & Halliday, 1994, pp. 26-27).

That's how my obsession with food began. My needs weren't met in childhood. I'm left with this "mess" to clean up and deal with that my family left me. I feel so inadequate with no skills and no tools to cope with life. I am angry that my family just dumped it into my lap. They did not take responsibility for meeting my needs, but instead abused me; a precious child of God.

I keep trying to achieve a sense of security and significance by my own efforts.

If we will be still and let God address our silent hunger, He will graciously show us that He never meant for us to find the fulfillment of our self-worth apart from Him. This undeniable, unavoidable longing for a sense of value is a sanctified hunger placed in me by God's design. But I will never experience inner peace until I face the truth that of this world -- my appearance, my performance, others' opinions of me, or my past experiences -- cannot fulfill my longing for security and significance. My silent hunger will persist unsatisfied until I can see myself not through the eyes of the world, but through the eyes of my loving Lord (Halliday & Halliday, 1994, p. 87).

Silent Hunger
February 7, 1998

Lord
My food
Is out of control
I'm overeating again
To fill up that hole

The one inside me
That drives me to eat
The emptiness
From childhood
That still feels incomplete
I had emotional needs

They were unable to meet

There was a house
Food and clothes
For me to wear
But their neglect
And abuse
Showed they didn't care

About me
Or what I need
I was wounded
And abandoned
Brokenhearted indeed (PS 34:18)

As a child
Food became
A source of love
For me
A way to survive
A way to flee

Painful feelings
Of loss
And loneliness (JER 15:18)
I did not know
How to express

Today I have the knowledge
Of what was
Done to me
And what I did to cope
I can clearly see

And yet
I still struggle
With this food addiction

Recovery

Has been on-going
My journey's
Just begun
Unraveling the layers
One by one

I need you
Lord
The silent hunger
Is for You (MT 5:6)
I want to be free
From the bondage of food (LEV 26:13 NCV)
I want to live
According to Your Spirit
And be renewed (2COR 4:16)

I can't do it
By trying harder
Or through legalistic control
Only Your grace
Will sustain me
And help me
With this goal (ISA 41:10)

This is a struggle
And a war
Between my flesh
And Your Spirit (EPH 6:17)
Your compassion
And unconditional love
Will enable me
To bear it (PS 103:8)

And come to a place
Of obedience
Out of my love
And gratitude (2COR 9:13)
I can have
Victory in Jesus

157

And not give in
to food *(1JN 5:4, 5)*

By *trusting*
His *perfect design*
And *allowing His Spirit*
To *work in me (2THES 2:13)*
I *can surrender*
My *will*
Make *responsible choices*
And *truly be free (PS 40:8)*

Only *You Lord*

Can *satisfy my hunger*
For *intimacy (JN 6:35)*
And *help me*
Grow *in Christ*
To *mature spiritually (2COR 3:18b)*

I *am in awe*
Of *Your power*
Wisdom
Love *and grace (PS 145:6)*
And *Your everlasting arms*
Will *be my resting-place (DEUT 33:27*

Journal Entry

February 19, 1998

Gary Smalley, came to speak at Saddleback Church and I picked the following book to read: *Joy That Lasts*. I wanted to learn more about the healthy things I could ask from God in prayer. The book suggests the following:

Ask God in prayer:
1. Ask God that I experience Him within me and that I might no longer expect anything other than Him to fill my life.
2. Ask God for healthy family relationships.
3. Ask God for knowledge and wisdom to be the best possible mother and potential wife.
4. Ask God for a mentor who could guide me to help me live an obedient Christian life.
5. Ask God to let me help others with my writing and speaking so I can share my insights from Him (Smalley, 2000, pp. 57 & 58).

God's Spirit alone fills my cup (Ephesians 3:19, NIV). to KNOW the love of God is to be *"filled with the measure of all the fullness of God"* *(Smalley, 2000, p. 77).*

"Prayer is what connects us to the source of life that charges our batteries and makes life worth living" (Smalley, 2000, p.197).

Okay, God, I will completely trust my life in Your hands and let You, in Your timing, fill my life and take care of my everyday needs.

Journal Entry
February 28, 1998
Pastor Rick's message today impacted me and I wrote down these questions to answer in my quiet time:

Do I want to be self-centered? Indulging my own inclinations and desires?

Do I want to be God-centered? Leading a life devoted to a growing relationship with God focusing on His plan and purpose for my life?

The struggle for me is the battle I face every day whether I want to be selfish following my own inclinations or letting God be the center of my life. I know God has a plan and purpose for my life and I do want to lead a life devoted to a growing relationship with God that focuses on His will for me. This struggle is very painful and I've shed many tears.

"You have seen me tossing and turning through the night. You have collected all my tears and preserved them in Your bottle! You have recorded every-one in Your book" (Psalm 56:8, Life Recovery Bible, NLT).

Journal Entry
June 4, 1999
I know my inspiration for my poetry comes from God. He's definitely given me this gift. He deserves all the credit. I never know when I'm going to be inspired. My Single Parents group was at coffee. We had just heard a speaker tell us that a good question to ask a potential partner is, "What are your issues?" I thought about how long I have been working on my issues. I definitely have issues, but I've never really listed them. So I sat down to contemplate them.

Issues

Codependence

Intimacy dysfunction

Fear of engulfment

Fear of abandonment *(someone connecting, then leaving)*

Trust *(inconsistency - someone being unstable as a love object)*

Lack of boundaries *(unable to say "NO")*

Detachment *(someone being emotionally inaccessible to me)*

Toxic shame *(I am flawed and defective - what I feel, do, or think is wrong)*

Communication problems *(no conflict resolution skills)*

Criticism and judgment *(unloving attacks upon my needy aspects)*

Abuse: physical, emotional, and sexual *(all are spiritual abuse – violations of my soul that destroy trust)*

Because of these issues, my bonding process was disrupted.

Coping Mechanisms

Fantasy/Romanticizing/Daydreaming *(not living in the present/reality)*

Isolation

Obsessive/compulsive tendencies *(addictions)*

Controlling, manipulation

Procrastination

I've Got Issues
June 4, 1999

I've got issues
Of that
There is no doubt
Looking at
Childhood wounds
Is what it's all about

And how
I learned to cope
Just to stay alive
I had to stuff
My feelings
In order to survive

Feelings were uncomfortable
I only knew to cry
But I was at a loss
I couldn't tell you why

Just that I was hurting
I felt unloved
And alone (PS 13:2)
I was a stranger
In the land
Of the unknown

Couldn't figure it out
It made no sense
To me
Still doesn't
That others can
Treat me so brutally (PS 35:4)
In the guise of care
Love and Christianity

Lies
All lies
I don't
Trust them anymore
There's a brokenness
Deep within my core (PS 34:18)

Healing takes time
Issues don't go away (PS 147:3)
They're triggered
In my
Relationships today

I get opportunities
To learn
New unknown skills
Which isn't easy
With my
Rebellious self-will (JAS 3:16)

I don't want to
This is too hard
I fight
This isn't fair
I don't like it
It's not right

I argue and rebel
But in the end
God wins
He knows my weaknesses
And all my secret sins (PS 90:9)

He's given me a Savior
To set me

Free from guilt (PS 146:7)
In the prison
Of my own making
That I alone
Have built

I'm already forgiven
If I could
Just do that for me (PS 103:2-4)
I could truly
Let go of the past
And totally be free (PS 118:5)

He who
Began a good work
Is not finished
With me (PHIL 1:6)
So my issues
Come up
One by one
For me to see

To deal with in a new way
If I can work it through
God never breaks promises
They always come true (HEB 10:23)

He'll never
Give me more
Than I can
Handle at one time (1COR 10:13)
He'll give me
The strength I need
To make
The uphill climb (PHIL 4:13)

He loves me
Just like this
No need
To be other
Than who I am
I'm His treasure
The apple of His eye
And His precious lamb (PS 17:8)

Journal Entry

July 8, 1999

My needs aren't getting met again. First it triggers anger and I snap. Then I sob and grieve the loss of not having those needs met. No one is coming to meet them. They weren't met when I was a child. This is so hard, Lord, to feel these feelings. I don't know what to do with them. I can't change the situation. I can't change things or people.

At any time something can happen to me that would hurt, that I can't stop and that scares me so. I don't know what to do about that. I'm just so scared. Something could happen to my body, my car, my job, and my children. Lord, I'm so scared. My mom sent me off to school with no protection. She left me at home alone with my brother with no protection. I was just a little girl, so frightened and alone. I was ridiculed for being scared and for crying. Crying is all I could do. It is still all I can do.

There's an Emptiness Inside Me
July 8, 1999

It's hard for me
To concentrate
On what I need to do
I have no motivation
I'm feeling depressed
It's true

My self-esteem
Is at an all-time
Disturbing low
My emotions
Are being tossed
Violently to and fro

My time is wasted
Each day
That goes by
I have no focus
No purpose
And my flesh
I just gratify (GAL 5:16, 17)
Anything at all
Just to pacify

This agitated
Annoying
Disgruntled feeling
That haunts me inside
The one I'm concealing
That no one
Talks about
So how can I?

So I stuff it
With food
In order to deny (PROV 23:20, 21)
What I'm
Going through

It seems so useless
I know so much
And continue
To eat in excess (PROV 23:2, 3)

God I need Your help
I can't do this
On my own (PS 18:6)
I feel totally abandoned
Disappointed and alone

Only You
Can help me
In the way that I need (PS 73:12)
Lord I'm wounded
Don't You care
If I bleed? (PS 22:24)

You've promised
To be with me Lord (MT 28:20)
I believe Your promises
I trust Your Word

Please lift me
Out of this hole I'm in

Give me Your strength
So that I can begin (ISA 40:29)

To take just one step
In the direction
You want me to go
Heal my brokenness
So that I can grow (PS 147:3)

To be all
You have
Created me for
To love myself less
And to love You more

You're all I have
That really
Matters to me
Nothing else
Counts eternally

I want to find rest
And peace
For my soul (MT 11:28)
My addictions
Keep flaring
Out of control

There's an emptiness
Inside me
Please fill up that hole
I'm tired of struggling
Isn't there
Any other way?
I pray for peace
Let me feel it today (ISA 26:3)
Give me Your wisdom
Your strength
As I pray (ISA 33:6)

You created me
To be Your own
Don't give up
On me now
Help me
To seek Your face
Through all of this
Somehow

Wipe my tears away
With Your gentle
Loving hand (REV 7:17)
Give me the strength
I need to rise up
And stand (ISA 40:29)

Knowing You
Are by my side (2TIM 4:17)
My Father
My Redeemer
My loving Guide

Be gracious
Be merciful
I bow at Your throne
I give up this world
And all I own

To be Your servant
To follow Your Will (2SAM 7:21)
Your divine purpose
For me to fulfill (PROV 19:21)

And one day
When this
Stressful life ends
A blissful eternity
With my Lord

I will spend (JN 3:15)

Open my eyes
So I can see (PS 119:18)
How blessed I am
To have a God
Who loves me (PS 90:14)

Totally without merit
Unconditionally
I am Your
Beloved child
Precious
And free (1JN 3:1)

10

Looking for "The One"

"Remind me each morning of Your constant love, for I put my trust in You. My prayers go up to You; Show me the way I should go" (Psalm 143:8, GNT).

Trying to Find Love

Meeting many men at Saddleback during this time was exciting. Although several male friends became very important to me, my efforts to move toward a romantic relationship just wasn't happening. My hope seemed plausible that at least one relationship would blossom into romance. My eyes turned toward one friend in particular. Affectionately called *"Little Glen"* because he was short, he attended a small singles group of about twelve men and women. They met every week for over a year. I joined that group right after the holidays. One of my New Year resolutions—get involved! Now there would be an opportunity to make my move on Little Glen; we were already good friends. After all, he could possibly be "THE ONE." So attempting to win him over became my strategy.

Knowing some of the people in the group already made it easier for me to fit in. Some other new people joined too. One night a new guy, tall and lean, came in and smiled. Immediately I thought, *Oh, he's good looking... ...maybe a potential mate!* By this time, every man I met became a potential mate.

His black hair, a stark contrast to his darkly tanned face made me look twice. Is that his true hair color? Watching him closely that night to see what he was like, I listened to what he had to say. He talked about his faith in God which was admirable, but his thinking sounded rigid. His inflexibility turned me off.

At the end of the night, group members hugged each other. He was next in line. Being so tall, I had difficulty reaching up to him. "You're too tall, I said, where's a stepstool to hug you?" My remark about his height made him laugh. He hugged me from the side. What a horrible hug! Accustomed to big ole bear hugs from the other guys, I thought, *"This guy doesn't even know how to hug properly."*

That same night two guys were introduced to me at the same time, Glen and Richard. Wouldn't you know it? I kept confusing their names. "Hi, Richard!"

"I'm not Richard, my name is Glen."

"We already have a Glen."

"I know. He's my best friend. He's Little Glen and I'm Big Glen or Big G for short."

Oh brother! Do you think I could remember that? He was Richard from that point on.

After several weeks, avoiding this guy was easy; him being too tall *(six foot three)* and me being a full foot shorter. His real name escaped my memory. Flashbacks of the name, Richard, kept coming to mind. Shy and quiet, he didn't say too much in group discussions. Now and then he would shoot a one liner – an unyielding statement obviously black and white with no in-between gray areas. He would say something like, "If you have problems, just give them to Christ. Just be together in Christ at the same time." That just rubbed me the wrong way. Oh brother did that sound unrealistic. He was not living in the real world. His answers to everything were so general and not true. I knew my life was a long, hard, painful time of working on my issues and healing my heart that took risking coming out of my comfort zone, seeking help from therapists and support groups. Christ had not instantly healed me. This guy knew nothing of the reality of life! So, based on what I knew about him *(not much)*, I deducted that this guy was not for me.

In spite of my disapproval, God urged me to pursue this guy. *Of all the men in the group, you really don't know him very well. What about asking him questions to get to know him better?*

Taking a big risk at the next group meeting, I asked, "Do you mind if I sit down to ask you some questions to get better acquainted?" His face lit up with the biggest, most handsome smile and he said, "Please sit down. Ask me anything you'd like."

Eager to answer my questions, Glen appeared transparent. That intrigued me. Not thinking any more about him, our group continued to meet each week.

Our church scheduled a Small Group Conference on a Saturday for half a day. All of us attended. Glen was already sitting and I asked to sit next to him. Again he flashed that handsome smile at me. Accepting his invitation to sit, his friendliness appealed to me. We chatted and laughed while waiting for the conference to begin.

Hungry by lunchtime, we both appreciated the box lunch provided by the church. We walked together to find a place to sit. Liking the idea that he wanted to have lunch with me, it gave me another opportunity to ask more questions. Determined to explore his personality in depth, the questions became easier for me. The conversation pleasant, Glen showed himself to be congenial and good-humored.

After lunch it was time to leave. "Glen, do you mind if I call you sometime?"

"Of course not, call me anytime."

The next day was the perfect time to take the plunge. Already experienced in calling and meeting men, there was no apprehension for me at all.

Working on replacing the pump for his swimming pool, Glen gladly took a break to talk to me. We talked for quite a while and ended on a good note. After hanging up, I thought how mechanically minded and ambitious he is to fix his own pool pump.

By Tuesday's group, it was obvious spending more time getting to know Glen appealed to me. I asked him to meet me at Midweek Service. We were seated at tables for discussion purposes which was perfect for me to hear more from Glen. One of our mutual friends was seated at a different table. She motioned to me that Glen and I were sitting together. I smiled. She smiled even bigger and gave me a "thumbs up." It excited me to share my new-found "friend."

So far, we were meeting at a few different church functions and continued to do so. Asking Glen to meet me for coffee after Wednesday's Service, he said, "I have to take my son home first. Do you mind waiting?"

"I'll wait. Meet me at Denny's."

Setting boundaries during the dating process, there were rules important to me. One rule included only waiting fifteen minutes for a date to meet me. Fifteen minutes had now passed while waiting at Denny's. It was decision time. Do I give him the benefit of the doubt? Something could have come up. Or do I adhere strictly to my rules and not let him take advantage of my soft heart? Half an hour later, I was ready to leave. The door popped open. His smiling face beaming at me made it worth staying.

"I'm sorry it took me so long to take my son home. There was a construction detour I had to go around. But you waited. I'm glad you did."

"So am I!"

We talked for two hours. He talked while I listened about his career as an Air-Conditioning/Heating Technician. He started his own business with a partner in 1979.

"Before going into business, I enlisted in the Navy," he said proudly.

A man in uniform always caught my eye. After all, my two ex's were sailors.

Now it was time for a real date. Might as well go ahead and ask him. My past experiences asking men out gave me courage. "Would you like to go to dinner with me on Friday night?"

"Yes, but I want to pick you up at your place and take you in my car."

"Okay."

We made arrangements and were on our way!

He picked me up, even came to the door of my apartment. Escorting me to his car, he opened the door of his red Ford Expedition helping me up to my seat. It was like riding in a bus. We didn't have far to go, so conversing about the day was easy to do. He politely changed the subject.

"Ardie, I like you. Getting to know you better is okay and we can become good friends. It won't go any further than that because I'm not attracted to you."

What? I thought... *What did he just say on our very first date? What do I say to that? My first reaction was to kick him to the curb! How dare he? It was rude and crude to say something like that. Oh, wait a minute, maybe he's just being honest with me up front, so give him a break. I have men friends. They're still fun to be with even though there's no romance between us.*

Although it felt like minutes of silence had gone by, I'm sure it was just seconds.

"Thank you, Glen, for your honesty. If friendship is what you want, I'll be your friend."

Despite Glen's brutally honest comment that he was not attracted to me, I decided to accept his offer of friendship. To me I couldn't lose since I had found a pleasant companion worth holding onto.

So we became a twosome, spending more time together, enjoying each other's company. Denny's restaurant became "our spot." As we were having dinner there one night, Glen asked me, "What's the color of your heart?" Sometimes he has this way with words that nobody else ever says. I had to stop and think what he actually meant but I did not have the courage to ask, for fear he might get offended, so I said nothing while contemplating what to say.

He added, "You know, *yellow* is the color of my heart." I remembered we had gone to a friend's wedding where he had rented a yellow tuxedo and was the talk of the reception. I wore a flowering print dress with yellow flowers to match. So I knew yellow was his favorite color.

"Oh you mean, what's my favorite color?" Back then, I was still working and wore acrylic nails with my favorite color, bright fuchsia. So I laid my hands on the table and showed him. Now and again Glen has shown me his signature gestures, one of which is holding his hand out for me to put my hand in his, so I did. His next move totally caught me off guard. With his free hand he began to stroke my hand ever so gently melting my heart like butter. He did that without saying anything for several seconds, then rested his hand on mine and looked at me intently with a look I had never seen before. Time stopped and we remained frozen as if in a freeze frame from a movie.

The server interrupted our interlude and we abruptly dropped our hands. Our conversation moved onto other things and nothing was ever said about what just happened. From that time on, when we walked together, he would hold my hand.

Finally, I asked him, "Remember our first date, when you told me, you were not attracted to me, you only wanted to be my friend?"

He nodded yes.

"What happened that night in Denny's? ...You began stroking my hand and you've held my hand ever since?"

"I realized that God took the blinders off my eyes, and I saw your heart." He hadn't professed love in so many words, but I knew then, that he loved me.

After several weeks of dating, I took him to meet my adult children for our Easter gathering at my oldest daughter Carla's house in Corona, CA. My girls and I talked while Glen got to know Carla's husband Steve Wilson.

"I really like him."

"Mom, don't you think this is happening too fast?"

"Yes it is, but we're older and know what we like."

After dinner, Glen and I went for a walk on the trail nearby. We were once again holding hands. Glen stopped, turned to directly face me and said,

"I have something to say, but I don't know if you're ready to hear it."

Now these are words I was not eager to hear, and knowing Glen's notorious one-liners, I was apprehensive at best. I thought I might as well get it over with.

"What is it?"

"Ardie, you're a great mother and grandmother, but you don't have to look like one."

Oh no! Zonked again! I thought, *what do I do with that?* Again, all I could say was "Thank you for your honesty."

When we got back to the house, Glen went outside to see Steve while I helped the girls with the dishes.

"You'll never believe what Glen just told me!" When I relayed the worst news I could have heard on a beautiful Christian holiday, the girls were shocked.

"Who says that to someone they supposedly love? First, he makes you dye your hair blond, now this. I say kick him to the curb!"

"Yeah Mom, don't let him do it. You're your own person. Be yourself, not what he wants you to be!"

"I don't know girls, maybe you're right, but then again, maybe I don't know the whole story. He was married before and maybe he never had a voice with her, so he's speaking up now. I'll have to think about it."

"Just don't let him bring you down, Mom."

We left soon after that and I was quiet all the way home. He knew that was hard for me to hear.

He dropped me off and said, "I'll call you tomorrow."

"Okay, good night."

I could hardly sleep that night. The very next day, I called Glen Ritchie "*Little Glen,*" his best friend from our singles group. I explained all that was said.

"Glen, be honest with me. Is it my being overweight?"

"Oh no, Ardie, he likes his women hefty. There's more to hug. He hates skinny women with their bones sticking out."

"So what is it?"

"Frankly, Ardie, it's how you dress. You always wear long pants, long-sleeved blouses with high collars. Give me a break, dress like a woman. He just wants to see short skirts and a little cleavage. You know us guys are very visual."

"Is that it? You're right. Since my divorce, I have dressed that way to protect me from men, so I wouldn't get hurt again."

"Yeah, he just wants you to be feminine."

"Wow that changes everything."

"Ardie, I've known Glen a long time. His ex, after six months of marriage, said she didn't love him. He stayed married for twenty years in a loveless marriage to raise their son, Dallas. He has such a big heart of love just ready to give to the right woman. I know that's you. Just give him a chance."

Things were going well between us and I was scheduled to give my singles testimony at the next big Singles group at church. As I thought about what I was going to reveal about myself and my struggles with sex, I panicked. Glen has not had a background of promiscuity that I've experienced. He might be shocked at what I was going to reveal in public. Frightened as I was, I knew I had to tell him first privately. I was taking a very big risk. I could lose him. I would have to trust God... ...If Glen was the one for me, he would understand my past. I'm no longer that person.

I picked a night to tell him and was quaking in my shoes. I not only told him what I would be sharing to the singles, but also shared my childhood abuse as well. After I finished, I looked at Glen. He was silent for a few moments, then looked directly at me and said, "I'm sorry you went through all that pain. Your behavior was who you once were. You're no longer that person. Christ has forgiven you. I can do no less. I'm not going anywhere. I love you for the long haul." As I threw my arms around him, I breathed a sigh of relief. I truly had met a wonderful godly man willing to forgive my horrendous past. Then he added, "Since you've had many sexual partners, have you ever been tested for STD's or HIV/Aids?"

"No."

"Then I would ask that you do. You see, I want to kiss you and you deserve to be kissed, but I won't until you get a clean bill of health." Wow, a man of integrity. I agreed. Upon receiving the news that I was negative on all counts, he felt he could pursue a romantic relationship with me.

That was May. On my birthday, June 19, we were sitting on a bench overlooking the Pacific Ocean where the waves were crashing against the rocks at the point at Dana Point, CA. Glen got down on his knees and proposed to me. I was thrilled beyond words. The kiss that we shared was truly monumental. Two weeks later we eloped on June 30, 2000, and were married at the Santa Ana Courthouse. While standing before the Justice of the Peace (JP), Glen was holding my ring. He was so nervous that he dropped the ring and it rolled across the floor and landed behind the JP. She picked it up and handed it to Glen. She said, "It's okay, take a deep breath." The vows the JP used were traditional. I was surprised, but very glad. When we walked outside, I started sobbing. Glen said very compassionately, "What's wrong, Sweetheart?"

"This is the most wonderful day of my life and no one is here to share in our joy."

"We are embarking on a new journey, just the two of us, and there's joy in Heaven that we found each other. All the saints that have gone before us are rejoicing with us."

Glen always has a way with words that cheer me up.

"Besides we will rejoice with our friends at a reception when we get back. This is *our* time!"

We drove up the coast and honeymooned in Cambria, a beautiful ocean resort, also known as Cambria, Pines by the Sea. It is a seaside village located midway between Los Angeles and San Francisco on the California State Route 1 *(Highway 1)* between Morro Bay and Hearst Castle. We stayed at Pelican Inn & Suites, oceanfront hotel on the second floor with a balcony. The view was incredible. There was a fireplace in the living room. Believe it or not, we used it. It was a cool June/July that year. I truly was in Heaven. When we returned, we had a reception for our friends from our singles small group where we had met. We were at the beginning of an unbelievable journey that has been truthfully indescribable. As Glen would say, "Together, as one, in Christ." Our hearts were filled with joy, laughter, and delight as God had faithfully brought us to each other!"

Glen and Me

I've been so happily married to the man of my dreams. I wrote our marriage purpose two years after we were married and he agreed with me. Here it is:

To magnify God. To love, cherish, honor, and enjoy each other, helping each other to become our best selves. To wisely develop and use our time, talents, and resources to help others. To love consistently, to learn continually, to live courageously, and to leave a legacy to our children with God's principles as our guide.

After a few years of our marriage, my issues started to come up and I began to feel like I made a mistake marrying this man that I barely knew. Glen looked at me and frankly said, "Look, I am not your father, brothers, or ex-husbands! I am me, your husband Glen. I love you and would never hurt you or treat you like they did. See me for who *I* am!"

He had held a mirror to my face and I stopped dead in my tracks. It gave me an opportunity to look at myself and my issues from the past, and take another step toward healing my heart. I thank God and my husband, Glen, for giving me that opportunity.

Over the years, Glen's signature one-liners continue to bring me laughter and joy as humor is now what gets us through some otherwise trying issues.

Glen and I have talked many times about things that happened early in our dating life; like when *I* asked *him* out. Glen revealed to me that he was tired of asking girls out. Mainly because of the rejection he continued to face. So he prayed that if God wanted him to date He was going to have to bring the girl to him and she would ask him out. Isn't that interesting? God always works these things out to bring two people together.

The two most meaningful things Glen has done to show his love for me has left a profound mark on my heart. The first one was just after my surgery. I was recuperating very nicely and considering going back to work. I would have to find a new job but I was prepared for that. We had always said that was the plan and we couldn't survive without that second income, or so I thought. We had never discussed any other possibility. One day Glen comes to me and says, "I really feel the Lord is leading me to tell you that you should not go back to work, but to work full time on getting your book written and published, and to also work full time in the ministry God leads you to. I've found a way to survive on one income."

I was shocked and totally surprised, but so loved this man beyond what I had hoped for. That is indeed what I have been doing these last thirteen years. Glen is incredible!

The second thing is my birthday last year. I'm a greeting card person. I've taught my children to give greeting cards and write something meaningful about me and our relationship. Glen is not a greeting card person. It's hard for him to pick a meaningful card, let alone write something. I always ask for a new phrase. These are a few samples of what he came up with:

Thank you for what you do for this family and for me.

Sometimes I don't show my love but it's always there. I will always love you Ardie.

Now we can go on more Saturday day trips.

I love you sweetheart always,

Your Big G. Glen

It's you and me to make our stand for Christ.

Thank you that you're my wife and you love me.

Love Always,

Glen

The one that topped them all off was this one, printed on the card:

To My Wife - I love being married to you
I'm proud to be your husband,
and I wanted you to know
That I see the special things you do,
The kindness that you show...

I see your strength and beauty,
And the talents that you share,
I notice, when a room lights up,
It's all because you're there...

And I can't imagine anything
More wonderful in life
Than all the love and pride I feel
Just knowing you're my wife.
Happy Birthday with All My Love

He wrote:

I love you so much what you're
doing for Christ. In this coming
year, you will touch thousands of
people for Christ who are struggling
with their past hurts. May your book
give them hope in Christ to deal with
their past.

Always love you Ardie,
Glen

He got it....he really got it. He hit this one out of the park!!!!

Journal Entry

August 10, 2002

I can't believe I haven't written any poems for over a year. Not even one attempt in all of the year 2000 even though it was a red-letter year for me for love, romance, and the man of my lifelong dreams.

I think fear has been blocking my writing. Even now I want to quit. Why is it so easy for me to give up? A lot of it is time. I am pulled in many directions. It takes time to write. It also takes peace and quiet. My life has had many ups and downs, anxieties, pain, and disappointment, then the opposite—joy and happiness. Guess I decided to just live my life instead of write about it. One friend of mine said, "I love your poems. I can hardly wait to hear your post-Glen *(the love of my life)* writings. For some reason that thought jolted me, but still I haven't written. Why? Again, the reason is fear. What if I can't write when I'm happy? What if I lost whatever it was that I had? I've lost my motivation. I've lost my style. I've lost my inspiration. In the past, I've only written from my pain.

Maybe I feel guilty or undeserving that God has blessed me so abundantly with love. So many wonderful things have happened. If I put it down on paper and make it real, maybe it won't last. God could take it all away. And what did I ever do to deserve all of this? And now Glen is building a room addition for me called the "Ardie room" solely for the purpose of my writing for me to publish my book. This is the happiest I've ever been. After surviving an abusive childhood family background, two failed marriages, two abusive ex-husbands, painful problems with my children, financial struggles as a single parent... ...after all of that, I have been blessed with the man of my dreams who truly loves me unselfishly and desires me just as I am. I am blessed with a beautiful home with a pool and spa, an Expedition car to drive, and no more financial struggles. I enjoy all these blessings. I am so grateful to God for providing all these answers to prayer, so why am I not happy? I've gained twenty pounds again. After all my struggles with food and weight, I still don't get it. I've stopped writing and started eating. I'm stressed and worried. My teenaged daughter and my job cause me stress. I don't know what to do with either problem, so I eat. I'm afraid I will lose

Glen *(he could die)* and I can't afford this house. I'll lose it too. I don't know what God wants me to do with my life. I don't know. I don't know. I don't know. If only I could stay home. Isn't there any other way, Lord? Father, You know that I love You. Are You telling me that I have neglected You? I don't feel satisfied. Food has become an issue again. I'm so sick and tired of this. It's just too much. Because of the construction of the room addition, the wall is gone. I've had to go without heat for so long, I'm going crazy. Plus all the upheaval of boxes and debris everywhere from all the construction going on in this house and a job at work that's changed so much that it's not my job anymore. I just can't take this. It's just too much. So I eat. I eat to forget. I eat to cope. I eat for comfort. I eat for pleasure. I eat, eat, and eat!!!!!

Journal Entry

August 12, 2002

I want to write. I'm staring at this blank page and don't know where to begin. I'm angry at everyone and everything. Now I'm crying. I don't want to live this way. I don't know what I want or what I need. I'd love to run away. It's too hard to figure out.

Oh Lord, I'm anxious and worried about so many things. I want to bring them to You and lay them at the foot of Your Throne. I don't want to carry these burdens anymore. First of all, I worry about Glen and his health. He's getting older and I'm afraid something is going to happen to him. I might lose him. He could die. I've only had a short time to be with him. I don't want to be constantly worrying that something could happen to him. Take this burden from me. Give me peace.

Another thing I worry about is the extreme expense of this home. If Glen dies, I cannot afford to stay here. This is our home together. He built this extra room just for me to write poetry and complete my book. This means the world to me. And then where would I go and what would I do? These things scare me. I don't have a sense of security. I never have—even growing up. I couldn't count on my parents to take care of me. Glen takes wonderful care of me, but he can't guarantee that he's always going to be here with me.

I overeat when I actually want to feel close to someone. There is no one to fill this emptiness. I want to recapture the feeling of being held and comforted as a child. Feeling unloved is a major theme in my life.

We can't erase pieces of our history—namely the dark, painful parts. Every piece of life is part of the journey that brought us to this place, and to miss God's plan and purpose... There is no healing without wounds, no freedom without chains, and no life without death. Lord, help me to write!

The Shelter of God's Love
August 12, 2002

I live
In the shelter
Of God's love (PS 91:1)
A love
That's freely given
From above (PS 86:5)

A love
That knows no limit
Has no end (EPH 3:17b, 18)
A love
I can't even begin
To comprehend (PS 103:11)

God's love calms me
As I go through change (1JN 4:16)
It's a love that I
Would never exchange (PS 86:13)

For all the "things"
On this earth (MT 16:26)
God's love for me
I cannot measure

Its worth (ROM 5:8)

He sent His
Only Son
To shed
His blood for me (EPH 1:7)
His death
On the cross
And resurrection
Is the key (ROM 4:25)

To heaven
My sins
Are completely
Forgiven and erased (MIC 7:19)
What awesome
Mercy and grace (EPH 2:4-7)

Jesus Christ
Is Lord
And Savior
I sing (PS 68:19)
Amen

And Hallelujah
To the Almighty King (PS 47:7,8)

My response
Is to live
A life of love
As Christ loves us (EPH 5:2)
His Holy
Sinless example
Is the stimulus (HEB 4:15)

That stirs
My heart to action (JAS 2:17)
Following Christ
Is the only satisfaction (JN 12:26)

That glorifies God
And honors
His Holy name (PS 29:2)

I am a
New creation in Christ
I'll never be the same (2COR 5:17)

Lord teach me
To do Your will (PS 143:10)
Let me listen
For Your voice
Help me
To be still (PS 37:7)

Great is the Lord
And most
Worthy of praise (1CHRON 16:25)
I will sing
Of His
Great love for me
All of my days! (PS 89:1)

Gratitude List

August 15, 2002

I'm grateful for my God who loves me. For my Lord and Savior Jesus Christ who saves me. For the Holy Spirit who leads me in the right direction and gives me strength to make right choices. For my husband Glen who loves me and takes care of me. For my children, Carla, Lori, Brian, Matt, Jenny, and Becca who love me. For my grandchildren, Eric, Kelsey, Aiden, Jonah, and Henry who bring me joy. For my best friend, Reggie Montei, who loves me unconditionally. For my small group couple, Dave and Jeannie Peeler, who listen with understanding and caring hearts. For my support group of four loving, caring women, Terry Pike, Sharon Bagan, Diana Hoard and Kaye Zienneker. For two ex-husbands, who I'm glad to call my friends. For material things that God has blessed me with: A beautiful home in San Clemente where the weather is wonderful; not one, but two nice cars to drive, money that I can bless others with, my husband's business, which is doing so well, my beautiful deck with the view of the hills, a computer to write my stories, the ability to write well and make my stories interesting and fun to read. The ability to laugh, especially at myself. The surgeon who saved my life. For the close relationship I have with my son Matt, even though there was only anger toward me for abandoning him when he was a boy—what a gift from God that Matt was able to open up his heart to me. For my health even though I'm experiencing difficulty right now.

These are just a few of the blessings I am grateful for. I will continue to write a gratitude list from time to time to remember all of God's blessings. God has been good to me!

11

My Daughter Pregnant at 16

"I can do all things through Christ who strengthens me" (Philippians 4:13).

Jenny's Story (and Brian's Story as a child)

The words I never wanted to hear from my sixteen year old daughter shocked and disgusted me at the same time, "Mom, I'm pregnant." I gasped for air as I said, "Oh Jenny, my baby."

Silently, I pleaded to God, I'm your child, Lord, and she's my baby. How can you allow something like this that is going to change all our lives forever? How did this happen? Where do I begin to look at why this happened?

I thought back to the circumstances of our family, her birth, and the events that led up to this day.

I was married to Bill, my first husband, for fifteen years trying to make a go of that marriage. Bill refused to get help for his drinking and I just couldn't take his numerous affairs any longer. We had four children and I shielded them from what was going on. I was at a loss what to do. I didn't know how I was going to survive. I had no job and my secretarial skills were rusty. Computers were being used in offices, not the typewriters I was familiar with. I knew nothing about computers nor how to use them. So when I decided to divorce Bill, I asked my brother, Lamar, if we could come live with him and his family in their big house in California until I could figure out what I was going to do.

In the middle of my divorce, I met Jeff at a sober Alcoholics Anonymous dance. At last I've met someone who is sober and getting help for his drinking problem. He was so attentive to my children and me, and I was starving for attention. It was inevitable that I quickly fell in love. We were married as soon as my divorce was final. Jeff didn't think he could have children, so he was excited to have a ready-made family. We were pleasantly surprised when I became pregnant. My children were not happy. In fact, they were disgusted that I was still having sex at my age *(thirty-eight!)*. Another baby was added to our already large family. The boys didn't much care, they were still young, but Carla and Lori were teenagers sixteen and fourteen and thought the whole idea was too abrupt. I hoped time would heal their feelings. All it took for them was to take one look at Jenny and their hearts melted. They became little mothers. It was so cute and I really needed their help, so it was perfect. In fact, because we were all so eager to hold her, we picked her up so quickly when she woke, that she never had a chance to cry. She knew one of us would come immediately when we heard her playing in her crib.

In the meantime, my son Brian, age ten, the older of the two boys, was my rebellious child and kept getting into trouble at home, at school, and in the neighborhood. He acted out in many ways including doing mean and cruel things to his brother Matt, who was eight years old at the time.

Another surprise, Becca, the youngest of my six children, arrived two years after Jenny.

When Jenny was a toddler about two years old, we had a pet, a cat we named Calico. Sometimes Jenny didn't know how to respect the needs of a cat and an incident occurred. I don't remember what it was, maybe Jenny pinched Calico, but I know that she was just an innocent child and didn't understand so I didn't punish her for hurting Calico. Brian did not like this and decided to take matters into his own hands. I was not aware of what he was planning. So with his younger brother Matt, eight, Brian planned *Operation Dragon Fire*. Later, I found these papers crumpled up under his bed describing everything. He wrote out his plan.

> Our mission is to make Jenny wish she never even
> hurt Calico. We have to put Tabasco sauce in
> Jenny's mouth while she's sleeping. She will never
> know what happened. We will get her back for
> what she did. We will do this at 9:30 tonight.
>
> VERY IMPORTANT NOTE: Do all this without
> being seen!!!!

Along with this note was a detailed map of our house with everyone's room listed and a trail starting at the refrigerator:

> 1. Get Tabasco sauce.

Arrows were drawn showing the path to Jenny's room and instructions:

> 2. Open Jenny's mouth (if not already open)
> and drop some Tabasco sauce in her mouth.
> All this without waking her. Then before
> she can identify you, jam back to our room.

He used Matt to do his dirty work for him. Poor Matt could not say no. By this time, Brian had already done so many hurtful things to him. Matt knew what Brian was capable of, if he didn't comply. He had no choice.

I never knew what happened to change his mind about doing this horrendous act, but I'm so glad Jenny was protected. This incident plus all the other things we caught Brian doing told me my son needed help. He showed me time and time again that he had no remorse for anything he did that hurt others. He just didn't care.

Then he started leaving the house in the middle of the night, stealing cars to joyride. He was in and out of juvenile hall and counseling as well. Three different times I enrolled him in behavioral treatment programs hoping the therapy he would get there would help him face whatever was driving his bad behavior. It broke my heart that nothing worked and to this day, my heart aches for him and what I couldn't give him as his mother.

While in treatment, my therapist who continued to work with Brian over the years, suggested I now reveal to him what happened to me as a little girl. His behavior was now triggering my issues since he had turned fourteen. My brother was fourteen when he sexually molested me when I was seven. This was difficult but I knew he was surrounded by therapists who could help him process the incident. I gave him no details just my feelings. Afterward, Brian said, "Oh Mom I'm so sorry that happened to you. It wasn't your fault; you were just a little girl. That should not have happened."

It was the first time I ever saw compassion in my son. I was so relieved. Little did I know he was wearing a mask. He had become very proficient at wearing that mask for the benefit of who he was with.

Two weeks later Brian came home for a weekend visit. We were told by his therapist not to let Brian babysit his brother or sisters at any time. He was not capable of taking good nurturing care of them. He had a history of abusive behavior with them. I went grocery shopping and left Jeff in charge of the children. I didn't know that Jeff took Becca our toddler with him to get his tire fixed on the car, but left four year old Jenny with Brian in the swimming pool. I would have reminded Jeff about the therapist's rule had I known.

A week later, Jenny innocently commented to Jeff what she had seen and what Brian said and did to her. It was obvious that Brian had sexually molested her. I was furious; first at Jeff for letting this happen, and then at Brian after I told him the damage molestation did to me. He must have been so angry with me to hurt me and Jenny like that.

We immediately called our therapist and Jeff called the police to do a 51-50 to have Brian permanently removed from our home. We got Jenny into therapy. Thank God she was young enough not to know and feel how bad and wrong that experience was with Brian in the pool.

I think that was the first of many incidences that had a detrimental effect on Jenny and her acting out.

After ten chaotic years, another divorce left me a "Single Parent." My second divorce made me realize the circumstances concerning my children. Two girls were grown and living on their own. Two boys were living with Bill, their father *(my first ex)*, in Mississippi. And two girls, Jenny, age nine, and Becca, age seven, were left shuffling between two houses here in California.

Becca 7 Yrs Old and Jenny 9 Yrs Old

Jeff, husband number two, filed divorce papers in 1995. I packed my bags and moved out of the house. My soon to be ex moved in with his girlfriend. He married her the day our divorce became final. A step-mother for my girls now a reality, Jenny and Becca chose to live with their dad and his new wife, Estrel. Disappointed, I understood their need for a complete family unit that I could not provide. Gratefully I accepted every other weekend to spend with the girls, plus some days during the week. Her father, Jeff, and I shared full custody with visitation equally shared. When she was eleven, her father kicked her out of his house and packed her bags. When he could not reach me when I went to bed and turned my phone off, he called my other daughter, Lori, twenty-five, to pick Jenny up.

I embarked on my new life as a "single again" woman. My girlfriend Sue and I decided to be roommates and moved to Lake Forest, located in South Orange County, California. I routinely accepted being a part-time single mother, sharing custody until one earth-shattering day.

One week after I moved into a two-bedroom apartment, my ex-husband called to say he couldn't continue having one of our daughters live with him.

"Jenny's angry outbursts are disrupting my marriage. Estrel and I can't take her hostility anymore."

Shocked, I didn't know what to say, let alone what to do.

"I'm not prepared to have her live with me. I don't even have a bedroom for her."

"You've got to. I'm not taking responsibility for her anymore. I've packed Jenny's bags. Lori has already picked her up."

No more discussion, decision already made, I reluctantly went to Lori's place to pick Jenny up.

Not that I didn't want her to live with me, but I panicked. How could I do this?

My roommate, Sue and I were only prepared for my girls every other weekend with a pull out sofa bed in the living room. An adjustment would have to be made.

Sue accepted Jenny with open arms. "We'll find a way to make it work," Sue assured me. Relieved about Sue's reaction, I turned to the overwhelming challenge before me.

I prayed to God, "Why allow this to happen now, after I moved into such a small apartment with a roommate?" I needed answers. How could I provide for myself, let alone for an eleven-year-old daughter full time?

I Need Answers
September 1, 1997

I just can't
See clearly
Right now
Single Parenting?
I just don't know how

I feel the weight
Of this
Enormous responsibility
I want to handle it
With confidence
And sensitivity

But it's too big
And overwhelming
I feel inadequate
Unsure and unskilled
I make mistakes
I admit it

My child's self-esteem

Is a treasure
As precious as gold
The words I communicate
Have the power
To mold (PROV 25:11)

To build up
Or tear down
It can go either way
To say what
She needs to hear
Is now what I pray (PROV 12:25)

To be an example
Of how God
Wants me to be
To guide and direct
God's Will
For her to see (DEUT 6:4-8)

I'm glad she's here

It's a privilege
And a joy
God's strength
And power
I now employ (PS 20:6)

To help me
Through the frustrations
I feel
I need answers
Your Will God
Please reveal (PS 143:10)

I don't know
How to do this
Asking for help
From others
Is such a big risk

But God's family
Of believers
Is here to help
Their tender
Loving care
Is genuine and heartfelt (EPH 4:16)

How grateful I am
To have such special
Caring friends
Time together
We'll continue to spend (PS 133:1 TEV)

Sharing our weaknesses
We build on
Each other's strengths (GAL 6:2 NLT)
Christ is our foundation
We're on the
Same wavelength (2TIM 2:19)

On Christ
The solid rock
I stand (1COR 10:4)
All other ground
Is sinking sand (MT 7:26-27)

"I can do
All things through Christ
Who strengthens me" (PHIL 4:13 NKJV)
This is His promise
And guarantee

No matter what happens
Or how quickly
Events change
Through His power
I'll be able to rearrange (PS 20:6)

My life
My circumstances
My attitude
And I know
That all these things
God will work together
For my good (ROM 8:28)

In spite of my fear of the responsibility I felt was dumped into my lap, I knew God had a plan for my life and would work it all out for my daughter and for me. I believed He would give me the strength to meet her needs, not just physically, but emotionally as well. The work ahead of me seemed insurmountable.

I joined the Single Parents support group at Saddleback Church. We had fun outings with and without the children which made it easier for me to cope with the challenges of parenting. Clinical psychologists Dr. Henry Cloud and Dr. John Townsend, both bestselling authors of the whole Boundaries series led many seminars at our group. They wrote *Boundaries with Kids - When to say YES, When to say NO, to Help Your Children Gain Control of Their Lives,* and *Raising Great Kids.* These are two great books. Drawing on the expert insights of these popular counselors, Drs. Cloud and Townsend quote, "If she (child) knows that the world requires her to take responsibility for her own personhood and life, then she can learn to live up to those requirements and get along well in life" (Cloud & Townsend, 1998, p. 18).

Persuading my daughter that I loved her unconditionally grew into my first priority. I worked hard to convince her that I would not kick her out of my house if she didn't live up to my expectations. A wall she had built up to guard her heart kept my love at a distance. Breaking down that wall turned out to be my biggest hurdle. Her basic needs expanded into more concerns. I could not give Jenny a room of her own, so I utilized creativity to make sure we each had our privacy.

Anger not only concerning the divorce, but how her dad treated Jenny compelled her acting out behavior. I knew Jenny needed to express the pain that existed underneath her fury. Validating her feelings, I created a safe place for her to begin opening up. I labored diligently to build up her crushed self-esteem caused by her dad's rejection. At first she didn't believe the positive affirmations I expressed to her. I continued to be the broken record until she could assimilate the encouraging words from my heart. Over time, not all at once, I communicated these affirmations "I love you just the way you are. I won't leave you, no matter what. Your needs are important to me. It's all right to say no. I'm glad you want to be you. You can be you and still count on my being there for you. It's okay to be angry. We will work out our problems together. In all the world, there has never been another like you. I love and value you." Finally, I caught a glimpse of hope.

Five months after coming to live with me, I shared my poem with Jenny. With tears of love in her eyes, she asked me if I thought she could write a poem too. "Of course, you can!" I smiled.

Living a New Life
Jenny Hamilton 11 years old
February 4, 1998

At first
I was afraid
Not knowing
What to do
I came to live
With Mom
Now I know
Why I am here

She comforts me
And gives me
Her support
It's what
I need now
More than ever

Sometimes
I can't explain
Just how I feel
That's why I know
She's there for me
I need her love
And care

I'm glad

I came
To live with her
That I got out
Of that mess (with Dad & Estrel)
Living there
Made me hurt
It wasn't exactly
The best

Now I'm happy
More than ever
That I came to live
With Mom
Now I feel
Much better
Knowing she
Makes me strong

It will take time
For the pain to heal
But as long
As I stay here
It's the best thing
For my care

What an incredible gift God gave me the day my daughter came to live with me.

You would think the worst was over, but there was more to this story.

She was a latch key kid. I had to work, so the rules began with no kids in the house when I'm not there. That was quickly broken. I believe Jenny had a rebellious streak in her again caused by her anger, but I didn't know how to help her. Consequences for breaking the rules became the norm. She began to smoke and then to drink, and I didn't know it until I discovered Sue's liquor in the kitchen cabinet was watered down. I found cigarettes hidden in the bedroom closet. I was at a loss what to do. It only got

Jenny Age 11

worse. She began to fail in school, and began having trouble fighting with the other girls. I removed her from school when she was so frightened of going that she cut classes. We changed schools three different times.

I made a plan to have her walk from high school to the library where I would pick her up after I got off from work. She was never there, always with friends fooling around or partying. I didn't know what to do.

In the meantime, I fell in love and married Glen, whom she liked. We moved into his house and Jenny finally had her own bedroom. I was so happy for her. Glen asked her to pick out colors and he would paint it the way she wanted. He let her pick out furniture to make her room her own. She was ecstatic. I thought things would calm down now.

Then she started sneaking out of the house in the middle of the night to go partying. When she finally came to me and confessed, "Mom, I think I'm an alcoholic just like my dad."

"Why do you think that Jenny?"

"I'm blacking out Mom and I got raped."

"Are you pregnant?"

"No, thank God, but I need help Mom."

I looked for a treatment program for teenagers with alcohol problems, but as an outpatient. We had to go as a family and of course her father was invited. He rarely made it, but Glen took on the role of father figure. I was so grateful. He became a hero to me that day.

Jenny had therapy. Glen and I had therapy with the other parents, then group therapy with all the kids and parents together. Jenny worked hard. I was so proud of her. She and I shared some deep emotions with each other starting with how it felt when she drank, stayed out all night, got drunk, passed out, and was raped. She had to share her feelings too. It was probably the first time she was honest. We both cried. Then it was up to her to make commitments from here on out. I finally believed she could do it. She did not commit to stop having sex. I wish now I would have addressed that issue.

She stayed sober for a year, and then started drinking again. And of course she continued having sex. She fell in love and was having sex with her boyfriend. She also was drinking, went to a party without her boyfriend, and she, again, was raped. She later announced she was pregnant. She thought it was because of the rape, so she didn't want to keep the baby.

At this point, my emotions built to an all-time high. I was exhausted and literally threw my hands up in complete surrender. I gave up. I didn't know what to do, so I called my mentor and explained what happened.

"I can't let her stay here. She's out of control and I can't provide the structure she needs. What do you suggest?"

"Let me make some calls Ardie, and I'll call you right back."

The phone interrupted my pleas to God in prayer.

"Ardie, I found a Christian home for pregnant girls with rules, school, skills, therapy, and options for the girls and their babies. It's all paid for by the state. I called and they have one opening right now."

What an answer to prayer! It was perfect with everything I could not provide.

Saying yes to this home was easy. Telling Jenny what I was about to do was the hard part.

"You can't be serious about this, Mom. How can you abandon me now? I need you."

"And that's exactly why I'm sending you there. What you need, I can no longer give to you. I'll come visit you. I'll take you to your doctor visits. I'll participate in family therapy. I'll do whatever I can to show you my support, but you can't live in our home until after the baby is born."

I knew Jenny would fight with me on this, but I didn't expect the rude comments and swearing she threw in my face. I had to be strong and kept my boundary in place. The next day I drove her to Mary's Shelter.

It was a large home remodeled to accommodate eighteen pregnant minors with a separate residence for those who already had their babies. Although Jenny was bitter about my decision and she had no intention of staying, where could she go? After realizing I was not going to change my mind, no matter how many times she called me crying and begging to come home, she settled down and took full advantage of all the classes, counseling, and life experiences Mary's

Shelter had to offer. I fully participated in all that I could, which was not easy. Mary's Shelter was an hour's drive from our home. I willingly did what I could to show Jenny my love and support. And when I was not able to come support Jenny, out of the blue, Pastor Rick Warren's daughter, Amy, came to mentor Jenny. I only prayed for a Christian mentor to help Jenny, but I never expected my own Pastor's daughter. God gives good gifts!

When I finally could relax to enjoy my life with Glen again, we decided to go on a date which included dinner and a movie. As we drove to the restaurant, I was reading an interesting article in a magazine out loud to Glen. All of a sudden I dropped the magazine and my body began to jerk and shake uncontrollably in all directions. I never lost consciousness, but my lungs locked and I couldn't breathe. I certainly couldn't talk. Glen pulled over and asked if I was alright. I couldn't say a word. I finally calmed down and my body stopped jerking, but I was numb on one side of my body. I didn't know what had happened but thought I had a stroke.

Glen asked, "Do you want to go home?" I shook my head no. "Do you want to go to the hospital?" I nodded yes.

When we arrived at the ER, they ran around quickly also thinking I had a stroke. They rushed me to get an MRI to find out what happened. Glen came into the room where I was and said, "You didn't have a stroke but you're not going to like what they found." The doctor came in with x-rays of my head. There was a big, dark spot that I could see clearly. "It's a brain tumor!" The doctor knew exactly what it was, "meningioma" and that it had been growing very slowly, probably thirty years, and that it is always BENIGN! I was so relieved! Two incidents of God's grace were so evident. First, that I was not driving when the seizure occurred, and the tumor was not cancerous! Gratitude overwhelmed me.

Now the tumor had to be removed. Surgery was scheduled one week later. I was given Dilantin to prevent another seizure and steroids for the swelling to go down. During that week, my numbness went away and my speech totally came back. It was a very difficult week for me anticipating that my skull was going to be opened on the operating table. Approximately four hours of surgery was scheduled to remove the tumor located on the outside of the brain and pressing against the speech center.

It ended up taking four and a half hours. The tumor was the size of a tennis ball and the surgeon had to dig deep to try to get it all. At the time, he didn't know if he had gotten it all or if he had dug too deep and injured my speech center. He didn't even know if I would ever be able to talk again.

When I woke up, my speech was awful, only garbled sounds. I couldn't form words, so I thought I'd just write down what I needed. The only letter I could write over and over was D. Great, I can't even communicate at all. My thinking was totally fine. I had to make hand gestures and do the best I could to ask for what I wanted and needed. Even when I could talk it was garbled and slurred like a drunk person and made no sense. I was miserable and cried pretty much every day.

Mary's Shelter allowed Jenny to come see me in the hospital, but she could see I was in no condition to help at this time. I was so glad God had placed her in this wonderful home to get her needs met when I couldn't meet them. Her older sisters, Carla and Lori, visited and took her to her doctor visits.

Eventually after working with a speech therapist and making it my full time job to speak again, I've learned how to talk. I was her most tenacious student because speaking is my life line. "The LORD says, *"So I will restore to you the years that the swarming locust has eaten"* (Joel 2:25, NKJV). It's very important for me to help other people to inspire them to overcome adversity. By sharing my story and sharing how God has worked in my life to heal my painful issues redeeming what the locusts have eaten is one of my purposes.

Jenny stayed seven months until just before the baby was born. We discovered her baby was not the result of the rape. Her boyfriend who decided to leave her during her pregnancy was not willing to be a father to his baby. He abandoned them both. Jenny knew she was not ready to be a mother, so the last half of her pregnancy was devoted to finding a loving family to place her son with. Our church, Saddleback, helped with the adoption and all the paperwork. She found a loving Christian home who had already adopted other children. Jenny still has contact with them. They send pictures and letters of his progress. It still is difficult for all of us, as each member of the family was affected by the placing of her baby. It was especially grueling for Jenny.

I was very pleased with the changes I saw in Jenny, and was glad to have her home once again. Although I wouldn't have wished for that experience for Jenny, she grew up emotionally and spiritually and her character changed for the better. She was a completely different person because of her experience. I think I grew too. I was stronger than I thought I could be. God was certainly with all of us and got us through a very tough time. *"And we know that God causes everything to work together for the good of those who love God and are called according to His purpose for them"* (Romans 8:28, NLT).

Jenny's Testimony at 17
February 21, 2003

> My name is Jenny Hamilton and this is my story of how God drastically changed my life. I grew up going to church every Sunday and went to private Christian school through fifth grade. I went on mission trips and joined Area Bible Study but living the Lord's way was so difficult for me. I went to parties every weekend, drinking excessively, and many times coming home at five in the morning. I never worried about the kind of danger I was putting myself into while being so intoxicated.
>
> One night I got scared when I blacked out from consuming too much alcohol. I told

my mom what had happened and that I
wanted help. Even in my most terrible state
God was pulling at my heart to change and
start living for Him. My mom knew I had a
drinking problem since alcoholism runs in
our family, so she put me through a rehab
program. I went through the motions of the
program, even though I hated being there. I
wanted to stop my party lifestyle, but I
couldn't do it on my own. Deep down I
wanted to change, I just didn't know how to
do it.

I took Saddleback Church's Christian Life
and Service Seminar (CLASS 101 Discovering
My Church). They are a series of classes
offered to provide members tools and
resources to take your next steps of faith, to
grow in your walk with God, to learn how to
serve others, and to begin to share your story
with those in your life who do not know
Christ. After taking the first CLASS, I began
to question if God could forgive all the bad
things I had done. The doubts I had about
my forgiveness prevented me from getting
baptized until a year later. I was nervous
and afraid. I didn't want people expecting
me to be a goody-two-shoes Christian once I
was baptized. I needed to wash away the
old me, to no longer drink, smoke weed or
cigarettes, or have sex. I also yearned for a
new attitude. Coming out of the water, my
desire was to have a clean white slate.
Nothing could have prepared me for how I

actually felt after I was baptized. In that moment I felt God's grace so strongly that I sobbed and sobbed. He had truly forgiven me and wiped the slate clean.

I stayed sober for six months but started drinking again one night with friends my boyfriend knew. While I was at the party I was given GHB (the date rape drug) and was raped. On May 7, 2001 I found out I was pregnant by a guy I didn't even know. I was frightened, confused, and even a little angry. I felt like my whole world was over. I even thought about killing myself at one point because I just didn't know how I was going to have a baby. I felt so alone. God knew the only way I was going to wake up and change my ways was if He allowed something drastic to happen to me. A verse I lived by when I was pregnant, "Seek His will in all you do, and He will direct your path" (Proverbs 3:6, NLT).

I knew I was too young to be a mother and yet abortion was not an option. How could God use this situation for my good? My reasons for giving my baby up for adoption were I could not provide for him in the way that he needed, he would not have a stable father and I was not ready to be a mother.

My mom sent me to a maternity house through the duration of my pregnancy. I hated it at first, but thought since I was going to be there for a while, I might as well get something out of it. I spent a good deal of my time praying and reading the Bible. I finally knew the only way I was going to make it through this was if I turned to God.

I wish I could say I stopped the bad things I was doing right away, but I didn't. It took me halfway through my pregnancy to realize just how much I needed God. "No one who lives in Him keeps on sinning. No one who continues to sin has either seen Him or known Him" (1 John 3:6, NIV). I wanted so badly to become a better Christian and start living for God. That was His plan for me all along.

While I was away from home, the other girls I was living with showed me just how fortunate I was. Hearing stories about their terrible lives and relationships with abusive parents made me a compassionate person that I never was before. I felt someone else's pain instead of just my own. I also became much more appreciative of my mom and started to restore our broken relationship. She became my biggest support during my pregnancy, next to God.

An event that made me rely fully on God and God alone was when my mom had brain surgery to remove a benign tumor. After her surgery, I couldn't come home as often or really talk to her because her speech was impaired. She was the one I went to for everything. Now the only person I could go to was God. I finally was drawing closer to Him which is what He wanted all along. It wasn't up until recently that I developed a personal relationship with God as my Savior and true friend.

Now I feel like a totally different person. God has transformed my life and my heart to see His purpose for me. I'm not perfect. I still get tempted to have a cigarette or to have sex but I choose to say no because, "I can do all things through Christ who strengthens me" (Philippians 4:13, NKJV).

Having a child at the age of sixteen and giving him up for adoption was the hardest thing I have ever done. It is not easy living without the child I gave birth to. Some days I miss him more than I can express. Other days I am glad he is with such an amazing Christian family. A month and a half has gone by and it still hurts that he's not in my arms. The pain of watching my child look to someone else as his mom is unbearable. I worked so hard to bring him into this world and that keeps me strong in my decision to live my life for God.

I am not the same person I was a year ago. Without God I never would have been able to survive all I have experienced. These trials have helped me to grow and I have received

all the blessings and benefits of God's grace.
I learned that I can and have excelled
academically. I am now aware of my God-
given abilities. I will be using these abilities
to serve God and others, rather than serving
my own selfish interests. I want others to see
just how much God can change even the
most disobedient person. If He can change
me, He can change anyone.

* * *

As a young lady of twenty-nine Jenny has grown into the woman she is today. I'm happy to say she has given up her party ways. She has a heart for God and loves to serve the Lord wherever she can. She's involved in charity work as well. Her job that started out as making pizza turned into becoming the youngest female manager employed in their company. She now has been operations manager of a dental office for nine years. She has recently married the love of her life and is a wonderful step-mother to his four-year-old son. I'm proud of her and delighted that she has done so well.

Me and Jenny

Jenny, Daniel and Jerry Flores

12

Reconnecting With Brothers

"We know that all things work together for good to those who love God" *(Romans 8:28, NKJV).*

How Anger Can Promote Healing

The emotional pain in my life had become unbearable. Why is pain such a motivating factor in my life? Pain teaches me valuable lessons. Pain is a gift. It tells me what needs healing and shows me how much I need God. Dealing with life without Him is impossible for me. Pain propels me to lean on Him for strength, *"I can do all things through Christ who strengthens me"* (Philippians 4:13, NKJV). Once having felt pain, accepting and embracing it, I can move through it. What awaits me on the other end of the spectrum is joy.

"There is no maturing without change. There is no change without loss. There is no loss without pain. Without pain there is no joy" (Pastor Rick Warren, Saddleback Church).

Tired of being a victim of abuse, I searched out help along the way on my journey to recovery.

In the late eighties, I started attending self-help classes to learn about myself and my need to overeat. I grew up fat and didn't know why, only that I ate too much and loved sweets. I began a journey of discovery about myself.

When I turned forty one, my son Brian's uncontrollable behavior compelled me to seek counseling for him with Dr. Vance B. Becker, a PhD in clinical psychology. Dr. Becker is an expert with adolescents. He was recommended by my niece Toni, my brother Lamar's oldest daughter, who is only seven years younger than I am. We're very close, more like sisters. I valued her recommendation.

I hesitated to get counseling because my mother and brothers were so against it. Counseling with my pastor was not working. Now that Brian was getting into trouble, I felt I had a good enough reason to go against the family and get Brian some help. Indeed my family agreed. As I began to work with Dr. B (*as I began calling him*), I learned about myself, and what happened to me in my childhood. It became clear to me that I needed further help with my own issues.

In the early nineties, I was attending a twelve-step group meeting in a therapist's office. On a bulletin board an ad for VOICES was posted. VOICES – Victims Of Incest Can Emerge Survivors. At last a group of survivors just like me. *"Incest survivors do have a choice... ...let pain from the past continue controlling and victimizing them, or choose consciously to leave the victim's role behind,"* was their mantra. I latched onto them for hope.

Once per quarter they sponsored one-day seminars focusing on different aspects of healing. My very first seminar was *"Learning to Love and Trust Your Body."* Terrified, I didn't know what to expect. There were so many women there; about one hundred in attendance. Speakers were all survivors of abuse, making me feel more comfortable. Of course, there were therapists as well, teaching on different subjects. We went to classrooms for group discussion and exercises. Anxious and nervous about what I was doing, this was the first time I acknowledged in public that I was a victim of abuse. I so wanted to be a survivor, not realizing I already was one. Put into a group of four, one being a therapist, I don't really remember the exercise. She reached over to me and put her hand on my thigh. Immediately I was transported to my childhood, and this was my brother touching me. The sobbing that came up from deep inside me was frightening but I let it come. When I stopped crying and realized I was in the present, I was petrified. It was like a trance or spell had just happened. I was told I had a regression, when I reverted back to an earlier childhood event. It is interesting how the body remembers everything it has experienced. What I could not articulate as a child, I could now express from my soul. But this time I had support, care, and understanding from safe people.

Another part of my journey began as I attended every class and group VOICES offered. I continued to learn and grow. One class was a journaling class where I wrote an angry letter to my brother Greg not intended for it to be sent. Anger can be a positive healing force. I never had gotten in touch with my anger... ...only my pain with tears of sadness grieving the loss of my innocence and childhood.

I handed my letter to the therapist who was the teacher. After reading it, she asked if I would be willing to read my anger letter at the next seminar, I was shocked. It's one thing to reveal to a therapist or small group what I experienced, but quite another to voice my truth to hundreds. Even though feeling fearful, I knew it was the right thing to do. It would also be healing for me and for others who would identify with my feelings.

I'll never forget the date October 26, 1991; forty four years old, I was about to read my anger letter to a public group of other survivors of incest. The title of the seminar was *"Anger: A Positive Healing Force; Survivors share their anger work."* Each woman survivor shared her story and her own writing used as a tool in her recovery.

As I waited for my turn to share, I kept looking for the friend I had invited to support me in this very big step. At last, I saw her in the distance outside the auditorium. I ran to meet her and hugged her tightly. As she held onto me, the tears I had been holding in with fear, now began to be released. I sobbed and sobbed for five minutes for that little girl inside me who was hurt and wounded by her brother in such a brutal, damaging way.

That's just what I needed to become the strong adult woman that I am, no longer afraid of my brother, even if he would have been in the audience listening to my every word. I was completely in control of this situation. I honored the little girl inside me and empowered her to tell her truth.

Anger is a natural response to abuse and a healthy response to violation. This is a letter to my brother who sexually molested me when I was a little girl.

Here's what I read to over two hundred in the audience.

I have a right to feel anger at what you did to me. I was violated, betrayed, and sexually abused. I discovered that my home was not a safe place. I learned that my saying "NO, don't do that" meant nothing to you. My sense of control over my own body was violated. I felt powerless, isolated, and alone. Terrified, I didn't understand what was happening and why it was happening to me. I wanted you to stop, but I didn't know how to stop you.

I was just a little girl. You were a teenager, seven years older than I. You had no right to touch me, abuse me, and molest me. I hate you for what you did to me. You disgust me. The sight of you makes me sick. When I see you, I see evil. I want to rip your eyes out. I want to hit you, beat on your chest, and scream at

you how much I hate you. There is
no excuse for what you did.

I was robbed of what was rightfully
mine—my childhood, my innocence,
and my happiness. I was thrust into
a world I wasn't ready for. You
robbed me of my right to learn,
grow, and explore my own sexuality.
You violated my boundaries,
making me question my ability to
say "NO" affecting all my
relationships with men. You robbed
me of my own identity and my sense
of self.

The extent of the damage done to
me is immeasurable, touching every
part of my life, and my sanity. My
world has been ripped apart. And I
have never been the same.

Yes, I am angry. I am outraged and
furious. I was hurt as a child and
I'm still hurting after carrying this
burden over thirty years. I am
innocent. I did not deserve what
you so brutally did to me. I looked
up to you with love and admiration
and I was betrayed. My innocence
was thrown in the street, trampled

over, and left to die. A part of me
did die; the little girl (inner child)
who was lost, abandoned, neglected,
and abused.

You deserve to suffer for what you
did. You deserve to be castrated.
Everything you love and value
should be stolen from you. Maybe
then you might possibly begin to
know what it feels like to be hurt
and humiliated.

Yes, I am filled with rage and fury
for the pain you inflicted on me.
Knowing I will always be affected by
what you did to me, I hate you for
that. I never want to see you or talk
to you again. And I won't allow you
to abuse me ever again.

I added to the audience, "Thank you for letting me share."

After a moment of silence, the crowd jumped to their feet and applauded my courage. I felt pleased that I followed through with my conviction to tell my truth. It's always amazing to me, that when I am willing to do the painful work involved, there's healing available if I want it badly enough. And I wanted to be free of the pain of my past. My journey to emotional and physical health and healing is my choice, something that no one can take from me. That day I began to feel proud and strong, sharing the truth of my past is the key to my healthy present and future. *"You will know the truth, and the truth will set you free"* (John 8:32, NIV).

Lamar's Passing (My other brother)

When I heard the news of Lamar's death, my eyes swelled with tears of pain. Fourteen years older, my brother turned out to be the father figure I needed when Dad gave more attention to his beer than me.

Lamar affectionately called me "punkin." I looked up to him with adoration. He was my protector, but I learned he couldn't protect me from everything.

I wanted to go to his memorial service, but wondered whether our brother, Greg, would come. The last words Greg said to me still echoed in my ears, "I don't ever want to see you or talk to you again!" That happened fifteen years earlier.

There were three of us, my two older brothers, Lamar the oldest and Greg, then me, the baby. We were each seven years apart in age. Lamar and Greg had a falling out many years before when they were in business together. I didn't get into the business when they asked me to work for them. *Yeah, right,* I thought. I knew better than to go into business with relatives. My brothers never worked out their differences and each swore that the other had stolen the business. They stopped talking long ago.

Lamar and I made our peace when I took Glen, my new husband, to meet my brother for the first time. I hadn't seen Lamar for fifteen years. When I confronted Greg in 1990 about his molesting me as a child, Lamar became angry that I even brought it up now that we were all adults. He said to me, "How dare you call him a child molester! If he is, then so am I!" I was shocked at his anger and fully didn't realize that what he revealed was the truth about himself; that *he* molested Greg! Tired of secrets, all I wanted was for the truth to be told about what happened to me.

As adults, Lamar didn't want anything to do with church, but Greg and I were Christians worshipping in the same church along with Mom and Dad.

Mighty Fortress Orthodox Evangelical Lutheran Church sounds

sacred doesn't it? That's certainly what Mom was searching for. Her quest for biblical truth became more rigid with each church she joined.

Mom attended so many Lutheran churches trying to find one that adhered to the truth of the King James Bible. She didn't believe in using modern translations. She thought they were incorrect translations from the original Hebrew and Greek. She started with Missouri Synod, then Wisconsin Synod, American Lutheran Church, American Evangelical Lutheran Church, and Evangelical Lutheran Church of America. All of them were Lutheran but differed in Biblical guidelines. Being highly religious, she needed accurate doctrine to justify her legalistic point of view. In the end, she discovered a small congregation not affiliated with any of the synods, Mighty Fortress, meeting in a Dutch Club in Anaheim, CA, that seemed to fit her needs.

That's when I arrived in Long Beach, CA. Prior to this time, I lived outside Chicago, at Great Lakes Naval Base in 1977 for three years; my first time living in snow country.

Experiencing the worst blizzard in Chicago's history, I moved back to CA. I longed for the warmth of Southern California and to be close to my family once again. In spite of what happened in our childhood, Greg had begun to show some caring for me and my children. In his own way I think he was trying to make up for what he did to me.

Missing them so much, I was eager to attend church with Mom, Dad, and my brother Greg. I loved him and tried not to think about what happened in our childhood. I gladly drove the thirty miles one way, from Long Beach to Anaheim to attend their church. I willingly became a member, although now I realize I could not have gone against the family system at that time even if I wanted to. There were silent rules with our family. Don't make waves. Don't stand up for yourself. Follow whatever they say. I did exactly that. But the agony of my childhood haunted me.

Unbearable emotional pain dominated my life. That pain coupled with the realization I lived as a victim, motivated me to find healing. I searched for help along the way on my journey to recovery. I learned our family maintained a cycle of silence. I hungered for the truth to be told but didn't know how to go about it.

As time passed, the memories of my childhood surfaced, memories that I tried hard to forget. I could no longer take communion at the altar, side by side, with the brother who molested me. Disturbing visions vividly haunted me of Greg walking around nude. I couldn't ignore the pain any longer. Finally, I chose to break the cycle of silence by talking about the secret no one else would. *No more secret,* I thought.

So without a support system, not even a therapist to help me, I called my pastor for counseling. I needed help. He advised me to confront Greg privately and ask for reconciliation. The pastor assured me that the air would be cleared. This was the right thing to do. God would bless our brother-sister relationship because the Holy Spirit would soften Greg's heart. My brother would recognize his need to repent of his sin against me.

"An essential part of healing from child sexual abuse is telling the truth about your life. Breaking the silence is a powerful healing tool" (Bass & Davis, 1988, p. 92). My recovery journey included telling the truth about what was done to me, then sharing the feelings I experienced caused by physical, emotional, sexual, and religious abuse.

I first wrote a letter to Greg detailing as best I could what happened. I used *"I statements."* Then I told him what I felt as a little girl of seven frightened of my teenaged brother. Being careful not to be graphic in case his wife read the letter, I did use the word molest because that's what he did. It was important for me to tell him the impact and residual effects that continued into my adult life.

It's devastating for a child to be violated, not once but repeatedly over several years. Touched inappropriately, I experienced severe psychological damage. When molested, the violation of my boundaries and sense of control devastated me. As a child blameless for the abuse inflicted on me, it was just wrong, I wrote.

I did not feel safe in my own home. My betrayed love and trust of family members alienated me. The adults I depended upon did not protect me from my own brother. I felt horrified, confused, and humiliated because the message I received was that *I* didn't matter. I didn't understand what happened. Why didn't my parents protect me? Terrified by the trauma, unavoidable inestimable scars wounded me.

Robbed of my childhood innocence and happiness, the nightmare forced me into a world that this *little girl* was unprepared for. In the same letter, I wrote:

Greg, you stripped me of my right to learn, grow, and explore my own sexuality. You violated my boundaries and made me question my ability to say "NO" which affected all my relationships with men. You cheated me of my own identity and my sense of self. The extent of the massive damage done touched every part of my life and my sanity. My world ripped

apart; I've never been the same since.

There. I said it! I revealed the secret that no one in our family wanted to talk about. Certainly Greg didn't nor my Mom who knew because I told her when I was ten years old. She never talked to me about it ever again. I wanted to be free of the pain. That day I felt proud and strong. I shared the truth of my past with others, which was the key to my healthy present and future. The journey to emotional, physical, and total well-being depends on me. *"No one will take that away from me!"* I reassured myself.

I wrote multiple letters to Greg, some he returned unopened. When he did not respond, I called him. I repeated what I wrote in my letters and pleaded my case. I wanted resolution so badly. I needed healing. I was shocked when healing didn't happen. What did occur frightened me.

He screamed into the phone, "How *dare* you bring this up now!?! We're adults for God's sake! That happened in our childhood and we were just playing doctor! It was nothing! How *dare* you call me a child molester! What do you want from me!?!"

His questions felt like stinging darts, but I answered what I could in the midst of my tears. His anger again intimidated me. What did I ever do to cause him to be so angry with me? I could have reported him, but didn't. Revenge destroys relationships. In spite of everything, I still loved my brother.

I wanted reconciliation after allowing the secret to be spoken and truth to be acknowledged. I just wanted him to say he was sorry for hurting me. I looked up to him as my big brother. I wanted him to look out for me, to protect me! Instead, I needed to be protected from my own brother.

After several heated arguments, a few emotional phone calls, and two more letters, neither one of my brothers wanted to talk to me or see me ever again.

All this time I had been counseling with the pastor. He told me to continue confronting Greg, and that God was with me. I didn't feel God anywhere, nor did I think He was even listening, let alone doing something in my behalf.

The pastor promised to be with me until there was resolution of the situation. He made one visit to Greg privately. I don't know what Greg could have said to him that would have made a difference, but the pastor told me that he had to decline himself from counseling me any further and I was on my own. The pastor didn't tell me anything further, but I suspected Greg brought up to him that I hadn't followed the biblical guidelines to confront the person who had given offense privately without telling anyone else what happened. I had told Toni *(my niece, Lamar's daughter)* who also was sexually molested by her stepfather. I was guessing but I didn't really know.

My heart sank. I felt lost, abandoned, and betrayed again. Riding an out of control speeding train for months, my world just exploded. This man had pastored me and my children for seven years with all our family's dysfunction. I counted on him to minister to me with all my problems. I needed guidance and direction. Now it felt as if I was going to die.

After much deliberation and soul searching, I couldn't get past this brutal betrayal. I left that church, the pastor, Mom and Dad, and both my brothers. It was the most terrifying time of my life, and I had nowhere to go and no one to talk to. I truly felt alone.

When the church I had been a member of for nine years heard that I was leaving, I received a number of phone calls and letters. I hoped my friends would wish me well, but again my hopes were shattered when I was ridiculed for leaving, calling me a pagan and condemning me to hell.

The pastor begged me to stay, that he would be held accountable to God for not keeping me in the fold. I said, "You should have thought of that before you so brutally betrayed me! I'm leaving!"

Although I was deeply hurt by how I was treated there, I still needed the support of a church I could trust. I tried many churches over the next few months, not finding what I was looking for. I needed to feel safe and cared for with love, support, and recovery from the hurts of my past.

Once again, I began to wonder, *"Is there a church that sees the benefits and value of recovery?"* I tried different churches, searching for something more than just good contemporary music and support of caring Christians. I was looking through the Yellow Pages of the phone book, calling Lutheran churches because that was the church I had been raised in. I asked for a church with recovery oriented support groups.

I called another church of the same denomination on the phone, told the secretary what I needed. Her answer shocked me.

She told me, "Our church doesn't have those things but you might try Saddleback."

"What's that?" I asked.

"It's a non-denominational church that has recovery groups and support groups for every known issue."

At the time I thought it was unheard of that she would suggest a church that wasn't Lutheran. I was frightened to leave my comfort zone that was familiar and what I grew up with. I asked my adult daughter, Lori, if she would be willing to go with me for support. When we drove up, the huge number of cars and the amount of people I saw there overwhelmed me. There were thousands attending this mega church. And when I saw the gigantic tent, I looked for jugs of Kool-Aid. I was frightened this might be a cult.

When I saw the big jugs at tables throughout the campus, I told Lori, "It's Jim Jones all over again."

I knew all about the Jonestown Massacre of November 18, 1978. "912 people died including 276 children by drinking grape flavored

Flavor-Aid (not Kool-Aid) laced with cyanide and Valium. It was a mass suicide driven by their cult leader Jim Jones" (Wikipedia, Jonestown Massacre, 2015).

Lori replied, "It's so hot Mom, it's probably just water."

To my relief, I found a wonderful church home. I enjoyed the upbeat and uplifting music, the messages touched my heart, and I loved that Christ-centered Celebrate Recovery was offered as well as various support groups. My prayer was answered.

After I calmed down, what I found was just what I needed. For many years growing up, I was just as deeply entrenched in religiosity as my mother. It was all I knew. God wanted more for me. He wanted me to have a relationship with Him, not a religion. When the pastor betrayed me so brutally, my pain propelled me to leave. It was God's idea all along. I know God allowed that pain for me to finally be able to leave. I wouldn't have left for any other reason and God knew that. I am so grateful that God always brings good out of tragedy. Saddleback has been my church home ever since and I didn't regret making that decision. I never looked back. That was twenty years ago.

I reflected many times about my brother Greg. What happened? I simply told the truth. I felt relieved and thankful I could finally breathe. My journey didn't end there. I continued to work hard to let go of my painful past. No matter what happened in the future, I needed to forgive Greg, not for his sake but, for mine. First I had to deal with all my anger, second my sadness of what I lost, and third grieve the loss of what could not be recovered.

* * *

After many years in therapy, when I could at last pray for Greg's healing, I knew I had healed enough to try one more time to reach him. Twelve years had passed when I felt compelled to write my brother one more letter.

December 5, 2002

Dear Greg,

I don't know if you have thought about me in all the years that have past. I have thought of you many times with sadness and regret.

I realize how much hurt and anger you have by what you experienced growing up in our family. When I told Mom at age ten what you did, she brutally attacked you physically. It humiliated you, damaged you emotionally, and wounded your very soul. I remember how terrified I felt to see such violence coming from our mother. I wanted her to get us some help. Choosing cruelty to punish you sickened me. Her harsh, ruthless, and callous rage caused me nightmares. Was she capable of unleashing that rage toward me? I thought. Another reason I did not feel safe.

I simply needed reconciliation, not further distance. You may still be angry, I don't know. How sad we couldn't talk as Christian adults about what happened, even if it wasn't handled Biblically. When I confronted you, I

never meant to hurt you. I just couldn't
continue living as if nothing took place
between us. It ate me up inside making
me nauseated. The answer never seemed
simple, but I needed peace.

I have peace now from our gracious
God. Three months ago I experienced a
Grand Mall Seizure. An MRI
unexpectedly discovered a brain tumor
the size of a tennis ball. The tumor
slowly grew for at least twenty-five or
thirty years. The impending five and
one half hour surgery one week later
removed it. The surgery results found it
benign. Praise God! I've had to re-learn
my speech and parts of my memory. Slow
and tedious, recovery takes time, but God
provides all that I need.

I don't tell you this so you'll feel sorry
for me, but to tell you what I've learned.
Because I received a second chance at
life, my gratitude is full to overflowing!
Precious and too brief, life swiftly slips
away. Relationships have more
meaning. Broken relationships must be
repaired and the only thing worth
spending time on.

I don't know how you feel today.

Things may not have changed for you. I hope that you can at least read this letter and give it some thought. I just wanted you to know I regret how much my confrontation hurt you. We've both suffered enough pain and heartache over childhood issues.

I intend to lay them to rest. Furthermore, I desire reconciliation with you, but I realize that may not be possible. At least I tried once more before God calls me home.

You and your family are in my prayers. Hoping you would like to talk, here's my new phone number.

Lovingly, your sister Ardith

I don't think I'll ever know if Greg read that letter, but I like to think God had me write it for a reason. God always brings good out of every tragedy.

* * *

In 2006, my oldest brother Lamar died. Would Greg come to the memorial service? I waited fifteen long years with no contact whatsoever. I hoped, but left behind any expectation that I would ever see my brother again.

As I greeted the relatives at the memorial service, I saw Linda, Greg's wife. She came up to me immediately, excited to see me and gave me a big hug.

"Are you here by yourself?"

"No, Greg is here." My heart sank.

"Where is he?"

"Over there." She pointed to a frail old man with very thick coke lens glasses, and seated in a wheelchair with one leg missing above the knee. My eyes swelled with tears as I approached my brother. I put my hand on his shoulder and bent down to quietly say, "Greg, do you know who I am?"

"No," he said, "I'm almost blind."

I said, "Do you remember your sister?"

He burst into sobbing tears. I threw my arms around his neck and sobbed with him for several minutes. "I want to see you later Greg. Are you going to the reception?" He nodded yes. "I will see you there."

So much just happened I could hardly concentrate on the beautiful memorial. Greg, a man I only knew to be strong-willed, controlling, and angry turned into a softened, vulnerable soul crying like a baby, I thought.

Afterwards, the reception buzzed with activity. Linda wheeled Greg into the far end of the room. I walked over to the table where they sat. I said a prayer, "God be with me and be there for my brother who needs me now."

I sat down.

Leaning closer I greeted him. "It's so good to see you. How are you doing?"

He explained his diabetes and resulting amputation. His going blind as well, another complication of the disease, saddened me. We talked about many things, but then Greg reverted to his old excuses for what happened in our childhood. I thought if he can do nothing more, I will accept it. I needed nothing further from my brother.

Greg sobbed again. Fifteen years prior his rage intimidated me. Now an old man crippled from the ravages of a horrible disease, my brother's fragility and vulnerability broke my heart.

Greg said, "There's no excuse for what I did. I am your older brother and should have protected you. That never should have happened to you." His tears turned to sobs as he added, "I'm so sorry that I hurt you."

As I wrapped my arms around him sobbing just as deeply as he, our hearts mended. I felt love and compassion.

On the ride home, I reflected on the day's events. I took a risk. Because I broke the cycle of silence my family maintained most of my life, I received a gift from God and from my brother I will never forget.

* * *

Two years later in 2008, Greg passed away at the age of sixty-eight. I can only imagine after releasing the burden that he carried for so many years, his heart must have overflowed with gratitude. I know my heart leaped with joy; we finally reconciled.

13
My Defiant Daughter

"For I know the plans I have for you," declares the Lord, "plans to prosper you and not to harm you, plans to give you hope and a future" (Jeremiah 29:11, NIV).

Carla's Story

Carla

Carla is my firstborn. I was a very naïve twenty two year old when she was born. There were many reasons why I didn't bond with my baby. I wasn't ready to be a mother. I was really an immature child myself. I didn't know what she needed or how to meet those needs. She cried, and I didn't pick her up to soothe her because the baby book I was reading *(that was popular at the time)* suggested I *not* do that. I didn't know she was just hungry. I didn't have any milk to breastfeed her because she had too much anesthesia from the birth and kept falling asleep instead of nursing. I just didn't know. The doctor wanted me to start her on cereal and formula at one month old, and of course she was so hungry by then she overate and vomited much of her food. It was a mess and she wouldn't stop crying. I felt so inadequate as a mother; I didn't know what to do. So Carla and I were not close, and I resented having a baby I didn't know what to do with.

Lori, who came two years after Carla, was my cooperative child, never giving me a moment's concern. She was very quiet and just a good baby and child. Comparing the two, Carla gave me many frustrations. That's where my resentment of her began and our relationship began to unravel.

As she grew she became my rebellious child, which made things worse. By the time she hit her teens, we were at each other's throats. When she was in high school, she wrote a paper:

> I wish my parents would understand my personal feelings. I wish sometimes that I could look at my mom and she would gaze intently at my pleading eyes and reconciliation would be made.

If I would have had some parenting skills, perhaps things could have been different.

My mother passed away in 1989 and I was grieving her loss. Then Carla decided to move out on her own. Instead of my being happy for her, I was sad for me.

I was very hurt that she chose the time right after my Mom's death to move out when I was still grieving. I really felt overloaded with facing the loss of my mother plus the loss of my firstborn daughter.

226

The empty nest syndrome hit me from both ends at the same time – not to mention the deep emotional problems with Brian. I know that wasn't Carla's fault, but I was overwhelmed by all of these circumstances.

I could see that my focus had to change from me to Carla. I did want the best for her, but as a mother I also wanted to protect her because I loved her so much.

I certainly learned from my relationship with my mother that I wanted so much more for Carla and me. I wanted us to be close. I certainly wanted to think twice before overreacting to any situation. I wanted no regrets. I wanted to be there for Carla and wanted to support, not criticize her dreams, goals, and decisions in life.

I thought our relationship would finally calm down now that she was living on her own... ...but it didn't happen. Instead we both continued to voice our feelings, and our conflicts escalated.

"Mom, this really hurts me. I feel completely rejected and abandoned by you."

"Carla, everything you said is true. I know I'm not the mother you would like me to be. I'm sorry for that and regret the choices I made."

"Mom, I'm sorry it's come to this, but I have to make this decision for my own personal growth and healing. So I want to divorce myself from the fantasy of the kind of mother I wanted by not having you in my wedding pictures. You can come to my wedding but not be in any of the pictures."

"I'm still your mother, whether I'm in your wedding pictures or not. I'll always be your mother."

"Mom, I'm not trying to hurt you, please know that. I feel I've made every effort to bridge the distance between us. Your process is different from mine. It's painful for me to reach out to you and experience rejection repeatedly."

"Carla, hoping to achieve a healthier, loving relationship on a different level is my hope, my dream, my want, and my desire."

"Where do we go from here?" Carla asked.

"My want for us today is to have an adult to adult relationship, not the "mother-child" relationship that you've always wanted."

Thinking back I see how harsh I might have been to expect so much from Carla who had no therapist to help her sort out her feelings, grieve her losses and relate to me differently. After all, I was the one in therapy and recovery. I had high hopes for Carla and me, yet our pattern was to forgive and move on, hug and love on each other for a while until the next conflict arose. She was getting nowhere in her personal life, and I was getting more and more frustrated and angry.

Carla was defiant. We were always locking horns. I was so angry with her for not taking care of her responsibilities. After all, she was now thirty three years old and should know better. We were always arguing. I prayed so hard for her to change. When that didn't happen, I prayed for me to change, for my heart to be softened, and for my anger to be taken out of my heart, so I could see Carla with compassionate eyes. We began to bond in a way that had never happened before.

I continued to pray for us both, and finally asked God to change my heart towards Carla, not expecting anything different from her. My eyes began to see her as God sees her, with eyes of compassion and unconditional love. God answered that prayer, and I began to listen to Carla and her problems in a different way. I was no longer angry. She began to see me differently because of my changed behavior. She let down her guard and began trusting me that I would be there for her in ways I never had been before.

What a miracle! We loved each other unconditionally, walked everywhere arm in arm, laughing and joking about private jokes that only she and I knew about. We were enjoying each other for the very first time. Our relationship changed and evolved into the most

228

loving ever possible... ...all because of God's grace. God grew me, matured me, and changed my attitude toward Carla, and I related to her differently. I was more understanding and loving toward her. We would affirm each other's love and marveled at the miracle God had provided when we both had lost hope. It was an unbelievable answer to prayer that we both were very grateful for.

Sunday has always been our family day tradition. Typically we would meet at church, have lunch afterward, then see a movie or rent a video. Family day has become even more important to me after two divorces. I wanted to provide family unity as best I could for my children. My two sons moved to Mississippi with their father and my four daughters remained here in California with me.

This particular Sunday in 2006, we intended to celebrate Lori's thirty fourth birthday. As a surprise, her fiancé Doug planned a party at a nearby restaurant with family and friends to greet her. My job: Invite Jenny and Becca, her younger sisters, and call her older sister Carla to make sure she would be there.

I called Carla on Thursday to confirm the details for Sunday. She agreed that she would meet us at church as usual; spend the day with me at home as she often did, and drive together to the restaurant for Lori's birthday surprise. Carla hadn't joined us for our family day the previous weekend, making me eager to see her.

Since losing her job two weeks ago, Carla hadn't been feeling well, probably a touch of the flu going around. She'd even cancelled her second job interview with another company because of her illness. Since Carla desperately needed financial counseling, I strongly encouraged her again to call the church which provided debt management. I was always talking to Carla about getting counseling to learn how to manage her money. I regretted that my words were harsh. She was doing the best she could as a single mother, raising her twelve-year-old son Eric.

As our phone conversation came to an end that night, I know I said, "I love you" which was our ritual before hanging up. This time I added, "Bye honey, I'll see you on Sunday for Lori's birthday party."

"I love you too, Mom. I'm looking forward to spending time with you on Sunday. Bye."

As I hung up the phone, I thought, I hope she calls the church for debt counseling.

On Sunday, I saved seats at church for us, as usual. The others were always late. Everyone but Carla had arrived. Coming from Corona to Lake Forest was a long trip for her, so I wasn't concerned. When she didn't make it, Lori and I speculated why.

She had started dating men again since her divorce. "Perhaps she spent the weekend with her newest guy," Lori commented.

"I don't think so, Lori. We made plans to be together this weekend. Besides, she would have called me."

Not knowing what happened, I really did think Carla would call me any minute with an excuse why she hadn't made it to church. She never called. So I went to the restaurant for Lori's party, fully anticipating that Carla would show up there. She and Lori were very close. She would never miss Lori's party.

Lori's party came and went. Carla was a no-show. Lori was so disappointed. Lori and I again speculated. "Where is she, Mom?"

"I don't know, honey. Should we be concerned that she hasn't called?"

"No Mom, she's done this before, remember when she was dating that guy and had gone to his place in LA? She forgot all about us that time."

"But what about Eric?"

"Oh he's at Dan's *(Dan is Eric's Dad)* for the weekend. He'll take him to school tomorrow. Carla will be back by the time he gets home from school."

I wished she would call so I could relax, but I knew I had to let her make her own choices.

I still continued to try to reach her by phone, but she never answered.

Monday evening I still hadn't heard from Carla, so I called Lori.

"Have you heard from Carla? Me neither. What should we do?"

"Why don't you call Christina? She lives right down the street."

Christina was Dan's new wife. She was nice and would be helpful.

"Christina, this is Ardie. Have you seen or heard from Carla? No? Would you mind going over there and see if she's home yet? We haven't been able to reach her by phone, and I'm worried about Eric, if he's home alone. Thanks. Call me when you get there, please."

The phone rang ten minutes later and I was relieved. It must be Carla, finally.

"Oh Christina, is Carla there?"

"No, but her car is in the driveway, and her purse and car keys are on the counter."

"Where's Carla?"

"I don't know, but Eric is here watching TV and Carla's bedroom door is closed. He told me that his mother, prior to today, instructed him not to disturb her when her door is closed because she hasn't been sleeping well and needed the rest."

"Please go in there and see if she's alright."

"Carla! Carla!" I could hear Christina calling out to her as she knocked.

"She's not answering, shall I go in and look for her?"

"Yes, please do."

She continued to call Carla's name and looked in the bedroom and the bathroom with Eric right behind her wondering where his mother was.

"She's not here."

"Okay, would you be willing to take Eric home with you and give him some dinner until we figure out what to do?"

"Sure."

"Thanks. I'll call you later."

I called Lori again to decide what we should do next. "Shall we call local hospitals to see if she's there? Maybe she called a friend to take her to the hospital because she's too sick to drive."

"I don't think she would have left without her purse and keys."

"Probably not. Where could she be? Maybe she was outside her home and fell in the ditch. I'll call Dan to go and check around her house." Dan agreed to call us if he found her.

Lori and I were very antsy by now, and decided to drive there and look for her ourselves. Fires had broken out near Carla's home and the toll roads were closed. We had to drive the long way around to get there. My husband, Glen, drove while Lori and her fiancé, Doug, were in the back seat.

Lori's phone rang. It was Dan. He was at Carla's house. The police and paramedics were already there.

"Dan, is Carla alright? Oh…" …her voice drifted off.

Lori, where's Carla? Is she alright? I was now in a panic.

"Mom, she's gone."

I'll never forget those words and how my heart felt in that moment. A heart-piercing wail of agony came up from the pit of my stomach that I could not control for twenty minutes.

We arrived and the police would not let me in to see Carla.

"You don't want to remember her like this, she's been dead for several hours perhaps overnight. It's not a pretty sight."

"I don't care, I want to see my daughter and hold her in my arms."

"I'm afraid we can't let you do that, Ma'am. It's just not a good idea."

Everything about that day is a blur. To say my heart was breaking is putting it mildly. I've never been through anything as painful as losing a child. I almost didn't survive. At least I thought I wouldn't. For two years, grieving became my full time job. I read as many books on loss and grieving that I could find. I went to every grief group available. I wrote in my journal every day. I read the Psalms over and over. I cried out to God in such pain and heartache. There's no describing the pit I was in, other than it was **HELL.**

Journal Entry
February 17, 2006
It has been eleven days since hearing the news of my daughter's death. I think I've cried a million tears and this is only the beginning. The waves of grief come and go like the ebb and flow of the waves crashing against the shore. Right now I feel so numb. I just can't believe that Carla is gone. I had her with me for thirty-five years, too short of a time. I feel so cheated.

We had a rocky relationship for thirty three of those years. A relationship burdened with conflict, stormy times, estrangement, times of forgiveness, and trying to reconcile but never quite achieving the mother-daughter relationship that we both longed for.

Then two years ago God laid it on my heart to reach out to Carla in a new way. I began to minister to her not in a self-righteous way as I had in the past, but in a heart-felt vulnerable way. She responded in the same manner. A love for each other began to grow that I hadn't experienced with her since I had not bonded with her as a baby. We were both amazed as our love grew and we bonded so closely together.

What a gift God gave to each of us. We often talked about the miracle we now shared of a renewed, restored relationship beyond our hopes and dreams. We never took our new love for each other for granted. Each time we were together, we took the time to say the words of appreciation and gratefulness for the gift God had given us. I'm so glad I let nothing go unsaid between us. I have no regrets. She knew how much I loved her and I cherished who she had become to me.

Journal Entry
February 19, 2006
I wish there was a way to avoid this grieving process I now find myself in. It is truly the deepest pain I have ever felt. After my mother passed away, my heart grieved the mother I would never have. But she lived a long and full life and was ill for several months. Her death was expected and a relief from her suffering and pain. This loss is different for me.

Carla was my firstborn child. I carried her inside me and felt her alive and moving until she was born May 15, 1970.

This pain is so deep and intense. My heart is breaking in a million little pieces. It feels as if lightning bolts are running through my body. Pins and needles are pricking my heart. There's a rush of heat to my head, then my body turns to ice. The tears come and go, but they don't stop. The tears keep coming. When will this pain end? Maybe it's a good thing to have my tears. I don't want to forget. I don't want to get on with my life like everyone else. This is my daughter and I don't want to forget.

Journal Entry
February 21, 2006

I still can't believe it's real. My daughter died. She's no longer here to share my life with me. That's where the sadness begins. The grieving process is not one I want to experience again. I've been here many times in my life whenever I've suffered a loss. This is, by far, the worst pain I've felt. I've got to ask the question "Why?" even though I may never have an answer. I think I would feel better if I could make some sense of all this. But nothing will take this pain away. I must feel this pain and I don't like it at all.

Journal Entry
February 24, 2006

It's been eighteen days since Carla's body was discovered. I've been in and out of a fog that is indescribable. I suppose that is a good thing... ...not being able to think or remember, just feeling numb.

Everything in life is meaningless after a loved one dies. Nothing matters. What seemed important before is insignificant now. People go on as if nothing happened. Something did happen. Something major happened and it happened to me. I lost my daughter. My daughter died. I was her mother. I hate that word *"was."* I **AM** her mother! I'll always be her mother. She will always be my daughter.

Mothers and daughters can have a strange and strained relationship as we each attempt to find our way as adults to be individuals. I had baggage from my childhood and from my relationship with my mother. I know that affected my not bonding with my daughter when she was a baby. I regretted that so much when Carla and I would have our conflicts. We could be brutal with each other. So many years were wasted that I could have been enjoying with Carla. How grateful I am that God granted us the wonderful gift of a cherished, bonded, close connection of a loving, nurturing, blossoming love relationship that I'll always treasure and remember.

Carla wrote this poem and gave it to me soon after she married Dan

Schmetzer and gave birth to her son Eric.

My Mother
1994

There is no one else like my mother
She is thoughtful, caring, kind to others
Thank you, Mother, for your care
And for always being there
For patience, wisdom, love so strong
For faith and hope to carry on
You are unique, an individual
A special person whose life is full
Of hopes and dreams and goals to reach
You've done so much and helped to teach
Me that I, too, can make a difference
You'll never know how much that's meant
Now that I'm grown with my own dear child
I look at him and feel so proud
To be a mom unlike any other
A mom like you
I love you, Mother

Carla, my firstborn, my special one, my precious one. There is no one like you, sweetheart, nor will there ever be anyone like you! I will miss you greatly!

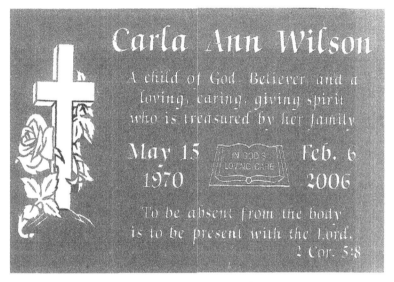

Carla's Grave Marker

14
Son's Addictive Personality

"Trust in the Lord with all your heart, and lean not on your own understanding. In all your ways acknowledge Him, and He shall direct your paths" (Proverbs 3:5-6, NKJV).

Brian's Story (as an adult)

Brian and Me

"Mom, I relapsed."

"That's okay, son. Everyone with an addiction relapses sometimes." I reassured my son, Brian, age thirty, so he would be able to cope with his disappointment. Yet, I wondered, *how many times would we have to go through repeated failures?*

I've spent so much time, energy, and money to get him the help he needed over the years. Ever since he was a little boy starting fires in the school trash can, behavior institutes for stealing checks from me and from our neighbor widow, various rehabs for psychotic behavior, not to mention juvenile hall when he would sneak out at night and steal cars to go joyriding. Of course therapy was included. My heart broke each and every time the steps I took failed. I cried myself to sleep each night as I prayed, *"Please God, help my son."*

I have to take responsibility for my inability to parent my children when they were young. I was an immature child myself, with no skills to handle children. And I certainly could not teach them how to handle problems or cope with life. I couldn't even do that for myself. I was empty and had nothing to give. Brian was the most disobedient of my children. Brian acted out and he quickly became the scapegoat of the family. At the time, I blamed Bill, his Dad, because of Bill's drinking. Bill also was in the Navy and overseas six months out of the year. He was an absentee dad. But now I know we were equally to blame for not meeting Brian's needs.

After going through ten horrendous years of disappointment and heartache with Brian, I was not able to handle anything more. Bill *(now my ex)* retired from the Navy and decided to take both Brian and his younger brother, Matt, back to his hometown in Mississippi to provide a better, more stable home life. Slowly but surely, Brian began to act out there too. First, with alcohol and then with drugs. Finally, when he needed more drugs, he robbed a liquor store with a gun and was caught. He went to jail and was convicted of armed robbery and sent to a penitentiary for five years. He was only nineteen years old. I thought, *what a waste of a young man's life.* Now he'll have a record that will follow him everywhere. But at least he would become clean and sober, and maybe have a second chance to turn his life around.

I was extremely sad to hear that Brian had been arrested for armed robbery. He had become an adult still making the same bad choices.

How tragic that the choices he made brought these results—where the precious freedom he had enjoyed prior to these circumstances had now been taken from him.

I grieved the losses between us. Sadly we didn't have a relationship. I didn't even know my own son. I have many memories of what it was like before he began to act out the family dysfunction. When he was three years old, he was so smart. He could memorize songs verbatim just by me playing the tape player again and again. One song I recorded to send to my mom. It was an old hymn. I still have the recording. It brings tears of joy as I hear his sweet little voice. But that was long before he acted out. I regret he took on the role of the family scapegoat. I did the best I could to get the help that was needed for all of us. I missed out on much of his teenage years, because of the distance *(both physical and emotional)* between us. That is very sad for me to acknowledge. Because I love him, I care about what happens to him. I have been praying for him for a long time. And I always have hope for the future. All of us can learn from our mistakes and that's important, as well as our love for one another.

I don't condemn him for what he did. I try *(to the best of my ability)* not to judge or criticize anyone. I know what it feels like to receive that kind of treatment. No one deserves that. I know whatever time he has to serve will give him the time he needs to think about what he did to reach this point, and to think about what he wants to do with his life. He always has choices to make and to figure out what he chooses for his life. He's smart, capable, and has abilities that he's not aware of yet. They just need cultivating. And he can do it. I believe in him. I know he can make positive choices that are in his best interest and I know he will.

Brian and I wrote letters while he was in prison declaring our regrets, our hopes and wishes for the future, and the kind of relationship we now wanted to have as adults.

It all sounded good, but I wasn't sure if Brian was capable of that kind of relationship. I sure hoped it was possible. He sounded sorry for the heartache he caused me, but I knew from his therapist that he was good at saying what I wanted to hear. I just couldn't trust that he truly meant it. He still sounded angry about the past and couldn't let it go. It broke my heart to hear him write,

I've missed you very much, Mom. Maybe now we can re-establish the relationship we so foolishly gave up on years ago. I just want you to know that you will always be my mother and that I will always love you no matter what has happened between us in the past. If you have not yet come to terms with us and our past, I sincerely hope that you do so during these next five years. For I look forward to seeing you once I am released and enjoying the bond that is naturally shared between mother and son. I love and miss you all.

Love always, Brian

I worked on my feelings about Brian from time to time in therapy. I wanted to be ready to move on from the past. And there was so much to work on... ...like the time he stole blank checks from me and cashed them for $200. The time he started a fire at school, I felt so helpless to do anything to help him. Then there was the time he pulled down a neighbor girl's panties. Her mother reamed me out for having a pervert for a son. I felt so bad. Another time we had a little kitten that Lori was attached to. Brian took that little kitten and drop kicked her into our back yard wooden fence right in front of Lori and laughed. I saw the kind of brutal cruelty he was capable of. And I found out many years later when Matt was an adult, that Brian was very heartless to him when they roomed together as boys. One example was that he urinated in Matt's shoes over and over again. I cried for all my children who were affected by Brian's malicious behavior. I was helpless so much of the time, but angry that Brian just didn't stop even with all the behavior institutes, various rehabs, and juvenile hall. These examples were just a few of the things he did. There was so much more for me to work on.

Our letters continued back and forth for many months. Then Brian found religion. Normally I would have said that's a good thing and certainly something that I prayed for, but the letters I began to receive from him after that were critical and judgmental questioning my very beliefs and values. Brian was definitely attacking my faith, beating me up with Bible verses I knew by heart, but he used them against me, seemingly in a way to hurt me. It tore me down rather than lifted me up. He called therapy *"worldly,"* judging me harshly for using it. These *"worldly"* things dramatically changed my life, so that I was able to have a closer, more intimate walk with God, and deepened my faith in a very profound way.

Having a relationship does not mean forgetting the past. The past has a funny way of haunting us in the present if it hasn't been dealt with and healed. Healing only occurs when responsibility is taken, and behavior is owned. Having a *'real'* relationship means being able to address anything in that relationship, especially if feelings were never talked about. I didn't do that with my parents, my brothers, or my ex-husbands. I didn't want to rock the boat, so I kept quiet. The past can't be swept under the carpet any more. It's not healthy and I won't do it. What about the hearts Brian broke in our family? I don't buy it that he was just an irresponsible child. He knew right from wrong. He hurt me, his sisters Jenny, Becca, Lori, Carla, and his brother Matt. Those hurts caused rifts in our relationships with him. Those rifts are still here today. This is not about forgetting the past. This is about mending broken relationships first, then the past can be put behind us, which is what we all want; me, most of all.

Brian was right about me still trying to relate to a fourteen year old. He has grown physically, but there's a young boy *(his inner child)* inside him that needs healing and he needs to restore relationships with family members.

He had every right to be angry with me. I was not the mother he needed me to be. I was not nurturing towards him. I was angry with him about his behavior and I abused him, rather than getting the help

I needed for me to be a better mother. I am sorry. I deeply regret how much I hurt him and I told him so in a letter. I know there's still a lot of sadness and pain inside him that needs to be grieved. Feeling the feelings is the beginning of healing. Those who mourn (*grieve*) will be comforted.

Beginning a new relationship is being able to ask each member of the family what the past was like for them, walking a mile in their shoes, and not being afraid to hear their feelings. That's what compassion is. When he truly loves each of us in the family in the way Christ does, I will be able to see, by his actions, his sorrow and regret over the past.

Until he can show his amends by reconciling instead of neglecting family relationships, he will not be able to let go of the past; something he so desperately wants and needs to do. As long as there is anger, bitterness, and resentment in his heart towards me, there's no *real* sorrow. Those feelings need to be worked through. It is hard work, but not impossible. "With God all things are possible" (Matthew 19:26, NIV). Healing is needed for his sake as well as for all of ours in the family.

These are the things I conveyed to him in letters hoping he could see the advantage of doing some new healthy behaviors toward me and the family.

* * *

While Brian lived in Mississippi, he married Nikki, and was involved in church at Crestview Christian Church in Memphis, Tennessee. He was playing the guitar and leading special music on Sundays in 2001. He was writing songs and sent me this beautiful song he wrote about the Holy Spirit. I was so proud of him and how God was working in his life.

Divine
Music and Lyrics by Brian Haley
November 26, 2001

You brought me
Into this place
Wonders all around
Such amazing grace
Thoughts of peace

Words of love
Spoken from above
Bringing release

Chorus:

I was asleep
But now I wake
Things are so different, changing
The chains of sin
That help now break
Weakening, seeking
His holy face.

I've never
Felt so alive
Filled with a peace
And love so divine

Everything's new
Leaving behind
Memories of pain and sorrow
Fading with time

He gives me strength
When I am weak
Your grace is sufficient for me
Your mercy and love
Are more than enough
When I'm down on my knees

I have to say Brian made a miraculous turn of events in getting his GED and going to nurse's school to get a certificate to become a nurse. He was able to talk to a hospital and they agreed, in spite of his record, to allow him to work there. He married Nikki, had a baby boy, Aiden, and was happy and successful for the first time in his life. I was overjoyed… …but my happiness was short-lived. Brian ruined everything by stealing drugs from the hospital and was caught. There went his career. One day while babysitting his ten month old son, his wife came home to Brian passed out with the baby crawling on the floor and playing with a hypodermic needle. That was it for Nikki, she had had enough. She left with the baby and soon divorced Brian. My son lost everything. Again, my prayer became, *"Please God, help my son."*

Then in 2006, his sister Carla passed away. Her enlarged heart from a virus, took its toll and caused a heart attack to take her life.

Bill, her Dad, and Brian came out to California from Mississippi for the memorial service. All my children were together for the first time in a very long time. We all grieved Carla's loss in our own ways.

Brian decided to stay here in California and get help for his drug addiction at a sober living home run by Alcoholics Anonymous. The rules were clear and Brian never could follow rules of any kind. After three months he was terminated. I didn't find out until I called to see how Brian was doing. Evidently he was living on the streets as a homeless person.

One day he called me to come pick him up and take him to church.

He had lost so much weight, and looked bad, but I was glad to see him and welcomed him with open arms. We took him to lunch after church and gave him some of Glen's old clothes and gave him a duffle bag. We dropped him off at the Orange County Rescue Mission. He stayed for a while, but once again left to stay on the streets. We didn't hear from him for six months.

Again he called out of the blue to have us pick him up for church because he had relapsed and had a car accident totaling his car.

After church we went to lunch.

"Mom, in the old days you would have been critical and judgmental. I was expecting that today as well. Instead, you were understanding, supportive, and encouraging. You showed me a different side to you I just wasn't expecting. Thank you, Mom, I needed that."

Now he was serious about getting help. He finally admitted he had a drinking problem and started going to AA. He got into a sober living apartment in San Clemente. They helped him find a job. He was excited about his life. So was I.

Then I got a phone call from the police department. Oh no, what next... ...another relapse?

"Ma'am, I'm sorry to tell you that Saturday morning Brian's roommate found your son, Brian, collapsed on his bed. The coroner pronounced him dead on the scene. There was nothing we could do."

After an investigation, the ruling was that Brian's death was an accidental overdose of morphine *(heroin)* causing his heart to stop. He had a heart attack, which killed him instantly.

My heart again broke into a million tiny little pieces. Now two of my children died only one year apart. It was almost more than I could bear. I relied on God to see me through what was the most difficult time of my life.

Journal Entry
April 4, 2007

Six weeks ago, on February 12, my son Brian died suddenly and unexpected just one year after Carla passed away. Now I'm grieving two losses. My heart is heavy with sadness and the pain, at times, is unbearable. I feel cheated. I didn't have enough time to explore who he had become as a man. He fathered two children I barely know. They live in Mississippi. Sometimes I feel that it isn't fair. God has taken two of my children. Other families are intact and never lose any children. Why me?

Journal Entry
April 5, 2007

Question: Think about the loss. If you listen to your heart, why did it happen and who is to blame? I want to blame God. After all, He is in control. He knows everything. He knew Brian was going to have a heart attack on February 23. God did not intervene and He could have, but He didn't. Is that fair? NO! Brian was only thirty-one. He had his whole life in front of him. He had a wife *(he botched that up and she divorced him even though she still loved him)* and two beautiful children. Now they will grow up without a father. Is that fair? NO!

Sometimes the pain hurts unbearably. My heart can't stand the pain. Prickly needles are stabbing my heart. Knives are piercing my heart over and over. How much more can a mother's heart take? I know God wants to heal my hurt. It's only by feeling the pain that healing comes. I am on this journey by myself. No one else can feel the pain that I feel.

Write out your expectations in a letter for the loved one you lost…

Dear Brian,

I wanted so much for you. First of all, I wanted you clean and sober having a length of sobriety so you could begin the process of recovery. Then you could look

back on your life and begin to clear up
the wreckage you were trying so hard to
avoid. What was so painful that you kept
running from?

I envisioned you conquering your
addiction and turning your life
around. I hoped for reconciliation for
you and your wife Nikki, creating a
peaceful family harmony for you and
your children Kelsey and Aidan. I
wanted you to begin paying back all the
money you owed to people who helped
finance you along the way. I so desired
that you take responsibility for your
actions, confessing your wrongdoings,
especially to Doug and Lori, asking for
forgiveness, and making it up to them.

Do you remember when I taught you
the A, B, C's of recovery? Acknowledge
your wrongs. Blame no one but yourself,
and confess what you did that was
wrong. That's how I envisioned you
taking responsibility for your life—all of
your life, including your past. I have so
many regrets about the way I parented
you, but when I got into recovery, I
changed how I responded and looked at
my own life thanks to Dr. Becker. I had
hoped that he could help you as well,

because he sure changed my life forever. That was a turning point for me. Your life could have, would have been so different had you taken advantage of what he offered you. It would have saved you from six years in prison. Instead, you lost your freedom, and I lost my son.

Journal Entry

April 9, 2007

I'm depressed. There's a heaviness surrounding me. There's a dark cloud hanging over me. I don't feel like doing anything. I've been pigging out on candy. I don't want to feel these sad feelings. I've been grieving all year for Carla, and I'm still grieving. Now I have to grieve Brian too. I don't want to. I have more regrets with Brian—more losses and it hurts. There can be no closure. I don't want to take time out of what I need to do to function on a daily basis. I feel overwhelmed. I'm feeling the emptiness from the loss of my two children. I seem to carry the emptiness everywhere I go. I don't acknowledge it most days because I don't want to feel the pain. But it's always there.

Lori gave me a gift at Christmas. It was a framed picture of Carla, Lori, Brian, and Matt—my four Haley children *(Jenny and Becca are my Hamilton children)*. I burst into sobs. Grieving comes in waves and shows up whenever there's a trigger and when I least expect it. My broken heart just needs to mend and more healing takes place by allowing the feelings to come up and feel them. Lord, be with me in the pain!

15

My Broken Heart

"Even though I walk through the valley of the shadow of death, I shall fear no evil for You are with me; Your rod and Your staff, they comfort me" (Psalm 23:4).

After Carla passed away in 2006, my heart was broken beyond what I can explain. Death was out of order, my children are not designed to pass before me. I'm not supposed to bury my children. But we live in a broken world that I have no control over. That was hard for me to accept. What was even harder for me was accepting that God allowed this to happen. My God whom I love and trust to take care of me and my family had allowed this hurt, this pain, when He could have intervened and protected her from death. She was only thirty-five with an eleven-year-old son.

I had no answers but only needed to grieve. I quit all my ministries to stay home and take care of myself. Grieving became my full time job. From all my years in therapy I had gained tools for grieving my losses. They were already in place, so I knew what to do. But this was the deepest hole I found myself in. I remember those days well, crying out to God, praying, reading God's Word, and journaling my thoughts and feelings. Much of my days were spent arguing with God. I felt that was the right thing to do, since He wants me to come to Him with all my burdens. God is a BIG God who can handle all my feelings, questions, doubts, and arguments. That's one of the things I love about God.

I joined a group called *Umbrella Ministries* for mothers who have lost a child. I gained so much love, comfort, and guidance through these women who had already walked this path of grieving their children. Slowly but surely, the severity of the pain lessened and my grief was manageable. Then one year into my journey, my thirty-one-year old son Brian passed away of an accidental drug overdose. My heart broke again into a million tiny little pieces. It was almost more than I could bear and I told God so. More anger, more grieving, and more trying to understand why God would allow this again. It was all just too much.

I have so many regrets since losing Brian in 2007. I never got to resolve all the things that happened between Brian and me as he was growing up. I wrote out my regrets during the grief group I attended. That helped me put those regrets to rest. Grieving is such a complex process. It takes time and is painful work. I grieved more as I wrote this story, but healing occurs each time that I shed more tears. It's what sees me through as I lean on God and trust His plan for my life. Even though I wrote these poems long before losing two of my precious children, these poems express my feelings now.

The Pain is Deep
September 14, 1996

I'm frightened and alone
I feel as if
I've been disowned

No one is coming
To take care of me
I wish there
Was some place
For me to flee

I'm just a
Little girl inside
For most of my life
I've felt terrified

When I feel
These feelings
I become little again
And there
Is no way
For me
To comprehend

What is going
To happen next
I can't breathe
The pain
Is in my chest

I think

I'm going to die
And all I can do
Is sob and cry

This hurts so badly
There's no relief
The pain is deep
I feel the grief

I am alone
There's no one here
Except God
Who is always near *(EX 312a)*
Comforting me
With His tender
Loving care *(PS 119:76)*

I rely on Him
To see me through *(1JN 4:16)*
His Word is sure
His promises come true *(PS 119:140)*

Psalm 62 says
"My soul finds rest
In God alone *(PS 62:1, 2)*
My salvation
Comes from Him

He alone
Is my rock
And salvation

He is my fortress
I will never
Be shaken"

David lists
Rest
Salvation
Protection and hope
I cling to these promises
So I can cope

With the struggles
And feelings
That come and go
Because through the pain
I continue to grow

God's grace is real
I know He loves me *(ROM 5:17)*
He led me
To recovery
So I could be free

So I relax
And know
I'm loved
Just as I am *(PS 31:16)*
God's very own
Cherished
Unique
And precious lamb *(ISA 43:4)*

Just As I Am
June 23, 1998

Here I am Lord
I come to you
Just as I am

The floodgates
Have opened
And broken the dam

251

Looking back
On all the
Wasted years
I'm exhausted
From crying
All these tears

I can't even think
My mind is worn out
So many messages
Voices and tapes
I'm thinking about

How do I let go
Of the past?
How do I hold on?
To peace
And make it last?

The pain is triggered
When I least expect it
I sob and sob
It feels as if
I'm in a pit

My head hurts
I'm tired of it all
I want rest
I'm walking
Through the process
I'm doing my best

I want a break Lord
I can't do any more
My eyes are swollen
My body is sore

You promised

Not to give me
More than I can bear (1COR 10:13)
I'm asking
"Where are You Lord?
Don't You care?"

I'm hurting
I need help
And I'm alone
I feel unloved
Neglected
And disowned

I'm at the bottom
Of my despair
I'm coming to You
Agonizing in prayer
Please take this load
I no longer can bear

I trust You
To do
What You've promised
I keep asking
For help
I will persist

You've always
Been my anchor
When I'm
In the middle
Of a storm
Hold me
In Your arms
Keep me safe
Keep me warm

I know and believe
You have a plan for me

From the chains
Of the past
I want to break free

Hold me close
To You
And never
Let me go
Your presence
Strength and power
I want to know

Deep inside
The emptiness I feel
Are the heartaches
And hurts only
You can heal

Fill me with Your love
The only thing
That is steadfast
The only thing
That will heal
The wounds
Of the past

And when
All is over

And said
And done
What matters
Is the victory
Jesus won

For me
Just as I am
His very own
Treasured
Precious
Cherished lamb (DEUT 26:18)

Because of Your
Undeserved mercy
And grace
Each day
I will continue
To seek Your face (1CHR 16:11)

Your love
Is everlasting
I love
To tell the story
I am grateful
I give You honor
Praise
And glory

Heavy Load Painful Road
August 9, 1998

These burdens I carry
Are a heavy load
I'm walking by myself
Down this painful road

I don't know

Where I'm going
Or why I even go
I'm alone
I'm scared
What to do?
I don't know

253

Where are You Lord?
I hate living this way
All I do is sob
And pray

I know
You've promised
To never depart
You're always with me
Healing my heart

Show me
Your love Lord
I need You
In my life

I want peace
I want rest
I want joy
In my soul (ISA 26:3)
I want freedom
I want healing
I want to feel whole

There's nowhere
Else to go Lord
Except to You
Alone
The path I am on
Is completely unknown

Only You
Can meet my needs
In the way
That fits me best
Your everlasting arms?
They're the only place
I find rest (DEUT 33:27)

Where do I go?
What do I do?
If I don't have You

You are the Rock
That is higher than I (PS 61:2)
You know
The innermost
Parts of me
I cannot deny (PS 139:13)

You created me
Sustained me
In all
I've been through
And all You ever wanted
Was for me
To know
And love You

When I was lost
And dying
You saved me
Through Your Son
Jesus Christ
Messiah
Holy
Sinless
Righteous One

I've done nothing
To deserve
This wonderful gift
It's free
You call me
By my name
You know
Every part

Of the "real" me (ISA 43:1)

I can relax
No need to perform
I can just "be"

I am loved
For who I am
I feel precious
And free (JN 3:16)

Life Isn't Fair
April 17, 1999

Life isn't fair
There's no predictability
Anywhere

When I least
Expect it
A tidal wave hits
It knocks me over
I can't breathe
Inside my emotions
Are beginning to seethe

There's no way out
I'm feeling trapped
All I want to do
Is collapse
Escape
Numb out

Anything not to feel
But that's exactly
What I must do
To heal

I wish there
Were an easier
Softer way
To make everything
Right

And be okay

But God loves me
And wants me
To grow (PS 86:5)
Within the storm
He wants me
To see the rainbow (GEN 9:13)

No matter what happens
God is in control (LK 16:30)
Drawing me closer
To Him is His goal (HEB 10:22)

If I can "be still"
And listen
For His voice (PS 46:10a)
I am filled
With His presence
I can rejoice (PS 16:11)

Great is
God's faithfulness
His promises are sure (PS 145:13b)
My feelings subside
Through the pain
I endure (HEB 12:7)

God brings me

Through each
Upsetting trial *(HEB 12:10, 11)*
All I have to do
Is be real
And stay
Out of denial *(1JN 1:7)*

I only need
To take
One step at a time
As I make
This challenging
Uphill climb

I am willing
To surrender to
God's Will for me *(1THES 4:3)*
To develop character
And to grow spiritually *(1PET 2:2)*

This isn't easy
Life is a test *(JAS 1:12)*
If I can hang
In there
I will be blessed

God gives me gifts
Of His mercy
And grace *(PS 25:6)*
His everlasting arms

Will be my resting-place *(DEUT 33:27)*

I can count
On Him
And what
He's done for me *(1JN 4:9, 10)*
He sent His Son
Jesus Christ
To set me free *(PS 146:7)*

I have nothing
To fear
I am reassured *(PS 23:4)*
God's faithfulness
Keeps me strong
And secure *(PS 91:4)*

"For in Him
We live and move
And have our being" *(ACTS 17:28)*
To Him
Belongs the glory
His praises
I will sing *(PS 147:1)*

I'm humbled
And I'm grateful
To my Savior
I will cling *(ISA 43:11)*

My Heart is Breaking
July 15, 2007

I have no mother
Father
Brothers
Now no son

Or daughter

Lord I need You
In my life

More than any other

I'm hurting Lord
And feeling the loss
My heart is breaking
My stomach
Is in knots

I stay
With the feeling
I know that is
The beginning
Of healing

This isn't easy
The pain
Hurts so much
Lord hold me
In Your arms
I want to feel
Your tender touch

You're the only one
I can truly trust
I'm tired of using
My addictions
As a crutch

As an escape
And a way
Of not dealing
With the pain
Avoiding my feelings
Only causes me
More stress and strain

If I can just
Hang on
And see

My way through
I come to a place
Where my hope
Is renewed

You're with me Lord
I feel You
By my side
Your promises come true
You always provide *(HEB 10:23)*

My life is a gift
You've given to me
Providing a Savior
Whose death
And resurrection
Has set me free

Jesus Christ
Emmanuel
My Redeemer
And my Friend
His mercy
And His grace
I just can't comprehend

Lord how thankful
I am
I praise
Your holy name
Your awesome majesty
I loudly proclaim

You are faithful
Accepting me
Right where I am
You are my Shepherd
I am Your
Precious lamb *(PS 23:1)*

To You
Belongs the glory
The honor
And the praise

And I will gratefully
Serve You
All the rest
Of my days

16

Longing for Another Son

"I will praise You, Lord, with all my heart. I will tell of all the miraculous things You have done. I will be filled with joy because of You. I will sing praises to Your name, O Most High" (Psalm 9:1-2, NLT).

Matt's Story

My husband Bill was content with three children. It was 1979, I was still young, only thirty two, and I wanted another baby. Carla, our firstborn, was ten years old. Lori was eight. Brian, our youngest just turned four. I longed for another baby. I prayed asking God for another boy. I knew what his name would be... ...Matthew. I would call him Matt.

Nine months later to my delight, Matt was born. I was so happy, but his dad had mixed feelings with another mouth to feed.

Somewhere along the line, after ten years of a very rocky marriage, things went sour. To say I made many mistakes as a parent would be right, but not nearly honest. I was a failure. I had no skills. I had no role models. I turned into my mother... ...an out of control yeller. I was an emotional basket case. Maybe because I was living with an alcoholic just like my dad.

By the time Matt turned five, I was separated from my husband of fifteen years and contemplating divorce because of his dad's *(Bill's)* infidelity.

Matt's first five years of life was filled with a father who was either out to sea for six months, on duty on the ship every third night and one weekend a month, or at home drinking. I was so focused on getting my husband sober that I pushed the kids out the door forcing the two older girls to babysit the younger boys. Parenting was the last thing on my mind. I now realize how wrong that was – it was abusive. Matt, as the youngest, lost his childhood. He had no father and he had no mother. This is hard for me to say, but it must be said because it's the truth: I abandoned my children.

If I had to do it over again, I would… …sure I would want to do it differently, but I now know I couldn't. I didn't have any knowledge of how to do it any other way. The *"what if's"* don't do anything constructive to change what couldn't be changed. It is what it is… …abuse, neglect, and abandonment, and I regret all of it.

So I take responsibility, name it, and confess what I did was wrong. Now I have a new opportunity with my grown children, who are all adults, to face our past together. Not that they have wanted to or welcomed such an encounter. They think and feel as I did in my pre-recovery days that the past is gone, over, done, can't be changed, and does no good to bring it up in the present. That's not true, it's a lie from hell for sure, to keep us from gaining what God has planned for each of us… …redemption and reconciliation. God is a God of second chances, third, fourth, fifth and as many as is needed for healing of past hurts and wounds.

Two of my daughters and I have had numerous opportunities to work out our differences. We've shared many healing tears together as I've heard their anger. It's also an important part of trusting me again, after abandoning them when they were young. One other daughter is still a little reluctant to face the past, but that's okay. I'm patient and will wait until she's ready.

Wanting to Reconnect with Matt

Swallowing hard, the questions stuck in my throat. Stuttering I finally said, "Matt… …will… …will you consider the possibility for us to re-build our disconnected relationship?"

This risk had to be taken, given my history with Matt. Divorcing his dad when he was only three, Matt left my home at the age of ten. First he lived in Mississippi with his dad, then to Florida to live with an Aunt and Uncle. I stopped writing letters to him when he turned twelve.

"Why now? Where've you been for six years, Mom? How come you didn't want a relationship with your own son? Why didn't you feel the need to reconnect with me sooner? I'm gonna be eighteen next week and you're just now starting to feel like you should own up to your responsibilities? How can I trust you now?"

"Matt, you have a right to be angry with me. You didn't have a responsible mother when you were growing up and needed me the most. I missed out on six years of your life I can never experience. That saddens me deeply. It took me all these years to feel that pain in my heart. I buried it and pushed it aside as long as I could, so I wouldn't have to deal with it. I regret that I didn't realize sooner how much I missed not being the mother you needed me to be in your life. I'm ashamed to admit I didn't want a relationship with my own son. I'm deeply sorry I hurt you."

"This whole situation reminds me of you, Mom, and your parents, how you would not talk to them, and I am in that same situation. I thought you would've done anything not to deal with what you had to go through. But I guess the saying *"history repeats itself"* is true; especially in families. Please remember where I am coming from and what I had to go through for the last six years."

"I know, Matt... You've been through a lot of hard, painful times without a mother. I can't go back and change that. I can't reclaim those lost years, but I can be here for you from here on out, if you're open to receiving my love and support. If you're not ready yet, I understand and I will wait for you. This is about your needs, not mine. I'm offering you what I have today."

"It would be nice, Mom, to have a relationship with my parents, but you can't just walk in and out of people's lives whenever you want. What if things get difficult again and you don't want to deal with them? Then what? Will you walk out again? Why would you allow things to take its course the way they did in our family? You didn't have a great relationship with your parents and brothers. I'll never understand why you decided to give up on me. I will always remember it."

"The damage is done Matt; angry and painful feelings are real for both of us. Amends are meant to heal broken relationships, and to repair the damage. Healing can take place. The anger and pain can be worked through to make both our lives better and happier. My desire is to stop the cycle of dysfunction and abuse in our family. Relating to my children in a healthier, more positive, and productive way is very important now. Matt, I wished I could've parented differently, but I had no tools and no skills. Now I do. And I'm glad I woke up in time to put them to use."

I really wanted to be there for Matt, but knew I would have to earn his trust. Would he let me back in his life?

Before Matt could answer, my mind went back to the time I divorced his dad.

I couldn't take Bill's lies anymore. I looked the other way for fifteen years. His drinking got worse and his affairs began to wear on me. Why did I stay with him so long and put up with all the abuse? His promises kept me from leaving. I hoped he could change and be the husband I longed for him to be.

But it never happened. He just couldn't give up his latest girlfriend and I stopped believing he would change. I decided to divorce the man I loved because I just couldn't take any more abuse.

The pain of losing my first love was too much to bear. I went looking for someone new. I found him and fell in love. Being in love was far better than pain over a broken relationship. I married way too quickly and didn't realize the mess I created for my children. After all, he wanted to marry me and I had four children, ranging in age from three to thirteen.

Matt never knew what happened to his dad. Jeff, his new step-father tried to be a good dad, but really couldn't handle the pressure. By the time Matt was ten, things escalated between the two of them until I could no longer take the chaos in my family. Jeff and I had two more girls of our own whom I wanted to raise in peace.

When Bill, the boys' father, said he would retire from the Navy and take Brian age fourteen and Matt age ten back to his home in Mississippi, I said, "Good... ...take them both!"

Although Matt and I wrote letters to each other at first, I didn't see him again until he grew up.

I divorced Jeff after ten years.

Now alone and working on my issues in therapy for several years, I could concentrate on renewing my connection with Matt.

"I know it's a lot to ask of you right now Matt, but I want a relationship with you."

"It saddens me Mom that I don't have much of a relationship with my immediate family and I wish that things could've been different. If you want to write and ask me about what's going on in my life, you can. But I don't know how else we can foster a relationship. Trust is a big part of every relationship and right now we don't have that."

"I understand. Thanks Matt. I'll write to you. I look forward to hearing from you again."

Single for four years, I married my present husband. When Matt graduated in 2002 from the University of Mississippi *("Ole Miss")*, Glen and I flew out to attend his graduation. He completed Officer Candidate School with the ROTC program his junior/senior college years. Commissioned as an officer in the Marine Corp the following day after graduation made me proud. Grateful that Matt included me in these two special events in his adult life, I became the fulfilled Mom I always wanted to be.

The Haley Kids
Lori, Matt, Carla, and Brian

That happened fourteen years ago. Since then, we've emailed more than talked. It's hard to know what to say. A boy has grown into a man I barely know. Asking the obvious questions, there's nothing more to say. It feels awkward and uncomfortable. Wanting a closer relationship, how do I get there? Call, send cards? It's still hard to pursue him consistently.

He's come out to California for a visit now and then. It's always great to see him, but he comes mainly to see his older sister Lori, who he bonded with when he was younger, more as a surrogate mother than a sister, and that's okay. Understanding how and why it happened, I still want a better relationship with Matt. Realizing it takes making him a priority, I've got to fight for it.

Several years ago, Glen and I visited Matt at his duty station in Florida. We actually stayed with him in his condo for a few days. Getting to know him better felt great. He's a well-mannered young man. He gave me respect and honor, more than I expected for a mother who's not close. And we had fun too. I really enjoyed being around him. After returning home to California, I called him in Florida more, just to see how he's doing and sent cards just to let him know: *"thinking of you."* I know that's what he's always wanted from me.

When it came time for a duty station move, he requested California, to be closer to his sisters and to me. Thrilled to hear he wanted to be close, made my day. When he got his request approved, I shouted for joy! He arrived July 1, 2009. What an exciting day for me! Although he chose to stay with Lori once again, having him near was heaven. Extending our guest bedroom to him when he needed it was all I could do. We've had so much fun getting to know one another. Having long talks where I really hear his values and goals for his life, my heart, as well as his, is healing.

He appreciated living with his sister and her family for two months, but longed for a place of his own. Sleeping on the sofa in the heat of the hottest summer we've ever had with no air conditioning became too much for him to endure one more night. Besides, Lori's one-year-old son Jonah needed lots of attention. Now another baby on the way would make the living situation crowded. Matt decided to leave his sister's home and find his own place. Looking at several apartments and rooms to rent, he hadn't found what he liked. One day Matt called me, "Mom, you know I'm going to Afghanistan in five months, is your invitation still open?"

"Sure, come on over Matt. Your room is ready. I've been waiting for you."

Will Shorecliffs Terrace Be Matt's Home?

Anticipating Matt's upcoming deployment to Afghanistan, I relished that he wanted to stay with Glen and I for the next five months. What I didn't realize was how many hurdles we would have to jump in order for him to live with us.

We live in a 55+ Condo Mobile Home Park, called Shorecliffs Terrace, in San Clemente, CA. It is a unique park in that we own the property and don't pay space rent. We do have a Home Owners Association with Rules and Regulations to follow and of course dues to pay.

The rules regarding overnight guests include: Only twenty consecutive days and no more than thirty days per calendar year.

When I called the office to see what I should do, the secretary promptly informed me I would have to write a letter to the Board of Directors. I began writing the letter, asking permission to allow an exception for our son, who is twenty-eight, to live with us temporarily, but longer than the specified rules state.

> This is our son's situation. He has been in the Marine Corp for eight years. During that time he served in Iraq for one year. As a Captain, he is waiting for orders to go to Afghanistan to serve our country once again. Looks like he could be deployed in January, 2010, but could be delayed until March.
>
> As a mother who has already lost two adult children to death in the last three years, I am afraid of the possibility I could lose another. It is important for me to spend as much time as I can with him before he goes to serve in another war. Living with us affords us that opportunity.
>
> We are hoping that you can help us in some way to resolve this matter and grant us our petition.
>
> Thank you for your time and consideration.

Having pled our case, I felt confident the Board would gladly and eagerly say yes to our request. Knowing the wheels and cogs grind slowly in even our small community bureaucracy, I had to wait.

Several weeks later, a neighbor stopped me while I was on my walk. She said, "It's a shame your son won't be able to stay with you." What? Did she know something I didn't know? I was not informed. I found out there was an upcoming Association meeting where we could discuss our request and then the Board would take a vote right there during the meeting. Little did I know, they already met to discuss privately and had voted no.

When Glen and I arrived, a big crowd had already assembled. There was much business to take care of before our name was called. We were allowed to plead our case once again. Many thoughts were

266

addressed and discussed, and it didn't look good. The Board was concerned that we could jeopardize our 55+ status by letting Matt stay for six months. After more discussion, pros and cons, the Board took a vote. All six Board members voted a flat no. My heart sank in disappointment.

I heard a gentleman speak from the audience, and very forcibly I might add, "You Board members should be ashamed of yourselves! Here is a young man devoted to his country serving to fight for our freedoms, and you would deny him time to spend with his mother before going off to war! You yourselves, are veterans in the armed forces and some of you served in WWII, the Korean, and Vietnam wars. You know what that is like. Come on, put your fears aside! This is only temporary. I am a lawyer and I will fight you tooth and nail and report what you're doing here to Channel 7 News! I don't think you want the cameras down here filming your actions. Re-think your vote!"

I was in shock... I didn't even know this man, but he was championing the cause for me and for my son!

The Board sheepishly looked at each other, then one spoke up, "I want to change my vote to yes! How many more would like to change their vote?"

One by one until it was unanimous to let Matt stay until he gets deployed! I couldn't believe it. In an instant, everything changed. I got up to thank this man who saved the day. He said, "No thanks necessary, we should be thanking your son." He got up and walked away with a cane, limping. Maybe he had served in a past war and had been wounded. He was my hero. I never saw him again.

How I enjoyed the next six months waking up to having breakfast with my son. After having missed out on so many years of Matt's growing up, this was such a blessing. We would play cards and games on the weekends, go to church and lunch, go to movies, take trips to share good times at the beach or mountains, but what I enjoyed the most was our deep talks, laughing, and sharing our hearts. I'll never forget those six months.

Glen, Matt and Me

I received a card just before he left for Afghanistan that said:

It has been a blessing to live with you and Glen for the past six months. It has been a joy to renew our relationship and share in each other's lives. Thank you for being there for me.

I'm thankful for our continued relationship and time together. I enjoy our conversations, venting, and laughter. I look forward to each occasion and I look forward to many more with you! I'm proud of how you continue to grow every year and develop into the talented and caring person you are!

You are important in my life!

When I am gone, always remember that anything is possible with God plus your willingness. Positive thoughts equals positive action. You can do it!

Time will go by quickly and I'll be home before you know it.

I love you!

Matt

17

My Daughter Uses Her Voice

"Be still, and know that I am God" (Psalm 46:10)

Lori's Story

Lori and I have had many ups and downs along the way. Our relationship was the closest for a long time. She was my compliant child and so became my "favorite." She always stood up for me, defended me to others, and was very nurturing, understanding, supportive, and encouraging. What I didn't realize was that I looked to her as *my* surrogate "mother." She did everything I would have wanted my mother to do. What I also did not realize is that I became "the child" and turned to her as a confidante, telling her things I should have been telling a therapist. I actually put her in a very destructive, dysfunctional relationship. It was bound to backfire at some point and did.

"Mom, I need to tell you something that's been bothering me for a long time. When you come over, you stay so long and whine to me about your life that I can do nothing about, but makes me feel uncomfortable. It puts a responsibility on me that I shouldn't have. Your visits have now become a burden to me, not a blessing. After your visits, I feel drained. I have a baby now with another one on the way. My children's needs come first. I can't continue to take care of you too. It's just too much. Don't come to me with complaints and vent to me about feeling unfulfilled and disconnected from God and your children. It puts me in an awkward place and is not healthy for me. I love you and care about what you're going through, but this has got to stop."

I already knew what she said was right, but still I was shocked. She had never stood up to me like that and I felt betrayed by my own daughter who I loved the most and felt the closest to of all my children. Now what do I do with that? My first instinct was to cry and run away. I held back the tears, and said I needed to leave. I didn't even hug her for fear of breaking down crying. She hurt me and I was not going to become vulnerable ever again with her. I cried all the way home.

Back in those days, my pattern was to distance myself from the relationship with conflict, so that's what I did. I journaled my feelings and tried to figure out what to do. I was in counseling and so of course I talked with my counselor who agreed that I could not turn to Lori anymore as a confidante. That was very unhealthy. I still didn't know how I was going to be different with Lori. I didn't know how to be a mother and not become the child.

So I wrote letters and emails back and forth to Lori. I thought I handled myself very well but Lori's answers baffled me. I thought she wasn't understanding me and I told her she was trying to parent me. I certainly couldn't see her side of it. I was still so needy myself back then and I needed more healing.

After several months, we came together face to face.

"Lori, what is it that you want? What's the one most important thing that you want from me? How do you see us resolving this issue?"

"Let me think about it, Mom, and next time we get together I'll have an answer for you."

"Okay, Lori, I'll see you next week."

I was not prepared for what happened on our next visit. She read this letter to me and handed me a copy to keep:

April 26, 2009

The Issue Between Us (as I see it)

You connecting on a consistent basis with
family members, reaching out
intentionally and proactively, asking
what *they* need or want that day…service
oriented. Don't just reach out for
yourself until you feel better or you
feel connected, or until you feel like
you don't need it anymore. Continue to
reach out even without encouragement from
the other person.

You asked me why I care or why is this so
important to me?

- Because it affects me.
- Because I need you to be there
  for me as mom, to be strong for me
  too, to be a role model.
- Because you care -- you tell me
  how you want a closer relationship
  with Matt and Becca and Jenny. You
  tell me how you only have four
  children left and you want to be
  close.

If you say it's not my place to "be the
adult" or "parent" you, then please don't
come to me with complaints and vent to me
about feeling unfulfilled and
disconnected from God and your children.
It puts me in an awkward place and is not
healthy for me.

How it could happen

Be intentional – have a plan:

- Mark your calendar in advance to
  call all children once a week
- Connect with grandson Eric
  (Carla's son) once a month – on the
  phone, make plans to see him for a

movie day or some other activity
once a month, initiate visits with
our whole family
- Ask what I need or want when you
come to babysit
- Think of others before yourself
- Do therapeutic things for
yourself AND the other person
- Focus on the positive before
sharing frustrations
- Offer to buy dinner or lunch for
whoever you're with
- Invite people over for dinner for
no reason
- Let the guests choose how to
spend the holiday (no expectations,
just enjoying the company and
togetherness)
- Offer to help with household
chores
- Be the first to suggest or offer
a nap for me or for me to get out
of the house
- Serve in a ministry but not as a
leader
- Bake cookies for Matt (son) or
Eric (grandson), send a care
package to all the kids/grandkids
- Pray for all your
children/grandchildren
- *Look* for ways to serve, be
creative
- Possibilities are endless!
- Rely on God for the strength to
do this and the consistency over
time
- Be intentional about growing
spiritually and staying plugged in
to God's power
- God will give you what you need
to build deep relationships with
ALL your kids/grandkids because He
gave this role to you

Let me quote Max Lucado's Bible study of
Philippians:

> "*Think of this: If the Father in
> heaven is not only with us, but in
> us, if He never abandons us, if He
> listens to us and cares about us
> and wants only the best for us,
> then all things are possible. We
> no longer have to scramble around
> trying to make life work. We can
> relax. We can go "off-duty." We
> can let go of the draining, joy-
> depleting habit of looking out for
> number one. Even better than that,
> when we are convinced that the
> Father is absolutely for us, we are
> freed up to focus all our attention
> and energy and efforts on living
> for Him by serving others. As
> surrendered servants, we can rest
> assured He will meet all our needs"*
> (Lucado, 2007, p. 49).

Positive things you're already doing:

- Praying for Matt fervently
- Washed the sink for me and Doug
  (husband), did the dishes without
  being asked
- Consistently babysitting Jonah
  (my son), wanting a relationship
  with him
- You have a real desire to connect
  with God and family
- Made an effort at Easter to
  provide for the family
- You think of Jonah when you're
  out shopping and you buy him little
  gifts. I love that!

WOW! What a list! I was overwhelmed. Again, my first instinct was to cry. How dare she tell me how to be a mom/grandma with my family?!? She really was doing exactly what I did with my Dad in my therapy session, but I couldn't see it or handle it well. At the time Lori presented this list to me, I hadn't grown enough emotionally or spiritually to hear her voice and respond in a healthy way.

Besides, that wasn't even the issue between us, but she certainly was making it so. I held back the tears and left. I could not believe what just happened. I went to a new counselor specifically to work on this list of Lori's.

The first questions from the counselor to me were, "Could you do anything that's on this list? Would you be comfortable picking out one or two things?

I answered, "I could if I wanted to, but I certainly don't want to under these circumstances. She's not going to dictate to me how I choose to act. That's between God and me."

My emotions were so charged at this point, it took me over a month to work it all out and calm down about this list. Every week, the counselor would ask me the same questions, "What are you willing to do?"

She said to pray about it and she would continue to also pray for God's guidance.

Finally she said that God revealed to her to throw out the list and continue praying what God wants me to do. I breathed a sigh of relief! I knew the things on the list were the right things to do, but I couldn't face it yet.

All I knew was that I was angry with Lori, and unconsciously punished her by withholding my relating to her. I now know that was so immature and unhealthy for me to treat her that way. I so regret doing that.

After some time passed and our heated emails stopped, we decided to test the waters and try meeting for short visits, not discussing or re-hashing issues or feelings. It was very uncomfortable at first, even awkward. Trust had been broken for both of us and it was not easy venturing out once again to navigate a new relationship. Slowly but surely, we won each other's hearts in a way that was healing for both of us as I showed Lori how nurturing, supportive, loving, and understanding I could be. When I could be unselfish and give to her, meeting her needs and not my own, things changed between us. It was a joy to me to finally be the mother I had longed to be.

I can't tell you what happened or when I changed and turned a corner. Maybe it was the fact that the counselor gave me permission to throw out the list, but I know God met my needs, soothing my wounds, and healing parts of me that prevented me from being the kind of mother Lori desired and I really needed and craved to be. Seemed like all of a sudden, I became that mother. It was not magically done in a moment, but over time, God worked with me, growing me up emotionally and spiritually. I wanted to follow God and do what He wanted me to do, which turned out to be the things on her list. That's the thing about God, He's not pushy. He lets me work it out with Him and gently nudges me in the right direction. I'm not perfect and I still make mistakes and say or do the wrong things, but I own my mistakes immediately if I can and I don't distance anymore. God has indeed brought me a long way. This card from Lori says it all.

From Lori
Christmas 2009

Printed on the card were the words:

Being your daughter has taught me so much over the years, and I'll always remember how you've encouraged me to be the best I can be. And I want you to know that your own life has been the best example I could have. And if anyone should say that I'm just like my mother, it would make me very proud and happy. Because I think you're one of the most wonderful people in this world!

She wrote.

This year has had its ups and downs for us but I'm so grateful for what we have and where we are now. I love you so much and am so proud of who you are - your joy and generosity for the whole family is so inspiring and just fills me with a joy of my own. I love you Mom.

Your daughter, Lori

On my birthday June 19, 2014, Lori gave me this card.

A Message For My Mother

When the world's telling me to be anyone but me,
I think about who you taught me to be…
I remember your wise words, your strong example,
and your unfailing belief in
who I am and what I have to give.
And on those days when I'm at my very best,
honoring the real me…
I hope you know I'm also honoring you.

She wrote

Happy Birthday mom! What a blessing it is to me to be celebrating another year with you, another birthday with my mom. I am grateful. I love you, appreciate you, and honor you today. I want you to know how much I value you and all you have taught me about yourself, about God, about love, and sacrifice, and for what you have taught me about myself. I hope you feel cared for and valued today because you are.

Your daughter,
Lori

Lori and I share a wonderful relationship today. I'm so glad she had the courage to stand up to me and tell me what she needed. Although I couldn't hear her voice at the time, God worked with me to meet my needs and I in turn could then hear Lori and meet hers.

As I look back over the timeline of our conflicts, I believe it really started to break down in 2003 and continued downhill until the volcano erupted in April of 2009 with "the list."

By Christmas we had moved on but many of our issues were still unresolved. There was a period of time, maybe six months where I continued my counseling working on my issues. What I was not aware of at the time *(we weren't sharing much),* was all the hard work Lori was doing, reading about mothers and daughters, boundaries, and letting go. When Lori gave up her expectations of me being any

Me and Lori

other kind of mother, something changed inside her that made a difference in how she related to me. She hadn't voiced it, but it was as if she threw out her list and let it go. It was about that same time that my letting go of my need for Lori to be any other kind of daughter, made me relax and accept her as she is: Beautiful, loving, caring, authentic, and kind. I started fulfilling the list because *I wanted to,* and God brought me to the place of healing I needed, to be able to fulfill giving unconditionally to Lori.

My gratitude goes out to Lori for using her voice to speak her truth. I never want anything less even if it hurts me or makes me angry at the time. We continue to be truthful and honest with our feelings and only share what's appropriate. I'm the mother; not the child. I think Lori and I are closer than we've ever been and we both love it. I'm so grateful to God for the wonderful gift of the relationship Lori and I now have and the way we can be real with each other. Our relationship keeps growing healthier and as we become closer, our connection just gets better.

The Hall Family
Lori and Doug
Jonah and Henry

18
Struggling to Connect

"When you call to me, I will answer you. I will be with you when you are in trouble. I will save you and honor you" (Psalm 91:15, GWT).

Becca's Story

Becca called to tell me about a poem she wrote for her English class. She won a certificate and medal. She would be honored at her school assembly. Would I come? She gave me a copy of her poem so I knew it was about me. I didn't have any mixed feelings at all. I was so proud of her for writing and being honest about her feelings toward me. Everything she said was true and I admired her capability at fourteen, to voice it so eloquently. I was also proud that she invited me to come see her accomplishment, no matter what the motivation behind it. I was glad to be included.

My husband, Glen, had a different reaction. "Why do you let your daughter disrespect you like that?"

"Honey, she's not disrespecting me. She's being honest with her feelings. I love her for that. She's saying she wants me to be her mom when I wasn't there for her. That's all true! I'm proud of her honesty and for sharing it with me. She had a choice and she did the right thing. I needed to hear this poem!"

As she read her poem to the assembly, my eyes filled with tears as I thought, *I have missed out on sharing her life all these years.*

Mom
As I look up at the midnight stars,
The tears start to roll down my face.
I think of you, about how you hurt me so.
I continually ask God why.
However, I do not get an answer.
Could I have been that bad of a daughter
For you not to have loved me?
What did I do wrong?
Did I hurt you?
I wanted a mom,
But you weren't there.
What did I do; was it I?
As I stare at the stars, I wonder,
Are you looking up at the same stars
Wondering what you have missed?

Becca age fourteen 2002

Me with Becca
wearing her medal

Regret swept over me like a wave. I congratulated her when the ceremony was over and we took pictures of her holding the certificate and wearing the medal proudly around her neck. I just basked in the pride I was feeling for my very grown up daughter.

Becca is my baby; the last of six children. She's the one I struggle with the most because we have no relationship really. When Jeff *(her dad)* and I divorced, she went to live with him and the woman he married *(Estrel)*. She was her step-mom, but more of a mother to Becca than I was. I really abandoned her because of my anger toward Jeff, and my uncomfortable feelings at first, with Estrel. So I just let them alone and I didn't contact Becca much at all. As I look back I've seen the damage it did, but I was in my own little world trying to heal from my childhood pain and abuse, two divorces, and children issues as a single parent.

Between 2001 and 2005 Becca and I began a dialogue through emails. This was an attempt on both our parts to share honestly with each other.

Mom, it hurts. I love you so much but you weren't there for me for four years.

Becca, I'm sorry our relationship is not working. I haven't been a nurturing mother for you and I'm sad about that and regret all the missed opportunities to be a part of your life.

Mom, I am not telling you this to hurt you or make you feel like less of a person or a mother. I am telling you this so that you know how I feel and can start being more of a mother to me and not just the woman who gave birth to me.

When we're together, Becca, after I've asked you all the questions I can think of, I don't know what else to say. I just don't know how to relate to you because I don't really know you.

Mom, I'm your daughter whether you like it or not. Every time I expect something from you, I'm just disappointed. I'm so tired of you hurting my heart, Mom. I don't know what to do anymore. I have feelings and the feeling of not mattering, hurts!

Becca, you have every right to feel angry and hurt about our relationship. It's okay to have those feelings toward me. You feel betrayed and don't trust that I can ever be there for you. I understand that.

Mom, I'm not a little girl anymore. I don't know if I should try to have a relationship and take my chances of being hurt again, or save myself the drama and pain of even trying.

I have disappointed and hurt you time and time again and there's no excuse for that. My heart breaks when I hear from you how much damage I've done.

In case you may have forgotten, Mom, I'm gonna be eighteen soon. I'm tired of hearing, "I'm sorry" or "I know" because if you really knew, you'd do something about it.

Becca, I can't go back and change the past. I wish I could, but it's gone. How I regret that! Will you please forgive me? I don't ask for your forgiveness in the hope that you will sweep this all under the carpet, let go of your feelings, and say let's be friends.

Mom, I'm angered to tears. You drive me crazy. I've already told you what I want.

You can still have all of your feelings,
Becca. And you can talk about them as much as
you need to. I will listen and NOT excuse
anything that I've done. You get to set the
pace of our relationship. 1) Do you want a
relationship with me? 2) What kind of
relationship do you want? 3) How do you want
to continue?

When I was eight years old, Mom, I met
a person that changed my life and that
was Estrel. She took care of me
because you weren't around. She still
continues to care. She talks to me to
see how I'm doing. I've been hurting
for ten years Mom! When my dad got
remarried, I just got pushed to the
side for some other time. Well...
...times up.

I was not there for you, Becca.

I'm too tired to hurt. I'm tired of
crying. I don't want to do this
anymore. I wish you could see how
much of an influence Estrel has had on
me. You could have too. You could
have seen me grow up, but you chose a
different path. God had a plan for me
and made me the person I am today
because you didn't care.

And I'm so glad Estrel was there for you
Becca. I see that she has changed your life
for the better. I like Estrel. I think she's
a wonderful woman and a better mother to you
than I've been. And I thank God for her. I
also praise God for the beautiful young lady
that He created and shaped you to be.

I hope that what I've said affects
you, Mom, but if it doesn't, then you
really don't care. I'm not saying
that I don't want anything to do with
you! So please don't take this that

way. I'm just voicing my feelings.

*Becca, I'm proud of you. In spite of me and
my lack of parenting, you've taken the higher
road of excelling in your life rather than
choosing drugs or alcohol. I have great
respect for who you are and how you conduct
yourself. You are a fine, upstanding young
lady with values and morals and I'm so very
proud of you!*

Mom, I love you dearly and I hope that
our relationship starts to grow.

*Do you have any ideas as to how to approach
having a closer relationship, Becca? I'm
willing to listen. To the best of my ability,
I would like to change to try to meet some of
your needs, if you'll let me, if I can.*

I wanted to show Becca how much she meant to me, but I also
wanted her to know I may make mistakes. I'm not perfect. How do
I show her that she matters to me? What would make her feel loved
by me? Maybe I just have to try different things and see what works.
The responsibility is equally mine not solely on her.
I wanted her to forgive me but I know that takes time to build up the
trust between us. My plans are to mend and restore our broken
relationship, if it is still possible. That is my intent because I do love
her. I know I've said that before. Now I want to show her.

I wanted to show Becca that she matters to me. I sent her this
Thanksgiving card:

Thanksgiving 2005
Verse printed on card: *"It is a good thing to give thanks unto the Lord…"*
(Psalm 92:1, KJV).

"Thinking of you with a grateful heart this Thanksgiving."

Daughter bookmark included in card ⇨

I wrote the following on the card.

I remember when you
were a baby you fell
asleep with a bottle of
milk. When you woke, I
would change your
diaper on the changing
table and would nuzzle
your neck and face,
tickling you, and you
would laugh. I would
say oh "vinegar baby"
because of the smell of
sour milk on your cheek.
Your toddler sister Jenny
would chime in "ginegar
baby" because she
couldn't pronounce it
right. We would all
laugh as we tickled you
including your sisters
Carla and Lori. You were
such a happy baby and
such a joy to our family.

When you
were born,
what a joy
you
brought to
the family.
It made us
so proud
when
people
said you
looked a
lot like us.

You've
grown
into a
lovely lady
now, but
nothing
would we
alter,
because we
are so
thankful
for our
lovely,
darling
daughter.

And then I signed the card with

Becca, you are precious to God and to me!

I love you!

Mom

Over the years Becca and I tried on and off to establish contact. I tried, but failed to be consistent. I still struggle with making better efforts to see Becca. I will continue to try. It comforts me to know that I must have made at least a small difference because this is what she wrote four years after the first poem:

This New Beginning
Becca age 18
January 17, 2006

You used to make me cry
And it seemed that you really didn't care
I had given up on you and me
I was too tired to cry any longer
But something has changed
Your heart and mine
God blessed us and what once was, is no more
I have hope in our new relationship
And our new beginning
We have taken on this journey
I'm trusting you and God
that this time it's different
I'm prepared to feel wanted,
To know I'm loved,
To have my mother back.

The year Becca wrote me this poem was the same year our family lost my daughter Carla, just one month later. A few months after Carla's passing I received the following card from Becca when we celebrated Mother's Day together. Maybe because of the loss, Becca's heart was softened.

***

Mother's Day
2006

(Printed on the card)

> *Mother, thanks for all the times you've ever prayed for me. So often in my life, and at the most unexpected times, I've felt a special grace surround me, helping me through a tough spot...I think, at times like that, that it must be you praying for me and God strengthening me in answer to your prayers. Mother, your faith has always been an inspiration to me....And though I don't mention it very often, I want to thank you for that faith, for all your prayers, and for always being such a wonderful example to me. God has made you an incredible woman and a thoughtful mother.*

She wrote

> *I know we've had our ups and downs, but I love you. Thank you for being there. I'm so glad we are trying a new relationship and it means a lot to me. You're my mom and please never hesitate to ask to spend time with me. Yes, I do have*

two moms, which makes me very lucky, but it also means that I need to make compromises in my time to spend time with each of them. I want you to know this Mother's Day that I love you and appreciate our relationship. I hope you never forget that.

Love always,

Becca

Becca and I met recently to discuss the story I wrote about her. I wanted her feedback and to talk about any feelings she had experienced while reading it. I told her how proud I was that she wanted to talk to me and that she made it a priority to do so. It was a good meeting and I felt I listened to all her feelings.

She told me some things I neglected to include in the story I wrote. I have since added those things. She handed me her paper written in 2011. I promised I would include it in the book no matter what it said. She gave me her permission. Everything she said in her paper was true. I regret that I did not treat her in the way she needed and have told her when I responded to her later. It made me sad to be reminded of how hurtful I was; especially to Becca. "I'm sorry" just doesn't seem to be enough.

I wish she and I would both be willing just to sit down and talk, heart to heart, and put our feelings out on the table for us to share openly and honestly what is real for each of us, to listen without judgment, without defenses, and really hear what is important to us both. Maybe we can begin to build a new kind of relationship... ...maybe one we've never even tried before. I hope so...that's what I would like... ...I hope she does too. Maybe someday soon!

Becca's Paper

This is the paper Becca wrote for her college course in Interpersonal Communication at Mt. San Jacinto College, dated fall 2011.

Listening Patterns in the Relationship Between a Daughter and Her Mother

A good relationship needs a balance of give and take. There needs to be equal listening and responding from both parties in order to be successful. When one side of the relationship has faulty listening issues, problems arise and it puts strain on the relationship. The relationship between a mother and a daughter is a vital part of a young girl's life.

Since I was born, my mom has not been around much. On many occasions, we have attempted to have a relationship, but it has never worked out. This paper is an analysis of my relationship with my mother and how her listening patterns have created relationship conflicts.

When I was born in 1988, my mother had already given birth five other times to my siblings ranging from the ages of two to eighteen. By the time I joined the family, my mom was tired of being a parent and relied on my dad and my two older sisters, Carla and Lori, to raise me. She felt that it was time to focus on herself, emphasizing on her spiritual and emotional growth. Therefore, during my young childhood, she was rarely around due to her involvement with church groups and therapy. When I was seven, my parents divorced. At that time, most of my siblings were older and living on their own. However, my sister Jenny and I were too young and joint custody seemed to be the best option. For about a year, we spent half of the week with my dad and the other half with my mom. When I was eight years old, my dad married my step mom and this really bothered my sister Jenny. For me though, I was very excited. It was the first time that I actually had a mother figure present in my life. Since Jenny did not like the new family dynamic, she went to live with my mom full time, resulting in me living with my dad and step mom full time.

Over the next few years, I had little contact with my mom. I would go over to her house for holidays and special occasions, but it always felt awkward, almost like I did not belong there. When I was 12, my mom and sisters went on a destination, Christmas in Big Bear, CA. She did not invite me and I felt much excluded. After they all returned, I confronted her and told her how her actions made me feel neglected and left out. Her reply was "I'm sorry that I made you feel that way. I thought it would be easier for me, that way I wouldn't have to worry about you and Jenny fighting the whole trip." My mother was being an insensitive listener. She heard the content of the message, but ignored the emotional aspect of it.

The next six years had little progress. My mother would tell me that she would want a relationship with me and would call every so often, but after a while, her attempts would fizzle and I would be left devastated by her absence in my life. When I was a senior in high school at the age of eighteen, my sister Carla passed away from a heart attack. This event brought my family very close. We all grieved with each other and relied on each other for support. My sister's passing opened my mother's eyes to the fact that life is short and that she could lose any of her children at any moment. My mom started planning family events on a regular basis. Plans like beach bonfires, trips to the apple orchard, or farmers market; activities that allowed us all to spend time together.

However, when these plans were being made, I

was excluded from the event planning. My mom and other siblings would decide which day and time was best based on their schedules and then I was invited after the plans were already made. After a few occurrences of this, I talked to my mom and let her know that it bothered me that my schedule and concerns were not being included in the planning. She felt attacked and immediately justified her actions by saying that I have cancelled multiple times at the last minute when my schedule was actually included in the plans.

Every time that I have expressed my feelings and emotions toward my mother about our relationship she has taken it as an attack and justified her actions in one way or another.

The biggest example I can give of her faulty listening issues is also the most recent development in our relationship. At the beginning of the year, I was at my wits end and did not know exactly what else to do; so, I wrote my mother a letter expressing my feelings and concerns about our relationship. I thought that a letter would be a good option because I could have better wording and the option of deleting or adding phrases in hope of avoiding defensive communication. After four months, she replied. I believe that this was only because I did not acknowledge her on Mother's Day and she was ready to retaliate. Her responding letter was full of justifications and attempts to put the responsibility of our relationship back in my hands. The part of the letter that most stood out to me was when she threw my feelings aside. She said, "I only see your letter as a venting to me about your feelings. Your feelings are always okay. All I'm saying is, "Where's the solution?"

My letter to my mother gave her an opportunity to see and acknowledge where I was coming from in regards to our relationship. The letter could have given us the chance to appreciate

and accept each other's feelings and move
forward in our relationship. However, my mom
was not able to grasp the information I was
giving her due to defensive listening.

My mom did not acknowledge my feelings. She
mentioned them, but never endorsed them. My
mother is looking at the content and words of
the letter, but is overlooking the meaning and
emotion of what is being said.

The quality of our relationship is very poor.
For most of my life, there was a serious lack
of any type of relationship and when there was
one, the listening issues created many
communication problems. I do not believe that
either my needs or my mother's needs are being
satisfied. She is looking for solutions and
answers that currently I do not have and I am
looking for support and recognition of my
feelings that she currently cannot give. Our
relationship needs a lot of work, time, and
energy.

Therefore, in order for me to see our
relationship as worthwhile and pursue a more
active relationship, I will need to see my
mother actively trying to improve her
listening skills. As of right now, I do not
know whether the relationship is worth
fighting for. I have never seen a consistent
effort from my mother. My history with her
though, does not give me much hope, but I will
not close the door completely.

The relationship between a mother and a
daughter is vital to a girl at any age.
However, that relationship needs to be healthy
and in balance. I can attempt to change the
patterns of the relationship by making my
mother aware of her listening issues. One
opportunity to do so is to share this paper
with her. Hopefully, by doing so, she will
seek to improve her listening skills and show
a consistent effort toward our relationship.

Once a relationship can reach a point where
communication allows both parties to be open
with each other without being defensive, it is
considered balanced and successful. It is my
hope that one day I will achieve this level of
relationship with my mother.

Becca's College Graduation 2015

Today

2015

Even though I told Becca *(before I even read it),* that I would include her paper in this book no matter what it said; after reading it, I found that I actually *wanted* to include it in this book. I am so very grateful to God that Becca had the strength of character within her, to write a college paper about *how* to heal *the relationship between us,* in spite of all my absences in her life.

I wish I could say Becca and I are extremely close now, but the truth is, I still struggle with connecting. After Carla passed away, I was grieving the loss of *Carla,* and didn't work on my relationship with Becca. Then Matt moved back to CA and I started working on my relationship with him. So once again, poor Becca, got lost in the shuffle. I wasn't even thinking, but I can see how I really only worked on one relationship at a time. All the rest of my children suffer, and I regret that. I've only just come to this realization.

I don't know why it continues to be so hard for me to pick up the phone and say let's try again. Maybe it's because I know she's tired of trying, getting her hopes up, and facing rejection all over again. I would be disappointed too and have been as well. There's no easy answer to building the bridge that I so haphazardly burned between us. I do know this: Nothing changes until someone reaches out to risk hurt and disappointment. I'm the mother and it should be me. My heart is there…I want to.

Now I have to show her, to earn back her trust, and just pick up the pieces and try again.

This time I will listen and I will nurture her in the way *she* needs to the best of my ability. I'm so thankful that Becca has not closed the door and that she wants a healthier relationship with me. I hope for that as well and will show her that I can be the kind of mother she's always wanted.

Me and Becca

19
Reconciling With Daughters

"You will find as you look back upon your life that the moments when you have really lived, are the moments when you have done things in a spirit of love" (Drummond, as cited by Neal, 2012, p. 129).

I've come a long way since confronting my dad in my therapist's office. At first, I parented just like my parents taught and modeled for me. So my parenting has not always been the best for my children, but as I've learned more about myself, grown emotionally and spiritually, my relationships to them have come to mean something more deep and meaningful than I ever thought possible. I keep working at it because I've seen the results of their healing from our past and how their hearts have opened up to me, which I never thought would happen. God has given me gifts with each of them as I continue to risk showing up with an open heart, being real with them, and looking out for *their* best interest. I've always believed it's never too late to do the repair work that's needed for them and for me.

My Daughters
Lori, Jenny, Becca and Carla

Family Trips

How I long for family times making memories. That's always been important to me, even when the kids were little. Trips to Disneyland and other fun places to enjoy together as a family were essential. Although my children have grown up and are living on their own, it still is important to spend time together even though we live some distances from each other. My daughter, Lori, and I take turns planning, arranging, and inviting the family. Whoever can make it is fine. We try not to put any expectations or judgments as to who shows up but understand that we all have busy lives. Still it is what we value to make time for the family gatherings not just for the holidays but anytime we plan an event.

In the fall, around September and October, Glen and I start thinking about Oak Glen, our favorite day trip for him and I to go on a date. I look forward to it all year. It's the time of year when the weather turns cooler, the air is crisp and clean, just the right temperature for picking apples.

Oak Glen has twelve apple farms, fifty unique gift shops, and five family restaurants to enjoy all year. We go in late fall when the crisp mountain air brings brilliant fall colors to the native oaks and sycamore trees – a sight to see! The apples on the trees add even more color to the hillsides – like a visit to New England, yet so close. Whether it's fresh apples and cider, a slice of hot apple pie, shopping, or just a visit to the country, mile-high Oak Glen has something for everyone (Wikipedia, Oak Glen – San Bernardino, CA, 2015).

At some orchards you can pick your own apples so I wanted my grandsons, five-year-old Jonah and four-year-old Henry to experience picking their own apples from a tree. I called Lori to see what she thought. "I think it's a great idea! Let's schedule a day and invite the family." We picked a date and gave enough time for everyone to make arrangements to be able to come.

I was thrilled to have a plan and really excited to be going together as a family. Day of, Glen and I met at Lori's house and she and the boys followed us in her car. Everyone else would meet us there.

There was a little difficulty finding each other, but that's happened before. Eventually it all comes together. We have cell phones to call. No problem, or so I thought. I swear my phone never went off and Lori's didn't ring either. So we were at the mercy of stumbling onto each other happenstance which was okay for most everyone. We all made do under the circumstances... ...except Jenny didn't.

When I finally stumbled onto Jenny in the General Store where we were waiting for them to lift the ban on picking any more apples that day, she was so angry with me. At the time I thought this was a bit of an overreaction that was not warranted. We were there specifically to pick apples and for the boys first experience doing so. In my mind I thought, *"Jenny, you're twenty six and old enough and mature enough to make do under the circumstances... ...get over it."* But I didn't say that. I apologized saying I was sorry it happened, but sloughed it off to again pursue getting a bag to start picking apples. I could see that made Jenny all the angrier, but didn't take time to smooth her ruffled feathers. This was about the boys picking those apples, at least for me.

After all was said and done, we never got to pick apples that day, but enjoyed the day anyway. By then it was lunchtime and we decided to go down the hill in our cars and meet again at the restaurant. When we all arrived there, my niece and her husband had to leave, but Jenny was not to be found. Lori announced that Jenny and her boyfriend left. I thought that strange but to me understandable since she was so upset with me. "I'll call her later and smooth it over." Let's eat!

When trying to call her for two days, she wouldn't answer. Boy, she really *is* angry. Finally I texted her and said, "Why did you leave?"

"I was so angry after looking for you for an hour. Why didn't you answer your phone?"

"I didn't hear it. This day was for the boys."

"I know, but you were so intent on picking apples, you didn't care if I was there or not, so I left."

"I'm so sorry. What could I have done to make this a better experience for you?"

"Have a plan where exactly to meet, have your phone on and answer when I call."

"You're right, that's a good plan. I'll do that next time. Will you please forgive me?"

"Yes Mom. I love you."

"I love you too."

I felt good about what had just transpired between Jenny and me, but something kept tugging at my heart. I felt it wasn't enough. Jenny hadn't said it, but I knew there was something deeper going on. I know Jenny and there's always some underlying issues and feelings that haven't been addressed or resolved. They will keep adding up, layer upon layer, until she explodes at me the next time something else happens.

Several days later, I called her to see how she was doing since our phone text.

"How are you Honey?"

"Good Mom. How are you?"

"I'm doing well, thanks."

"Have you reflected on what happened between us at Oak Glen?"

"Yes, I was so angry with you!"

"How frustrating that must have been for you to be looking for an hour and not finding me. Then when you couldn't reach me by phone, how upset you became."

"Yes it was. Mom, you didn't care about me at all. I wasn't important to you. You neglected me and abandoned me."

"Just like I did when you were growing up."

Next time I saw her for lunch, I reiterated how sorry I was to neglect and abandon her just like I did when she was growing up.

Sobbing like a baby, I held her in my arms and comforted her. What a healing moment for both of us.

The following week, a Girl's Night was scheduled at Mariner's Church, so I went to Lori's house early to talk about what had happened between Jenny and me. As I did, I began to think about some conflicts Lori and I had experienced in the last few years. All of a sudden what came out of my mouth surprised even me.

"Our conflicts have not been easy for you. When I was so against you and Doug buying your house, I should have realized it was *your* choice. After all, it's *your* life. I was wrong. I never should have stood against you just because I wanted to be right. You're my daughter, I love you, and I care about what happens to you. I'm so sorry. I WAS WRONG."

She sobbed like a baby, I hugged her and we cried together. Another healing moment for mother and daughter.

I can't tell you how many times I was glad I pursued something deeper with my girls. It has paid off in so many blessings, gifts that I am grateful for. God always wants healing for us from the wounds of the past.

* * *

How I wish I could tell you that my parenting has finally reached a point of perfection. It certainly is better in the sense I can say I'm more nurturing, understanding, and supportive. Even my kids would agree with that statement. But I still make mistakes. I say or do the wrong things and cause my children disappointment and heartache. The difference is, I can *own* my mistakes today and I can make amends. I don't make excuses or get defensive. At least I *try* not to. And I certainly allow my children their feelings whether angry or hurt, and I give them what they need. There is healing for my children and for me from our past.

God has certainly been with me through everything I've experienced and continues to redeem what was lost and has reconciled my family where disconnection took place. I've even made amends to my two ex's, Bill and Jeff, and we're all good friends.

I learned in recovery how important it was to make amends to those I had harmed. It was not easy with my ex's, since I felt I was wronged. Once I did my work in therapy, I could let go of the hurt they caused me and start working on my amends to them. I thought back to Bill and how ambitious he had been regarding his career. When we were married, I wasn't able to appreciate that quality in him because of my own neediness. I see that quality in him today as a positive.

I am so sorry that I hurt him and told him so. That made me very sad. He didn't deserve that from anyone, let alone his own wife. There was no justification or excuses for abuse, neglect, passive/aggressive behavior and distancing, triangulating, cruel remarks, blaming, and nagging. I did all of those things. I am sorry that he was the recipient of my acting out. I wasn't the kind of wife that I wanted to be and hoped I would be. Since then, I learned that unconditional love really is accepting and valuing the other person enough to feel the sadness over wrongs incurred, rather than blaming the other person for what he did or didn't do.

I realized how I injured him in so many ways. I hoped he heard the sincerity of my heart, for I truly meant it.

The other things I wanted to acknowledge were the positive things he gave me. He was an anchor of stability when I was at my worst emotionally regarding my family and he supported me. He was more objective than I was, because I was so enmeshed with them. When he stood up to my mother, there was a part of me that was so proud of him. He was able to stand up to her when I couldn't. Watching his example was a first step in helping me make the break from them later, when I was strong enough to do so. I thanked him for that.

I hoped there was peace in his heart regarding the past. He did the best he could. I'm glad we shared our lives together for the fifteen years we had. Good times and bad, it was worth being together. I'm glad and thankful he was a very important part of my life.

Bill had this to say.

I appreciate you, Ardie. During our marriage, I appreciated you doing all that massive recruit laundry and making big mac runs and delivering it for 86 people in Illinois for my recruits when I was Company Commander for the Navy. Throughout the bulk of my career you were a strong, stable support system helping to make any achievements I had possible.

For all the grief I gave you, I am glad you feel there were some positive things I gave you. The truth is, Ardie, you had them already, but I appreciate you giving me any credit in helping to bring them out. I'm also glad you feel the fifteen years we had together was worth it. I feel that way too. I look back today and realize we were really a couple of God's kids each in our own way just trying to do the best we could with what we had for coping skills at the time. Just like you said, there's no excusing or justifying, but today there is understanding, appreciation, and abiding love for one another. For that I am grateful!

These words meant so much to me. I value who we both have become. I'm so grateful that God gave me the strength to make the amends needed for both my ex's.

Jeff was surprised that I made amends to him and appreciated it, but didn't have much else to say other than we have two beautiful daughters to show for it. And that is very true. I'm grateful for them.

I'm especially grateful to Glen who always makes my ex's feel welcome in our house when the opportunity arises. He's such a loving man, gracious, and forgiving of the hurtful things done to me in the past. These are all gifts God has given me and I am so grateful. Thank You Lord!

20

A New Day

"This is the beginning of a new day. God has given me this day to use as I will. I can waste it or grow in its light and be of service to others. But what I do with this day is important because I have exchanged a day of my life for it. When tomorrow comes, today will be gone forever. I hope I will not regret the price I paid for it" -Anonymous

My prayer is that you have hope in these pages. There is healing for your past hurts. I hope you've been inspired to pursue taking a proactive step in your own recovery. God has a plan and purpose for your life. He loves you and wants the best for you. I do too. May God bless your journey!

To quote one of my poems:

"I will look to the Lord for strength, and seek His face always And joyfully sing praises to Him all the rest of my days."

* * *

I have come to know a deeper relationship with God through all of my experiences. I believe solely in the Trinity, Father God, His Son Jesus Christ, and the Holy Spirit.

I have a Savior, Jesus Christ, who was willing to die on a cross for me so that I could have life everlasting. That fills me with so much gratitude and love. I have joy in my life, a peace, and serenity I've expressed on these pages. I have learned so much about my struggles and myself. God has been good to me. Healing has taken place. What a gift!

I want to express my deepest gratitude to my Heavenly Father, who has repeatedly picked me up and carried me, when I couldn't take another step. To Him belongs all the praise, honor, and glory, for He has done mighty and wondrous things beyond my comprehension and beyond my fondest hopes and dreams.

My humble gratitude belongs to the Holy Spirit who continually nudges me, gently leading me in God's path of truth. But even when I rebel *(as I so often do)*, the Spirit never lets me rest until I come to a place of surrender *(which I need to do)* to follow God's way *(always the BEST way!)*.

My story isn't over yet. It is a continuing process of growth and healing until the day I die, so I continue to journal and write my stories. I look forward to what the Lord has in store for me, here on earth, and forever with Him in Heaven.

If you've related to anything I've written here, I would love to hear from you. You can write to me and please feel free to do so:

Ardie Hamilton Sarris
24 Mira Las Olas
San Clemente, CA 92673

Or email me at: ardiesarris@yahoo.com

Ardie Hamilton Sarris

My Poetry

And

Journal Entries

Precious and Free!

"Then the way you live will always honor and please the LORD... ...All the while, you will learn to know God better and better" (Colossians 1:10, NLT).

"It is through a deeper relationship with God and others that hope and encouragement will flood your soul" (Arterburn & Mintle, 2004, p. xiv).

I started writing poetry to express my feelings when I found my voice in 1989, but the first poem I ever wrote was written as a seventeen year old senior, at Pioneer High School, Whittier, California. My English teacher, Mrs. Schryver, would not give A's without doing extra credit work. Of the three choices I had, I thought the one I could probably do was write a poem. I had never written anything but term papers and book reports, but somewhere inside me I thought I could do this. I not only received an *"A"* for the poem and for the class, but my poem was published in the High School literary booklet entitled *"Reflections."* Twenty four years later, my poetry came to my rescue when I needed it.

What Else is There Left?
Ardith Wilfinger (maiden name) Age 17
May 1965

How often I sit	*As they twitter by*
By my bedroom window	*Their song*
Watching the birds	*Fills my head*

'Til it's well overflowing
What else is there left
For my eyes but to cry?

The sun shines
Its rays
Down on me
As on others

But somehow
I feel
I'm all alone
The birds
Hush their singing
And all turns quiet
What else is there left
For my heart but to groan?

'Tis spring
Say the flowers
The trees
And the grass

'Tis spring
All around me
In all that I see
The smells
Are so sweet
The wind
Is so cool
What else is there left
For my soul but to be?

Nature blooms
All the while
No stopping at all
Just as I
On my way
Must continue
To go

Finding out who
What
Where
When
How
And why
What else is there left
For my mind but to know?

My eyes
How they cry
My heart
How it groans
My soul can it be?
My mind can it know?

All these things
I ponder
And wonder
And feel
What else is there left
For myself but to grow?

Who Am I?
December 26, 1989

I don't know
Who "Ardie" is

To figure this out
Is such a quiz

309

There's so much
Going on inside
My feelings
Can no longer
Be denied

I want to listen
To the little girl
Who has felt lost
In a world
Of confusion
Helplessness and
pain
Trying to fill
The "black hole"
In vain

I'm scared
I want to run away
Not really wanting
To go
I stay

But I don't know
How to be me
And really
Let you see
The truth
And what is real
Is that I have
A right to feel

Whether joyous or
sad
Angry or glad
There's no such
thing
As a feeling that's
bad

Or right
Or wrong
Weak or strong
A feeling just is
You don't
Have to be a whiz
To figure it out
Although
I have some doubts
About trusting you
Will you
Leave me too?

I cannot stand
To be alone
I have no life
Of my own

It's hers
What she picked
out
For me
A wife and mother
I must be
And suffer dutifully

That which is my
fate
Never mind
If I'm feeling hate
And disgust
Toward my mother
But alas
I also love her

Her message
Girl, do what you're
told

And you better not
Be bold

That's not allowed
In this family
I didn't know
I had the ability
To say "NO"

Because they beat
Me down
With words
Like quicksand
All around

I was slowly
Pulled under
Everything
Was torn asunder

Her insides
quaking
The little girl cries
Her heart is
breaking

Listen to me
Is her plea

Just let me be
Who I am
Is "Ardie"

I'm special
Unique
And lovable
And knowing that
Is powerful

I can be strong
I can be free
Believing in myself
Is the key

The little girl
Doesn't have to hide
I take her hand
And gently guide

With acceptance
Compassion
And loving care
Growth
Healing
Inner peace
Is my prayer

Freedom
April 17, 1991

A simple life
That's what
I've wanted
Without the strife
That's always haunted

Me from childhood
If only I could
Be someone else
Someone who tells

Without fear of hurt
Even if she
Has to blurt
It out
To tell the truth

Even if the roof
Caves in
The truth
Will be told
And she
Will be bold

She will be strong
Climb up the ladder
Rung by rung

Freedom at last
From the past
A life
That is mine
I choose the design

Within me
Is my happiness
I will accept
Nothing less
Than the best

For me
I deserve to be
Happy and free
Free to be me!

Are You There Lord?
July 1, 1991

Can anybody see?
Does anybody hear me? *(PS 5:1)*
Are you there Lord?
Its heaven
I'm looking toward

Asking for help from you *(PS 18:6)*
I don't know what to do
Can I ask?
Are you real?
This pain hurts
That I feel *(PS 34:18)*

Where are you Lord?
I'm in need *(PS 10:1)*
I'm waiting
For you to lead *(PS 27:11)*

Me
Into the quiet calm
Please hold me
In the palm *(PS 37:24)*
Of your hand

And never
Let me go *(ISA 41:10)*
Your love
I want to know *(PS 33:22)*
And feel

I'm hurting Lord
You seem far away *(PS 13:1)*
Let me know
You're here today

With me
Helping
Healing the pain (PS 25:17)
My tears are falling
Just like the rain (PS 56:8)

I want to
Feel your hand
Wipe away the tears (ISA 25:8)
And hold me
Until all my fears (PS 34:4)
Fade away
And I can see
A ray of hope
And once again
I can cope

With the daily struggles

I go through
What I see
Is a beautiful view

Of my caring Savior
Walking with me (PS 139:1-10)
Kind and gentle
As only Jesus can be
Filling me
With joy and peace
Nurturing that
Will never cease

A priceless gift
Is mine today
The Lord is
In my heart
To stay (1COR 6:19)

Dedicated to
Pastor Paul E. Miller
Prince of Peace Lutheran Church, Anaheim, CA,
April 17, 1992

I see your face
Light up
When I come
Near to you

I feel warm inside
Because your love
Is real

And in my heart
I know God
Is speaking to me

Of His love
Touching me
Warming me
Healing me

And tears
Come to my eyes
Joy and sadness
Mixed together

This is what
I've always wanted
And missed so much

313

Of my life

First to have
Someone know ME
Who I really am
And love me
"Just as I am"

Then to believe
And feel
In the deepest
Part of me
God's love is real
For ME personally

I thank
And praise God
For His greatness
Wonder and majesty

He's awesome
Beyond words
He has revealed
His love for me

Through friends
Like you
One of many blessings
He continually
Showers upon me

As I journey
Through the pain
And trials of this life
And even in those
Trying struggles
He has shown me
Grace and mercy
Beyond compare

He led me
To this church home
To find a new family
Of loving
Caring
Understanding brothers
And sisters in Christ
I truly am blessed

Journal Entry
March 24, 1994

I drew and colored a drawing I called "NO RULES" -- I describe it as free flowing, colorful, playful, dazzling shapes and sizes. The sky is the limit. No rules, no fences, no posts, and no ropes. Run free little Ardie. You can be curious and explore. The whole world is there for you. No one here will say, "No, you can't do that" - because you can. You're free – free to be whomever you were meant to be. You can be the person who makes you happy; not who they told you that you *should* be, just to make them feel okay about themselves. You are so creative, Ardie, an artist and a poet! How special and how precious you are! Be free!

Be Free
March 24, 1994

Be free
As the birds
Spread my wings
And fly
Listen to these words

Fly high
As the sky
I can do it
Nothing
To stop me now
I won't quit
This is my vow

I'll always be here
To champion
For you
When you're feeling
fear
And when
You're feeling blue

Your feelings are yours
I give them honor
A special place
That soars
Full of life
And full of wonder

No more
The victim place
Take back your power
You've won the race
No need to cower

We'll walk
Through the fear
I'm right
By your side
I'll always be here
Together
We will abide

Grieving the Loss
January 24, 1995

I know it won't last
I've got to hold on
And wait for the dawn

I'm feeling
My feelings
Grieving the loss

Of a little girl
Whose need

Was just
To be heard

To be nurtured
With love
To be shown
She was enough

I didn't get
My needs met

All the years
Have stockpiled a debt

That will never
Be paid
My inner child
Has been betrayed

And so I cry
These tears of pain
Knowing as I do
I gain

Healing for me
And for
The child inside
Whose feelings
For too long
Have been denied

I know
What I feel
This pain is real
When I feel it

I can let go
And with the release
I feel a glow

Of the passion
Of feeling alive
And once again
I can strive

To face each day
With joy and zest
Because I know
I've been blessed

I'm grateful
For recovery
It has been
A unique discovery

Of who I am
And how I've grown
Today the little girl
Is not alone

She is precious
Creative and free
And I look
At her lovingly

And I know
In my heart
We'll never be apart

She and I
Walk together
Hand in hand
Loved and supported
Re-united we stand

This truth I know
Is most certainly true
Together there's nothing
We can't do!

I Know God Cares
March 24, 1995

Nature and I
Are one
I feel the sun
It warms my skin
It warms
My heart within

I know God cares
I know He's aware
Of the pain I feel (PS 34:18)
He wants me to heal (PS 147:3)

From the wounds
Of my youth
Feeling His presence
Begins to soothe
And comfort me

When I am distressed (PS 119:76)
He gives me gifts
I know I'm blessed (ROM 6:23)

When I feel
Out of control
And I'm falling
In that big black hole

The tears I cry
He cries with me (ISA 38:5, PS 56:8)
I don't have to flee

To my addictions
To escape
From there
It only escalates
Into depression

Hopelessness and despair

I'm in the lion's den
Waiting
For the devouring to begin

If I stay
How do I fight?
I surround myself
In God's white light

In order
To feel protected (PS 116:6)
In the past
When I was neglected
I abandoned myself
By stuffing my feelings
Today I have tools
That give me healing

It's not always easy
Life is difficult
It's not about blame
It's nobody's fault

God never gives me more
Than He and I
Can't handle together (1COR 10:13)
Each day
The quality of my life
Gets better

Although there are changes
In my mood
I am filled
With so much gratitude

And I know that God
I'm special *Loves*
Unique *And cares*
Precious as can be *For me (1PET 5:7)*

My Feelings Are Mine
May 26, 1995

I have a sense *I pleaded*
Of peace within *Their approval*
On this page *Is what I needed*
My feelings are written

And I would do anything
Ever more recorded *To get their love*
For generations to come *Because by myself*
My experiences *I wasn't enough*
That started in the womb

I couldn't survive
Never feeling safe *I would have died*
Afraid and terrified *And that is how*
All I wanted to do *My true feelings*
Was hide *Were denied*

I tried to say *So I kept them*
What was true for me *Locked inside*
All I received *And my inner child*
From my family *Began to hide*
Was criticism
Ridicule and blame *It has not been safe*
Faultfinding was *To come out*
The name of the game *In full view*
Until now
I was wrong *I can tell*
I was sinful *My truth to you*
I was bad
And my family members *I am precious*
Were mad *Lovable*
One of a kind
"I'm sorry, I'm sorry" *In my journey*

Of discovery
Now I find

I have a voice
For all to hear
Whether I laugh

Or cry my tears

My feelings are mine
They're a part of me
Expressing them
I now feel free

Journal Entry

June 22, 1995

Here's another one of Pastor Rick's questions to get us *(his church members)* to think:

What does "restoration to wholeness" mean to you?

When I think of wholeness, I think of being complete, filled, fulfilled, integrated, balanced, healthy, happy, and at peace. I long for these gifts. Growing up in a chaotic, alcoholic home, I remember being in emotional pain, most of the time feeling lost and alone, unloved, crying a lot, frightened and terrified of people, places and things. I felt very empty inside and can remember that when I ate food, especially sweet, sugary desserts, and candy, that emptiness would fill up. I could feel "full" from food. That's when my obsession with food began, trying to fill up that empty hole inside. I still feel that emptiness and want desperately to be restored to wholeness. I know and believe that the God of my understanding is the only one who can restore me and yet I keep God at a distance. I know God is here guiding me. God brought me to recovery. Nothing has happened to me by accident or coincidence. I truly am grateful but something is preventing me from pursuing a closer relationship with Him. Perhaps I am afraid to ask for wholeness; afraid I might not be restored. Maybe I still don't believe *(on some level)* that I deserve to be restored to wholeness. What I know in my mind must be felt inside my heart as well.

Where Are You God?
June 22, 1995

The gaping hole
Inside me
Cries out to God
For ease *(PS 5:2)*
Not knowing
How to fill it
Food obsession
Became my disease

Feeling empty
And alone *(1PET 1:18, 19)*
Brought me to tears *(PS 6:6)*
I only knew to cry
In spite
Of all my fears

I nurtured myself
With food
It was all
I knew how
I knew
It tasted good
And each day
I would vow

Never
To do it again
I would be

Strong and diet
Win their love
And then
The family
Would be quiet

Leave me alone
Stop hurting me
Soon I'll be grown
Older I'll be
On my own

Where are You God? *(PS 4:3)*
Help me please *(PS 5:1)*
I can't
Do it alone *(ROM 7:18)*
This
Is a powerful disease

I'm relying on You *(PROV 24:25)*
For healing
And wholeness *(JER 33:6)*
Fill me
With Your love *(PS 13:5)*
In
All its fullness *(PS 32:8)*

Journal Entry
August 10, 1995

There is such contrast between what I'm taking in at my Twelve Step meetings *(acceptance, understanding, support, and love)* and what I live with at home. My husband is judgmental, critical, sarcastic, and angry. I don't deserve this kind of treatment. I'm feeling the pain and the sadness of being unloved, unsupported, and neglected. That hurts really badly.

However, I know I built up this fantasy inside of me.

The Way
August 10, 1995

It's difficult
Not knowing
What lies ahead
For me
I don't know
Where I'm going
I don't know
What's to be

One step at a time
Is all I can do
Each step I climb
Brings me
Something new

It's scary
Yet exciting too

Challenges are waiting
I change
My point of view
I'm no
Longer hating
My life
Or what I do

I've got support
And love
Surrounding
Me today
God blesses me
From above
He's showing me
The way

My Specialness
September 7, 1995

Today I have support
and caring
Closeness as a result
Of sharing

I've opened up
And let you see me
Your acceptance
Allows me to be

Myself
With all my strength

And weakness
I can be
At my best
Nothing less

Than
To take loving
Nurturing care
Of all
My specialness
I am aware

I've discovered
My value
I know
This to be true

I'm capable

And strong
Precious and free
I know
Who I am
And I'm glad
To be me

Journal Entry

October 5, 1995

The feelings coming up are overwhelming. I'm hurt and feeling rejected and abandoned. I'm scared. There's so much that I have to do to work these issues out. My inner child has all these feelings and I'm having difficulty functioning and letting my loving adult parent the wounded inner child.

Lord, what am I going to do? I'm powerless and I'm weak. I'm relying on You to get me through this very difficult time. It's very painful and hard to keep putting one foot in front of the other after having a memory of the circumstances of my birth. My Mom told me she was ready to deliver me, the doctor hadn't arrived, and the nurse was instructed not to let the baby be born without him there. She held my Mom's legs together because I was already crowning. I had mixed emotions; sad for my Mom, but angry too that I wanted to be born and someone prevented me from doing so when I was ready. Besides I could have been injured as well as my Mom. It's just not right nor fair!

One Step at a Time

October 5, 1995

One step
At a time
I have to climb

Seems like
An endless mountain
Will it stop?

I don't know when

I feel overwhelmed
With feelings
When they're triggered
It sends me reeling

It's difficult
To feel this pain
But I don't want
To run away again

A lifelong journey
So I stay
Of learning and growing
In the process
The best part
My past
Of all for me
I continue to address
Is knowing

Healing
Who I am
Is now my goal
And what I like best
God's love
Living my life
Will fill up that hole
With passion and zest

I try to fill
And if I may
With my addictions
I'll share with you
My experience
Recovery is on-going
Strength
I'll never be done
And hope of recovery too

Exploring a Healthy Relationship
May 25, 1996

Intimacy and closeness
And I can take care
I don't know
What that is
Of myself
But exploring
In any relationship
A healthy relationship today
I'm trusting the process
Is my emphasis
I don't have a script

It's an exciting adventure
This isn't easy
Creating what fits
But the promises
Honest
Do come true
Open-minded
Today I have
And willingness
A brand new
Are the prerequisites
Point of view

Yes my fears
I love
Are evident
Nurture
I am aware
And support myself
Today I have choices
To be all I can be

And doing the same
For my partner
We both can
Feel free

Free to choose another
Or to choose
To be with each other

Real love
Is unconditional
Not binding
Creating what fits us
Our own designing

There are feelings
To walk through
There is no blueprint
This is all new

It's worth the challenge
This definitely feels right
Whether feeling anger
Pain, joy, or fright

We both have tools
And a program
Of recovery
By clear communication
We are discovering

We both
Can be heard
And understood
With no rescuing
Fixing
Or telling the "shoulds"

What a relief

There's room
For growth and healing
Learning to be
Accepting
Of all our feelings

Yes this is an adventure
Taking it
One day at a time
There isn't a hill
Or a mountain
We can't climb

Together yet separate
Individuals are we
Practicing new behaviors
With healthy boundaries

I'm grateful
For the gifts
I have now
This continues
To be an opportunity
For that I'm proud

To be a participant
And enjoy each day
Dealing with
Whatever comes
On the pathway

Don't know
What will happen
As we go on
From here
But one thing
For sure
Is perfectly clear

We've learned
Many lessons
And shared so much
Through emotional connection
Our hearts
Have been touched

These have been
Gifts of priceless value
Healing has come
From this relationship too

In providing this connection
I've not known before
God continues

To shower blessings galore

I'm grateful
I have peace
I feel whole
I feel loved
Whether in a relationship
Or not
I am enough

I will continue
To be all I can be
And today I know
I am precious
And free

Feelings
June 10, 1996

Sometimes
I don't know
What to do
A scary place
I don't have a clue

The feelings are intense
I'm in a lot of pain
It feels as if
I'm going insane

I'm asking for help God
Please see me through (PS 18:6)
This bottomless pit
I'm begging you

I trust the process
Feelings come and go
The only way is up
When I'm feeling this low

So I hang in there…

Feel the feelings
And use the tools
In order to heal
I break the rules

From my childhood that says
My feelings don't count
Now I can freely express them
In any amount

My feelings are important
And I know
This too will pass
They really are temporary
They really don't last

What's more important

325

Is the support
I have now (ROM 12:10 GWT)
Criticism and judgment
I just don't allow

In my life
Today I know the difference
I trust my intuition
And my common sense

I know my capabilities
The gifts that God
Has given (1COR 7:7)
Today I have serenity
I'm no longer driven

By hysterics
Chaos or insanity
My life is peaceful
And I'm glad
To be me (1TIM 2:2)

In spite of feelings
That come and go
That's life
Just the ebb and flow

I like how that sounds
It feels good
I can let go
And the solution
Will appear
When it's time
For me to know

Whatever the problem
Whatever the fear
God is listening
I know that
He will hear (1JN 5:14, 15)

Me
When I pray
Guiding me
Every step of the way (EX 13:21)

He's awesome
Unconditionally
Loving me (PS 25:10)
I am His child
I am indeed
Precious and free (1JN 3:1)

Journal Entry

July 3, 1996

I'm experiencing loss again, and I'm feeling so much pain. My partner ended our six-month relationship last night. We talked for an hour, and I felt overloaded. I started feeling the pain when he left. This is a major loss for me of the healthiest relationship I've ever had. I love him and I will miss him. I've shared with him a very deep soulful connection. I've also learned many lessons risking and growing, walking through feelings. I've not only enjoyed his presence in my life, but I've learned the value of unconditional love. Now I have an opportunity to put it into practice. Because he wants a "spark" and is uncomfortable with the way our relationship is deepening, I'm going to let go and give him freedom by ending the relationship and saying goodbye.

God's Rainbow Shines
July 3, 1996

The storm had come
I overwhelmingly feared
The clouds parted
And a rainbow appeared

Beautiful colors
Shining and glistening
I feel like a new ship
At its christening

Embarking
On an exciting voyage
The struggle is over
I can disengage

Move on to
Whatever's coming next
No matter
What it is
I'm blessed

God has been
Good to me
Even in pain
I have an idea

God knows
And feels what I feel
And is willing
To hold me
While I heal

I have faith

And strength
To carry on
To feel my feelings
Is a phenomenon

And still have peace
And serenity
And not give in
To self-pity

My life is full
I feel loved
And God's rainbow
Shines
In the heavens above

Reminding me
The promises come true
When the pain passes
I feel renewed

I'm working
My program
Today I have tools
I no longer feel
Like I'm drowning
In a pool

Of overwhelming
Devastating feelings
The lessons
For me to learn
God is revealing

327

Pleasant
Yet painful
This is bittersweet
Yes I have peace
I feel whole
And complete

I know
I will get through
This pain
Strength
And courage
I will gain

God is great
God is good
I know
I'm loved
And understood

God's will
Not mine
Is best for me
Today
I know
I am precious
And free *(ISA 43:4)*

The Dark Side of Night
July 4, 1996

When I'm alone
And the night
Sets in
My world
Of feelings
Starts to spin

I'm walking the road
Less traveled
Going within

Each layer unraveled
Shows
How this hole
Inside me came to be
Unmet needs
Cruelty and abuse
I've come to see

Is the emptiness
I feel

The tears
And the pain
Are very real

This hurts so much
Will the pain subside?
Nowhere to run
Nowhere to hide

I trust the process
This I can do
Somewhere
Inside of me
I always knew

There was a way
To have
Peace of mind
Even though
My family of origin
Was blind

I see clearly now
And I know how
To use the tools
God has given me
Embracing the pain
Is the key

The wounds do heal
Only scars remain
Peace
Serenity and strength
Are mine again

I am blessed
God sees me through
The dark side of night
Turns into daylight

It's true

I feel stronger
I feel renewed
The happiness
I've always pursued

Outside of me
Is here in my heart
And even
If a loved one
Departs

I can grieve the loss
Embrace the pain
And know
I will be
Happy again

Broken and Wounded
August 28, 1996

I'm tired
Of this burden
I want to
Know when
This pain will end
And my heart
Will mend

Time heals
All wounds
I hope
It will be soon
There's not much more
I can take
Lord you promised
Never to forsake
Me

Or leave me alone (JOSH 1:5)
From a child
To an adult full-grown

You've been with me
Every step of the way
Even
When I've gone astray

Your promises are sure (HEB 10:23)
Your love
And grace will endure
When everything
Earthly fails
Your Word
Will prevail (MT 24:35)

From above

It's you
And me Lord   *Your compassion*
When by others *Mercy*
I'm feeling ignored *And tender*
I come to you   *Loving care* (PS 103:8)
In prayer   *Is what I need*
My tears   *To repair*
And my sadness
You're very much aware *My broken heart*
      And woundedness
The hope that I receive *In spite of my hurts*
Comes in the form *I continue to express*
Of peace (JN 14:27)
Praise   *My gratitude*
Honor   *And faith in God*
And glory to you
Will continue   *Who unconditionally*
To increase   *Loves me*
      His own cherished child
All I ever need   *I am precious*
Is your love   *And free* (1JN 3:1)
Filling me

Journal Entry

August 29, 1996

As I was driving home from Single Parent's night at church, I began to think of the song my mother taught me as a child: "Jesus Loves Me." These lines just came into my mind. *Jesus Loves Me. I sang it as a child, I know Jesus heard me sing and smiled.* I immediately thought, *here's another poem.* I went home and wrote it.

Jesus Loves Me
August 29, 1996

"Jesus Loves Me" *Heard me sing*
I sang it as a child *And smiled*
I know Jesus

He said
"Let the children come to me" (MT 19:14)
His unconditional love
Has set my heart free (ISA 61:1)

I feel that freedom
In a different way today
God has revealed
A lot to me
Along the pathway

Of my life
Filled with chaos
Conflict and abuse (PS 7:9)
My heart
Has been broken
Betrayed and bruised

God
In His grace
Gives me healing (JER 30:17)
Whenever
I feel my feelings

I've denied
For so long
Running
And hiding only prolonged

The process
Causing me more stress

Yes the feelings hurt
I really feel the pain
And this too shall pass
I'm at peace again (JN 16:33)

God
In His mercy
Knows what I can bear (1COR 10:13)
Instead of despair
I go to Him
In prayer (PS 55:22)

I draw near
To Him
And He draws
Near to me (JAS 4:8)
Uplifting my soul
With the sure hope
Of eternity (TITUS 3:7)

This earthly journey
Has been rewarding
When I get to Heaven
You know
I will triumphantly sing

"Jesus Loves Me"
Like I did as a child
And how glorious
It will be
To see Jesus smile!

Journal Entry

October 13, 1996

The Twelve Step program of Codependents Anonymous has had a powerful impact on my life. As I celebrate my Two Year CoDA Birthday, I look back and see what changes have occurred in me through what I learned in CoDA. I received awesome gifts from the people in those meetings that changed my life forever.

Two Year CoDA Birthday
October 13, 1996

These last two years
In the scheme of things
Have had an impact
On my heartstrings

I've gained so much
That touches my heart
Friendships have grown
As I've taken part

In this
Twelve step program
Here I've been accepted
Just as I am

I've taken risks
I've shared my feelings
Here I can talk
About anything

I feel freedom
I feel love
God my Higher Power
Blesses me from above

I work the steps
Peace
And serenity are mine
Even though recovery
Is not a straight line

I have ups and downs
I experience the pain
Of my past

That has been
Such a strain

But today
I have healing
I'm at peace
My growth
Continues to increase

Yes my life
Was unmanageable
When I walked in that door
Beyond manageability
I gained so much more

I found myself
I learned
To take care of me
I discovered
I can grow to be
All God created
And intended
Me to be

I can take action
To set my boundaries
Anger and resentments
I can release

I can be vulnerable
When I feel safety

I listen to
Appreciate

And respect my body
That has kept
My feelings
Safe inside
I've expressed them here
You showed empathy
When I cried

I allowed myself
To grieve
In order to
Make way
For the joy
That can't be
Taken from me

Nothing can destroy
(Unless I allow it)

My heart
Is full of happiness
Many gifts
From God
I now possess

I'm grateful
For my life experiences
That brought me
To the place
Where I am today

God orchestrated
My life
Directing
And guiding me
On the way
To recovery

And healing
From past abuse
Giving me talents
I know
He's going to use

To help others
Who are hurting
And needing love
And care
That's why my poetry
I continue to share

To give away
What's been
Given to me
So that together
We will know
And believe
We are indeed
Precious
And free

Journal Entry

October 31, 1996

Just weeks ago, I wrote the poem, "God Has a Plan." I believed it then and I believe it now. I've just been laid off from my job. After working five years for Disneyland in Anaheim, California, they decided to restructure, re-focus, and eliminate my position. It was such a shock. I had no warning and no notice. Again, this is another loss that I'm grieving. This is an extremely painful place and incredibly familiar.

I wish it would get easier, but it doesn't. It still hurts deeply. Thank God I have tools today. I thank Him for what He continues to give to me. In the long run this will be for my good. I believe that and I know God will open another door. In the meantime, I will feel my feelings and express them the best way that I know how -- through my poetry.

Over the years I have been laid-off from countless jobs, but the first is always the most devastating. As I wrote in my journal in the above entry, it became clearer to me that God is in control over all aspects of my life, including my job.

Loss
October 31, 1996

Loss
I've been through
All kinds
As I walk
Through the pain
God reminds (JER 15:18)
Me

Nothing is secure
Outside of Him (DEUT 33:12)
When I rely
On something else
I'm putting myself
Out on a limb (2COR 1:9)

And when that limb
Comes crashing down
I hit hard
When I hit the ground (PS 7:15)

I'm feeling the loss
The pain
And the fear (PS 5:1, 2)
And all I can do

Is cry these tears (PS 6:6)

I am by myself
I'm on my own
Yet I know
In my heart
That I'm not alone (MT 28:20)

Jesus my Savior
My Shepherd
My Friend (ISA 43:11, PS 23:1, JN 15:13)
On His power
And strength
I will depend (ISA 40:26)

He comforts me
When the pain
Is so bad (PS 61:2)
I think I'm going
Stark raving mad (DEUT 28:34)

I read His Word
I see His face (PS 119:105, PS 31:16)
His love

Comes shining through
His mercy
And His grace (PS 25:6, 7)

I'm blessed
Beyond measure
For nothing I've done (ISA 41:1, 2)
His death on the cross
My freedom He's won (COL 1:20, LK 4:18)

He calls me by name
I'm His very own child (ISA 43:1)
He paid the price
I've been reconciled (1COR 6:20, ROM 5:10)

I rejoice
And am grateful
For what He
Does for me (PS 13:5, 6)

Continually guiding
And directing me
To be all
He created
Me to be (PS 25:4,5)

And one day
I will see Him
Face to face (REV 22:4)
In that very glorious
Special place (PHIL 3:20,21)

Where there
Is no more crying
No more pain (ISA 25:8)
And I won't shed
Another tear
Ever again (REV 21:4)

Journal Entry
November 6, 1996
I have no job and no structure to my life. I'm lost and wandering aimlessly.

Wandering Aimlessly
November 6, 1996

I'm lost
I'm wandering aimlessly (PS 119:176)
I feel like a refugee

No place is safe
Plans fail
I can't think
Even the smallest detail

Is overwhelming
What am I to do?

How am I
Going to get through?

This unbearably painful
Place to be
I keep trying to flee

I'll do anything
Not to feel this pain
But fighting it
Is such a strain

I give up God
I'm on my knees
I'm asking for
Your help please (JOSH 24:7)

This is so difficult Lord
I need You
Where do I
Go from here?
I don't have a clue

If You are putting
My faith to the test (MT 24:7)
In the midst
Of what I'm feeling
I'm doing my best

To rely
On Your promises
They're the only things
That are true (PS 71:6)
Your love and grace
Will see me through (1COR 15:10)

When everything else
Seems out of control

Relying on Your strength
And power
Is my goal (PS 68:34)

When the storms of life
Are raging (JON 1:4)
You can calm the sea
Inside of me (PS 107:29, ISA 4:6)
And You give me peace
And serenity (JN 14:27)

Your love is real
I feel it in my soul (PS 136:4)
When I am most broken
You can make me whole (JER 23:9)

Mold me
And shape me to be
The best I can be (JOB 10:9)
This is a day of rejoicing
A day of jubilee (NEH 12:43)

A day of excitement
And opportunity
My life is just beginning
And my heart is free (PS 118:5)

All my life I have been on a quest to find answers.

What Will the New Year Bring?
December 31, 1996

As the year
Comes to a close
It's time to reflect
In a poem
I compose

I've experienced
Many losses
During this past year
Loss of a marriage

Loss of a home
Loss of loved ones
And loss of a career

It's been painful
Feeling the sadness
But feeling my feelings
I've made
So much progress

In becoming healthier
More whole
And complete
Healing must occur
So my past
I won't repeat

God is awesome
Wanting
What's best for me
Surrendering to His Will
Is the key

For me
To have peace
And joy in my heart
It's not found
Outside of me
Nor apart

From my connection
To my Lord
And Savior
Jesus Christ
His perfect life
And death
On the cross

Paid the price (ROM 4:25)

For me
To live eternally
My home
Will be Heaven
One day
But for now
I continue
On this earthly
pathway

Learning my lessons
God strengthens me
In my time
Of need
His promises come true
They're guaranteed

My joy is full
I'm grateful for
What He's done
He knows me
I'm His
There's no need
To run (ISA 43:1)

Whatever happens
Whatever
The New Year
Will bring
In the everlasting arms
Of Jesus
My Savior
I will cling (DEUT 33:27)

The Broken Parts of Me
January 16, 1997

I'm sitting by myself
Contemplating my issues
Codependency
Abandonment
Lack of trust and abuse

It wasn't easy growing up
I was hurting
So much pain
Trying hard to figure it out
Was always such a strain

It made no sense
They "loved" me
Yet abused me
"God please stop the pain!"
Became my plea (JER 15:18)

I would do anything
Not to feel that pain
Food, drugs, alcohol, and sex
Became my domain

To mood alter
Feel the high
The thrill of escape
That's how my fantasy
Of romanticizing
Began to take shape

Reality was too painful
To face
Living in the moment
I just could not embrace

I know and understand

My childhood
And my past today
Although I thought
God didn't answer me
When I prayed (PS 4:1)

To stop the pain
He did much more for me
I've learned to
Embrace the pain
That is the key (HEB 12:11)

Healing comes from grieving
Tears need to be shed (PS 126:5)
I don't have to run
To my addictions
Instead

I can run to God
He's here waiting for me (ISA 65:24)
To hold me
In His arms
Lovingly (ISA 40:11)

When I am feeling
Lost and alone (LK 19:10)
At my most needy place
He makes Himself known (EZEK 38:23)

He's compassionate
Accepting
Truly my Best Friend (PS 103:8)
He knows
All the parts of me
And understands (ISA 43:1)

My issues
And how they
Came to be
He not only cares
He wants to heal
The broken parts of me (1PET 5:7, JER 30:17)

How grateful I am
God is good
God is kind (EPH 2:7)
I am an awesome
And wonderful design (PS 139:14)

He created me
And He helped
Me to survive (PS 139:13)
Today I have peace
I have joy
It's great to be alive! (PHIL 4:7)

God walks with me
My path is clear (LEV 26:12)
God holds me
When I cry my tears (2KINGS 20:5)

Although abuse is evil
God turned it into good (ROM 8:28)
Today I feel accepted
Totally loved and understood (JER 31:3)

I have peace
Inside my heart
I feel serenity (ISA 26:3)
Because of God's
Grace and mercy
I feel precious
And free (2THES 2:16)

Journal Entry

January 23, 1997

I have some pretty incredible friends at Saddleback Church's Single Parents Support Group. I am in awe of God who continually meets my needs even before I know that I need them. When I need to grieve and express more tears, I need love and support to feel safe enough to do that. God is the source; people are the channels. Two very loving, special people in my life, Rick Sianez and Vicki Daniels who became Mr. and Mrs. Sianez on September 20, 1997, inspired me to write this poem.

Healing Comes in Many Forms

January 23, 1997

Healing comes
In many forms
When I least expect it
When I'm discouraged

Sad and blue
And feel like a misfit

God sends someone

To connect with me
And shows me
Compassion once again

As this person
Holds me
And I feel safe
That is exactly when
The sobbing tears
Of release
I can express

Physically
This is another
Human being
But I'm here to confess
In that moment

I feel God's arms
Securely holding me
Allowing me
To feel the pain
Hurt and disappointment

Only He
Truly knows
Understands and feels
And with His arms
Around me
Again and again
Heals

Those broken parts
Of me
Giving me strength
To carry on
His grace
And mercy
Is far beyond

Anything I could imagine
Or conceive (EPH 3:20)
Many gifts
Including love of friends
Daily I receive

How precious
Is this family of God

Befriending each other
In Christ's name
Showing Christ-like compassion
To one another
Changes us
We're not the same

In the moments
That we bond
And have connection
With each other
"There is a friend
That sticks closer
Than a brother" (PROV 18:24)

"Greater love
Has no one than this
Than to lay down
One's life
For his friends" (JN 15:13)
What a friend
We have in Jesus
Truly a "Godsend"

He loved me
So much
That He died
And rose again
For me (ROM 5:8, 1THES 4:14)

In thankfulness
More like Him
I can strive to be

When I see
Someone hurting
And needing a friend
I can hug
I can listen
I can help
A broken heart
To mend

Yes
Healing comes
In many forms

And when
We least expect it
We see
The love of Christ
In each of us
And reap the benefits

I am truly grateful
For the gifts
God continues
To give to me
My heart is healing
I feel precious
And free *(1JN 3:1)*

Journal Entry
February 11, 1997

Sometimes the love that I have for my Creator is overwhelming. When I feel this wonderful love and gratitude, I want to express it in the form of praise. This next poem was my way of expressing that praise. But out of all the poems I've written, this one was the toughest. I fully believe that the distractions that came up for me were no accident, but I was determined to write and finish this poem, no matter what struggles I had to experience.

Gifts Beyond Measure
February 11, 1997

My soul
Has been touched
In the deepest part
By God
Whom I love
With all my heart *(MT 22:37)*

He is my Creator
The reason I'm here *(DEUT 32:6)*

His unconditional love
For me
Is perfectly clear *(JN 3:16)*

He's with me
Even when
I think He's not *(PS 46:1)*
When I was beaten down
Discouraged and distraught *(PS 22:1)*

God
In His mercy
Showed me the way *(PS 143:8)*
He's given me gifts
Beyond measure
I can never repay *(2COR 9:15)*

He gave His Son
Jesus
So that I could live *(EPH 2:4, 5)*
He's my Savior
And Redeemer
My sins
He did forgive *(JN 1:29)*

Everything I've done wrong
Is gone
Wiped clean
White as snow *(PS 51:7)*
The love
Inside my heart
Continues to grow *(EPH 5:19)*

This is true happiness
That comes only
From my Lord
And Savior
He continues
To heal my wounds
My brokenness
He will restore *(PS 147:3)*

The Psalmist says
"My heart leaps
For joy
And I will give thanks
To Him in song" *(PS 28:7)*

I'm no longer
On my own
To Him
I now belong *(JN 15:19)*

Praise
Honor and glory
To my sovereign
And majestic King *(PS 66:1, 2)*
To my Lord
And Savior
Joyfully
I now sing *(PS 13:6)*

A life of service
Whatever I can do
In His precious name *(ROM 15:17)*
To be His tool
To fulfill His Will
His praises to proclaim *(2TIM 2:21)*

God is gracious
Abounding in love
And mercy *(PS 86:15)*
My heart is uplifted
I have peace
And serenity *(PHIL 4:7)*

I will look
To the Lord
For strength
And seek His face
Always *(PS 105:4)*
And joyfully
Sing praises to Him
All the rest
Of my days *(PS 104:33)*

What is the Answer?

May 3, 1997

God what is the answer?
So many questions
They all become a blur
I want clarity
I want wisdom
What is Your Will?

I'm surrendering my will
Your will
I want to fulfill
Just tell me
What it is
Show me
In some way
What to do
What is Your plan
I will obey

Your plan
Is far better
Than anything
I would do (JER 29:11)
My sight is limited
You see
The bigger view

I come to You
With questions
Not with doubts
I know
You are working
All of this out (ROM 8:28)

For my good
Not because
Of what I've done

But solely
Because of the victory
Jesus has won

How precious
To have a Savior
A Shepherd
And a Friend
Unconditional love
That I can't
Even comprehend

I'm grateful
God has given me
Wonderful gifts
I have peace and joy
My heart He uplifts (ISA 26:3)

I am in God's
Tender loving care (PS 103:8)
He will not give me
More than I can bear (1COR 10:13)

God is greater
Than any challenge
I face
As a child
Needs a father
I embrace

The loving arms
Of my Creator (PS 103:8)
With all my heart
I worship
And adore

God has
All the answers
That I ever
Need to know
By learning
To wait patiently
I will continue
To grow

Relying on
God's strength

To see me through
His Word is sure
His promises come true *(HEB 10:23)*

I am in awe
Of God's power
And majesty
I am His child
I feel precious
And free *(1JN 3:11)*

Journal Entry

October 2, 1997

I'm sitting here lethargic. I don't want to move. Nothing interests me. I don't care about anything. I'm apathetic. I hate when I get like this. I get sarcastic. What is sarcasm? Anger! What am I angry about? I have no job again. It is the second time within a year. Same reason as before. My position was eliminated. Broken promises again. I hate this. It's not fair. Why do I have to suffer through this? God, why are You so hard on me? I hate having to go outside my comfort zone once more and put myself out there under the critical eyes of bosses. I feel so ugly right now, old and fat. Who will want to hire me when there are younger, prettier, slimmer women who look good? This is so difficult having to sell myself in the work place. This isn't the only thing I'm dealing with. I have been struggling with money, no life companion, my book not being published, Jenny coming to live with me full time, another child being a victim in crisis mode, two sons that have shut me out of their lives, and having to deal with two dysfunctional ex-husbands. When life becomes too overwhelming for me to deal with, I eat, and continue to eat. Bingeing becomes a way of life. I feel bad and I feel bitter. Where's the hope that my life will be any different? I have no job, no way to pay bills, let alone debts that I owe, and big debts that have accumulated. I have no answers. I keep looking to God for the answers, but they don't come. Life goes on for everyone else, while I sit here alone and hurting. I'm tired of hurting. Where is everyone? No one calls me on the telephone. Don't I matter to anyone? Haven't I made a difference in anyone's life?

Where's the Hope? Where's the Joy?
October 2, 1997

Where's the hope?
Where's the joy?
These days
Things just
Seem to annoy
Me

I'm disillusioned
Discontent

Nothing satisfies
I'm doing my best
To visualize

That God
Is in control
Trusting in Him
Stepping out in faith
Is the role

He's given me
To face

Whatever life brings
No matter
How it hurts
No matter
How it stings

God will never
Give me
More than
I can bear *(1COR 10:13)*
He promises
That He will hear
My every prayer

I'm crying out
To You now Lord
I'm feeling lost
Alone and ignored

This isn't fair
I'm angry
What do You
Want me to do?
I don't know
The answer
I wish I knew

Is there
A lesson here
I'm not learning?
This keeps happening
Inside I'm churning

Show me the way
I want
To do Your Will
This is so tough
It's like climbing up
A very steep hill

Nothing outside of You
Is safe or secure
When plans fail
Here's another detour

You've promised
You'll turn it into good *(ROM 8:28)*
Even though the outcome
To me

345

Is not understood

Give me the strength
To take
One day at a time
If I have to go uphill
Please help me
To climb

My life
Is in ***Y****our hands*
Y*ou have*
Far better plans (JER 29:11)

Than I could
Ever hope for
Even though one
Has closed
There will be
Another door

Give me the courage
To open it
And walk through
I just don't know
Where it is
I don't have a clue

I'm relying on ***Y****ou*

Because of the victory
Christ has won
I don't have to rely
On anything I've done

The choice is clear
There's nowhere
Else to go
Nothing else
In this world satisfies
That I know

My Creator
My Redeemer
My Savior
And my Friend
No matter
What the problem
He'll help me
To transcend

Although it's hard for me
To smile sometimes
There's hope
Inside of me
And joy
That lasts a lifetime
Because Christ
Has set me free

Journal Entry

December 30, 1997

My life feels like a shambles. I feel the upheaval, the fact that everything's undone. The work is unfinished. It needs cleaning up, but I don't know how. It's overwhelming to me. I think of all the reasons why I don't want to face it. I don't want to clean it up. It's hard work. I don't know where to begin. I'll never finish. I can't start it if I can't finish it today. Then the mess is all over the place and I have to look at it all the time and be reminded how painful it is to have this mess in my life. So I want to have fun, go places, and be with people, and forget about the mess. I don't want to deal with this mess. I'm sick of messes. I'm always having to clean up my parent's messes. Why should I have to clean up *their* mess? Why should I have to live with it and look at it day after day? I want to enjoy a "mess-free" life. Don't I deserve to be happy? I want to be happy. I'm tired of pain. I want to let go. I don't know how. If I fall, who will catch me? There's no one there. God, where are You? I need You. Why won't You help me? I don't know what to do.

My Life's a Mess
December 30, 1997

I'm feeling
That unsettled
Uneasiness again
I've been trying
To hide
Trying to pretend

That everything's okay
I'm fine
Nothing's wrong
I can handle it
I can be strong

But that's a lie
I need help
I can't do this
On my own
When I isolate
My needs to others
Are not known

I must risk
Talking about
The mess

I've created
And how I feel
So defeated
And frustrated

I have no answers
To solve my problems

I'm afraid
I'll be judged
And condemned
My life's a mess
I should be able

To clean it up
But if I begin
The process
The volcano will erupt

It's easier to act
As if things
Aren't that bad
Or ignore
That these problems
Make me feel sad

I don't know
Which way to go?
What do I do?
God I'm asking
Where are You? *(PS 84:26)*

I know I can't
Do this alone
I keep asking
For Your Will
To be shown

I want to surrender
I guess
I don't know how
I want to
I need to
Can I begin now?

What's the first step?
Where do I begin?
Rather than
Outside of me
I know
It's here within

Lord You know my heart
I'm completely
In awe of You *(PS 139:23)*
Your power
And majesty
And all
You can do *(JER 10:6)*

You are my God
My Lord
And Savior
I know this

To be true *(PS 63:1)*
But when it comes
To "letting go"
I don't have a clue

If I surrender
And truly "let go"
I'm afraid of falling
I know

And no one
Will be there
To catch me
When I fall
So there's no use
Shouting out a call
For help

There's no one there
I feel hopeless
I sink into despair *(PS 88:15)*

To not feel that pain
I fill up with food
It's easier
Distracting
And sure tastes good

I know better
And I do it anyway
It's as if I don't care
I want to disobey
No matter
What the cost
I will have to pay

What is the
Underlying drive?
That started out

As a way
To survive

But now
Is causing more pain (PS 38:17)
There's so much
To face
That I can't explain

Or understand
Or know
The reasons why
Sometimes I feel as if
I just want to die (JON 4:8)

But that's
Not an option
God has a plan (JER 29:11)
A purpose
For my life
That began (EX 9:16)

Long before my birth
From the beginning
Of time
If I can
Be patient
Trust God
And start
The uphill climb (HEB 11:40)

God will reveal
His purpose
For me (PS 57:2)
And show me
What He wants
Me to be

He'll use my talents
And abilities
In a way
That will be
Best for me

Everything I've been through
He'll work together
For my good (ROM 8:28)
No hurt is wasted
Or misunderstood

God in His mercy
Is kind
And full of grace (PS 25:6)
He wants to hold me
In a loving embrace

His arms
Are always open
He is waiting for me (DEUT 33:27)
His unconditional love
Is a gift
It's free (ROM 6:23)

I am His special
Beloved child
Unique
And precious
As can be (DEUT 33:12,1JN 3:1)

And I know that
My Heavenly Father
Cherishes me
Ardie (PS 17:14b)

Journal Entry

March 21, 1998

Instead of feeling sadness or pain, I'm surprised I feel a peace, a calm in my life. I'm enjoying the blessings God has given me.

Joy in My Soul
March 21, 1998

I am calm
And peaceful
Knowing God
Is constantly with me *(ISA 26:3)*
I have joy
In my soul
My heart is alive
And I'm free

I love the Lord
With all my heart
Soul and might
He loves me
I am precious
In His sight

I was created
In His image
His Spirit
Lives within me
Because of the gift
Of salvation
I am totally free

He sent His Son Jesus
Because He loved me
So much
From the curse
Of sin
He wanted me
To feel

His healing touch

I have so much
To be grateful for
God's been good
And kind
He's given me joy
And peace of mind

I behold the glory
Of God everywhere
The glorious beauty
Of His creation
Shows me He cares

My life is enriched
With each blessing
He sends
Each challenge
That makes me grow
His love never ends

The more I let Him
Live through me
The more I can grow
To be what
He wants me to be

I listen with my heart
As well as my mind
And trust that

God knows best
His plan is divine
It's at work
I'm secure
I'm relieved
Now I can rest (JER 29:11)

My joy
Bubbles up
In waves of delight
His Word guides me
And continues

To give me
More insight

I am blessed
I have peace
I know God
Loves me
Unconditionally
I am His beloved child
I feel precious
And free (1JN 3:1)

No Roadmap No Answers
April 18, 1998

My heart
Is heavy
I feel sad
I'm alone
The path
Set before me
Is totally unknown

There's no roadmap
No answers
Which way
Do I go?
I'm required to
Step out in faith
If I am to grow

I believe
There's a
Divine plan
In place (JER 29:11)
I feel the fear
But I rely
On God's grace (PS 56:3 TLB)

At every crossroad
He's been there
To guide me
Continually (JOSH 1:9)
To give direction
If I wait
Patiently

Although God doesn't
Make a problem
Magically go away
He strengthens me
And gives me
Peace
When I pray (ISA 40:29 NLT)

"Lead me in Your truth
And teach me
What I need to know" (JN 16:13 NLT)
Help me through
Each challenge
To learn

And to grow (JOSH 1:5 NLT)

You are the Potter
I am the clay (ISA 64:8 NLT)
Mold me
And shape me
As I surrender
And obey

I am peaceful
God is in control
He is the
Sure Foundation
The salvation
Of my soul

He sent
His Son Jesus
To redeem me
From sin (1JN 4:14)
It's a free gift
I can hardly
Take in

He loves me
Totally unconditionally (PS 86:15)
The prison doors
Are open
And I am
Set free

How awesome God is
I am filled
With peace and joy
That Satan
In all his attempts
Can never destroy (JAS 4:7 NLT)

God deserves

All the glory
Gratitude
And praise (DEUT 10:7)
For His awesome
Mysterious
And wonderful ways

In everything
Around me
It's easy to see
Beautiful examples
Of His
Sovereign majesty (NUM 14:19 NLT)

I love the Lord
With all my heart (1TIM 6:15, 16)
He's always with me
He'll never depart (PS 36:7)

Out of love
I praise Him
And give Him
Honor (ISA 25:1)
God alone
Is the Lord
And King
I worship
And adore

My heart is filled
With ecstasy
The joy
He's given me (PS 28:7)
I am
His beloved child
Uniquely
Unrepeatable
Precious and free (1JN 3:1)

Journal Entry
June 7, 1998

Lord, I need You now more than ever. I feel so lost and alone. This isn't just about not having a job. It's about my value and worth as a person. I want to be appreciated and paid accordingly for what I bring to the workplace. Paid, not just for my skills *(I know I have them)*, but for who I am; my character, my values, for what I believe to be important, and how I live my life. I want these to be acknowledged and appreciated. I want to contribute. Lord, where do You want me? Which way do I go? I need Your guidance and direction. I'm lost and I'm hurting. I'm letting go of the job that I wanted because You said "No." I'm grieving and I'm scared. I know and believe that You will provide. You always have and I thank and praise You for that. Help me now. I need to feel Your arms around me, holding me, comforting me, and uplifting me in my time of need. Only You can give me the peace I seek. Nothing outside of You is secure and I know that. You're my anchor and my rock. Hold me close and give me rest and courage to walk the path that You have chosen for me. I know You know what's best for me. I humbly bow before You and surrender to Your will. Praise, honor, and glory belong to You! I love You Lord with all my heart, soul, and mind!

God's Mercy and Grace
June 7, 1998

My soul wells up
To sing (PS 108:1)
Hallelujahs
To the Almighty King (PS 24:10)

The Lord God
Of all the earth
Creator of the Universe (GEN 1:1)
My heart is so full
Of love for God
I could burst (LK 10:27)

My finite mind

Just cannot comprehend (ECCL 8:17)
My Creator
Redeemer
Father and Friend (ISA 44:6)
The Everlasting God
Who has no beginning
And no end (REV 1:8)

I sit in awe
Of God's
Power and majesty (1CHRON 29:11)
Who loved me
So much

He sent His Son
To die for me *(ROM 5:8)*

Jesus rose again
To give life everlasting
And life
more abundantly *(REV 2:8; JN 10:10 KJV)*

How blessed I am
To receive
Such a wonderful gift *(ROM 6:23)*
My heart
And my soul
He continues to uplift *(JAS 4:16)*

I am at peace
I am filled with love
And joy *(ISA 60:5)*
That Satan
Continually tries to destroy *(JN 10:10a)*

But nothing
Can pluck me
Out of
God's loving hand *(JN 10:27-29 KJV)*
His power
And strength
Will help me
To withstand *(PS 29:11)*

Any trials
Or temptations
I must go through *(1COR 10:13a)*
He'll give me a way
To escape
If I let Him
Show me
What to do *(1COR 10:13b)*

God's mercy
And grace
Are overwhelming to me *(EPH 1:7, 8)*
In gratitude
And humility
I fall to my knees *(1PET 5:6)*

I am so weak
So human
Undeserving
Full of sin *(MT 26:41; PS 38:18)*
Jesus said,
"I am The Way
The Truth
And The Life"
I take that truth within *(JN 14:6)*

And "The Truth
Shall set you free"
Is a precious gift
To me *(JN 8:32)*
God continues
To show me
How Christ-like
He wants me to be *(PHIL 2:5)*

Nothing
Can adequately describe
How joyful
I feel inside *(HAB 3:18)*
His unconditionally
Loving arms
Are always open wide *(DEUT 33:27)*

My Lord
Loves me
Beyond anything
I could ever know *(EPH 3:17-19)*
His unmerited grace

354

And undeserved blessings
Continue to overflow *(EZEK 34:26)*

I will worship
And adore Him
For His mysterious

Wondrous ways *(PS 100:2)*
I will give Him
All the glory
Honor
Gratitude
And praise *(PS 100:4, 5)*

His Plan for Me
August 22, 1998

I wonder about
The meaning of life
And God's purpose
And plan for me *(PS 16:11a)*
The past
Does not dictate
Who I am
Or who I can
Strive to be *(ISA 43:18)*

I am
A new creation
In Christ
A privilege
To be called
God's child *(2COR 5:17)*
God sent
His Son Jesus
To be my Savior
So I could
Be reconciled *(ROM 5:10)*

Behold
The Lamb of God
Who takes away
My sin *(JN 1:29)*
Jesus died
And rose again
Victory

Over Satan did win *(1COR 15:57)*

For me
What a gift
I'm washed clean
By His blood *(1JN 1:7)*
I'm completely
Forgiven
What awesome mercy
And love *(PS 103:3, 4)*

In gratitude
I dedicate
A life of service
In all ways *(EPH 4:12, 13)*
And humbly trust
His Plan for me
Every one of my days *(HEB 11:40)*

This is an in-between time
For me
I know not
What lies ahead *(ECCL 3:1)*
God is faithful
Never breaks a promise
I believe
What He has said *(HEB 10:23)*

"For I know the plans

355

I have for you
Plans to prosper
Not to harm you" *(JER 29:11)*

That all things
Work together
For my good *(ROM 8:28 NKJV)*

Although God
Doesn't show me
A preview
Through Christ
I can wait patiently
My hope is renewed *(PS 25:5)*

God gives me grace
God is so kind
His love
Is awesome to me *(2COR 9:8)*
I am
His cherished child
Loved and forgiven
I feel precious and free *(1JN 3:1)*

And I know

My Soul Hungers and Thirsts
November 27, 1998

I need to feel
Safe and secure
If I focus on fear
I become unsure

Hungers and thirsts
For You it's true

The emptiness I feel
I want Your Spirit
To fill inside me
I want to be
The Christ-like person
You intended me to be

Of me
What can I
Possibly do?
When I fix
My eyes on Jesus
I get a
Brand new view *(HEB 12:2)*

I have a reverence for life
I want to make a difference
I'm sick of
Gratifying my flesh
I'm tired of
Sitting on the fence

Of my caring Savior
Steadfast and sure
He's my anchor
In any storm
I feel reassured

I want to be "sold out"
For God
He's my Best Friend
He's here
Waiting for me
To spend

Lord I long
For sacred communion
With You
My soul

"Alone time" with Him

He wants me close
His providential provision
Of all I need shows

How much
He showers me
With His mercy
And grace
I am completely enfolded
In God's loving embrace

He knows my concerns
Even before
I put them into words
I am more valuable
To Him than many birds (MT 10:31)

He sees me
As precious
A possession

He treasures (DEUT 26:18)
His unconditional love
For me
Can't be measured

He gave me a Savior
Who saved me
From eternal
Death and sin (JN 10:28)
It's a free gift
Of grace
With gratitude
I can begin (EPH 2:8)

To surrender "self"
And to walk
In His ways (EPH 4:2, PS 25:4)
To sing praises
And give God
The glory
All of my days (PS 104:33)

This Maze Called Life
January 2, 1999

I have worries
And doubts
About where
My life is going

Each day
I face my fear
Of not knowing
Where to go?
And what to do?
Problems
Overwhelm me

How do I
Get through?

This maze called life
With choices to make
I don't know
Which path to take

Left on my own
I could fall
Into despair
But I turn to God

Who hears my prayer

God is with me
Ready to take my hand
He knows my fear
And understands

He holds me safely
In His loving embrace
His gift to me
Is His amazing grace

He loves me
He sent His Son
To bear my sin
Jesus shed His blood
To cleanse me
From within

I am grateful
His love envelops me
I'm His precious child
I feel free (ISA 43:4)

I don't know
What lies ahead
But the future
I no longer dread

God's guiding light
Shines on me
Directing me to be
The best He intended
Me to be

There is no need
For me
To be stressed

Whatever happens
Will be
In my best interest

God has promised
To work
All things for good (ROM 8:28)
I feel loved
Supported
And understood

God will never fail
His promises are sure (HEB 10:23)
If I have the faith
Of a mustard seed
I can endure (MT 17:20)

If I keep my eyes
On Jesus
My path is clear (HEB 12:2)
He gives me courage
To walk through
The fear

Life is an adventure
I will seize the day
Even when I feel
There is no hope
God will make a way (1COR 10:13)

I will make the most
Of what God
Has given me
And gratefully
Give Him all the
Honor
Praise and glory

Journal Entry
June 6, 1999
Through my experiences I have learned about my struggles and myself. No, I'm not perfect, I make mistakes. Yes, I am a sinner, and God loves me with a love so deep, abiding, unconditional, and everlasting. God's grace is a free gift. Healing from a broken, wounded heart continues to take place in me. I'm grateful for these precious gifts.

Satisfy My Soul
June 6, 1999

Lord I'm coming
To You
With all my needs
I know I've
Failed Your tests
With my misdeeds

I'm sorry Lord
I turn to other things
I've experienced
The heartache
And disappointment
They bring

Along
With discouragement
And hopelessness
Every time I am faced
With stress

I'm longing Lord
For You
To satisfy my soul
To lean on You
And trust You more
Is my goal

Surrendering my will
And selfish desires
I want Your Spirit
To put out the fires

That are of
My own willful flesh
And prideful sin
Your Word
Your Will
Your Spirit
I want here within

My heart
My soul
My body
And my mind
So I can be
All You
Magnificently designed (PS 139:14)

I want You
To be
My first priority
To think more
Of You
And less of me

I know
I can't do this
On my own
What I need to do
Is completely unknown

But You know Lord
What I need
And how to get it met
Help me to be patient
When I don't
See the answer yet

As Pastor Rick Warren says
I dig my own well
And then deny
I had anything
To do with it
Then I suffer
The consequences
Of being in a pit

Lord You have a plan
And purpose
For my life (JER 29:11)
I'm tired
Of all the struggles
I'm tired
Of all the strife

Lead me
And guide me
To where You
Want me to go (PS 31:3)
So I can step
Out of denial
So I can grow

So I can
Serve others
In unselfish ways (GAL 5:13)
And give You
All the glory
Honor and praise (PS 34:1)

I know
You love me
And forgive me
Unconditionally (PS 44:26)
If I can love
And forgive myself
Then I truly
Will be free (PS 119:32)
From the guilt
Of past mistakes
I've been trying to flee

Avoidance
And a quick fix
Is what
I was looking for
Anything not
To feel the pain
Has always been
At the core

Thank You Lord
For providing a Savior
Who has
Set me free (PS 25:5)
I am forgiven!
The crown of life
Is waiting for me (REV 2:10)

I Was Planned for God's Pleasure

June 13, 2003

Without God
Life makes no sense (EPH 1:11 MSG)
Created by God
His love for me
Is evident (EPH 1:4a MSG)

I'm not an accident
God never
Makes mistakes (ISA 44:2 CEV)
He has a reason
For everything
He creates (JAS 1:18 NCV)

It's not about me
It's about living
For God (COL 1:16b MSG)
God is real
Even when I feel odd (HEB 13:5 TEV)

I was planned
For God's pleasure (EPH 1:5 TEV)
This is a truth
To build my life on
And it's secure (PS 19:4a TEV)

Bringing pleasure to God
Is called "worship" (PS 147:11 CEV)
The first purpose
Of my life
Is to exist
For His benefit (COL 3:23)

What God wants
Most from me
Is a relationship (MT 22:37,38)
My task is to discover

How I can do that (EPH 5:10 MSG)

God smiles
When I love Him
Supremely (GEN 6:9b NLT)
He says
"I want you
To know Me" (HOS 6:6 LB)

God smiles
When I trust Him
Completely (HEB 11:7 MSG)
I will thank
And praise Him
Continually (PS 69:30, 31)

Wholehearted obedience
To God
Is done joyfully (PS 119:33 LB)
And is pleasing to God

Because it proves
My love (JN 14:15 TEV)
When I express
My gratitude
He smiles from above (PS 147:11 TEV)

Real worship
Is rooted in the Word (JN 4:23)
"Loving God
With all my mind"
Is commanded
By the Lord (MK 12:30)

Is pleasing God
My deepest desire? (2COR 5:9 TEV)

The smile of God
Is the goal
That lights my fire (PS 14:2 LB)

The heart of worship
Is surrender (ROM 6:13b TEV)
God wants my life
All of it
It gives Him splendor (ROM 12:1 TEV)

Surrendering to God
Brings freedom and peace
(ROM 6:17 MSG; JOB 22:21 NLT)
Experiencing God's power
In my life
Will only increase (JOSH 5:13-15 NIV)

God wants to be
My best friend (PS 25:14a LB)
I pray my self-will
And stubborn pride
Will end (GEN 3:5)

Can I trust God?
Yes
He keeps His promises (JER 29:11)
He sent His Son
His love towards me
To express (ROM 8:3)

The sacrifice
Of Jesus' death
On the cross (ROM 5:8 NRSV)
Was for me
So I could be saved
I'm no longer lost (ROM 10:13 NIV)

My sins are forgiven
I have a Savior
Who loves me (PS 86:5)

If I obey Him
Wholeheartedly
I will be free (LK 1:38 NLT)

Of the bondage
Of fear
And stubborn pride (1JN 4:18 NLT)
If I let go
And let God
Be God
He is edified (ROM 14:18 NLT)

Real worship
Is falling in love
With Jesus my King (JN 15:14 KJV)
I will worship Him
By surrendering
Everything (ROM 12:1 TEV)

Tribute to My Family

"Moreover, no man knows when his hour will come" (Ecclesiastes 9:12).

"I have fought the good fight, I have finished the race, I have kept the faith" (2 Timothy 4:7).

I am sixty-eight years old and thinking, *"Where has my life gone?"* Sixty-eight years; gone in a blink of an eye. I may have many more years left to live, but I don't know that. I want to live each day as if it were my last, which means saying how I feel right now in this moment. Especially about the people in my life who mean the most to me.

To them I would quote the words from a wall hanging I have in my living room:

Living Life

Me Age 68

Life is not a race but indeed a journey. Be Honest. Work hard. Be choosy. Say 'thank you,' and 'great job' to someone each day. Go to church, take time for prayer. The Lord giveth and the Lord taketh. Let your handshake mean more than pen and paper. Love your life and what you've been given, it is not accidental. Search for your purpose and do it as best you can. Dreaming does matter. It allows you to become that which you aspire to.

363

Laugh often (Mohr, 1997).

Glen, my wonderful husband and companion, "I love you dearly with all my heart more than you're ever gonna know," because I'm the originator of that line... ...only *you* will get the meaning and I'm sure will laugh over how much we share joy and humor in our marriage. You are the best thing that happened to me and such a blessing and gift from God I'll always be grateful for. You are a rock I can lean on in times of crisis. I've learned so much from you. You bring out the best in me and adore me in a precious way. Your face lights up when you see me and you call me your sweetheart or sweet one. I always feel loved. Thank you my Gen *(nickname; not typo).* I love you like crazy. You're *MY* hunk a' burnin' love! I love you with all my heart!

My children deserve so much more than I can say here, but I will try, mentioning them one by one.

Carla and Brian are waiting for me in heaven, having left this world way too soon.

Carla, you're my firstborn and have a special place in my heart, which came to fruition only two years before your untimely death. I'm grateful for the gift of your love, in spite of all the mistakes I made raising you. This world was a better place because of your caring heart, hospitality, generosity, warmth, and loving smile. I long to see you and to be in your presence once again.

Brian, you lived such a sad life and I let you down in so many ways, but I always had hope wanting the best for you. I just didn't have the skills to teach you how to face life and cope with the struggles of this world. I'm glad I had the privilege of being with you in California at least some months before you died. I was able to share my love, my heart, my home, and be the nurturing parent I always wanted to be. I long to see you again too.

Lori, you have always been my encourager and my cheerleader. I've felt the closest to you probably because you filled a need in me left void by my own mother. I regret that I turned to you to meet those needs, because doing so put our relationship in an awkward place, creating an unhealthy connection. You know how hard I've worked to right that wrong, and I hope I've made a difference in how I mothered you even through all the conflicts we've had. It's never too late to change and take a risk to do things differently. Say your truth even if it hurts the mother who needs to hear it. That's the only way change can happen. Through it all, I've grown up emotionally, and I'm proud that you were able to speak your real feelings to me.

Jenny, you have been the catalyst for most of my growth, since we weathered many crises together. I handled each crisis to the best of my ability at the time, so I have no regrets. I couldn't have done it any differently, but I have many feelings about how each one affected you. To hear you say to me directly what it meant to you is a privilege and I'm glad you were able to tell me the truth about the anger and the hurt you felt toward me. How precious it is to be able to hold you and cry with you and hear your pain, soothing you even knowing that I caused the pain. It's not easy to do, but I'm so grateful God gave me the ability, strength, maturity, and the opportunity to be able to handle it.

Becca, I have many regrets and I'm still unsure how our relationship can be any different. There's so much missing between us and I'm older now. You're my baby and have been raised by your father and stepmother; only visiting me now and then. My heart has always wanted the same for you as well as all my children: To be able to say directly to me how you feel, and for you to want to work things out between us. I'm willing, and even though I know you are in a life stage that doesn't easily facilitate that, I still have hope that someday soon, we will have an opportunity. I know God wants reconciliation for us. So do I.

Matt, I left you for last because again, we've had a tumultuous relationship. I've worked long and hard to win you back into my life after abandoning you when you were ten. It took me eight years to realize I wanted to have a relationship with you. You had so much anger toward me, but you were willing to tell me and share what it was like for you for the eight years I wasn't around. I wrote a story about the interactions between us. It made a great story, but one that was true and filled with emotion. Again, I'm grateful that God worked in both our hearts to give us what we needed... ...each other in a more deeply bonded and loving relationship.

Although I'm sad that my decisions, behaviors, and actions have negatively affected all of you, my dear children, I am grateful for your willingness to let me back into your lives, and for God to allow opportunities for reconciliation to occur. Love is all that matters. Relationships with loved ones are more important than money or things. I hope, in the end, that you, my children, will see and feel my heart, that I truly love you and only want the best for each of you. I hope you will be happy, will let God lead your lives, and will remember I was proud to be your mother. Even though I made mistakes, I truly was sorry I let you down, and tried to right the wrongs as best I could.

I love you Carla, Lori, Brian, Matt, Jenny, and Becca with all my heart. Know that I did the best I could as your parent. Although I lacked skills and failed miserably to meet all your needs, I have gone back to repair the damage I caused, and did it out of love and willingness to have a better relationship with each one of you. I hope you will look at my life through this book and understand where I came from. I hope you will have compassion for me as the mother God gave you, to bring opportunities for your healing as you look at your own lives and the choices you've each made. I've done my work, now I hope you go on to do your own work, and have better lives than I did for your own sakes and for your children. May God be with you and bless you as you continue the legacy I am leaving with all of you!

I leave you with these words written on a wall hanging in my kitchen.

Home Rules

> *Always be honest (Proverbs 12:22)*
> *Count your blessings (Psalms 34:1-3)*
> *Bear each other's burdens (Galatians 6:2)*
> *Forgive and forget (Micah 7:18)*
> *Be kind and tender hearted (Ephesians 4:32)*
> *Comfort one another (1 Thessalonians 4:18)*

Keep your promises (Romans 4:21)
Be supportive of one another (Acts 20:35)
Be true to each other (Revelation 15:3)
Look after each other (Deuteronomy 15:11)
Treat each other like you treat your friends (Matthew 7:12)
But most important LOVE ONE ANOTHER
deeply from the heart (1 Peter 1:22)

- Carole Taylor

I love you my sweet children. Always remember the words that Nonny used to say:

"Love one another."

Lovingly,

Mom
2016

Resources

CO-DEPENDENTS ANONYMOUS
www.coda.org (CoDA)

The Twelve Promises of Co-Dependents Anonymous

I can expect a miraculous change in my life by working the program of Co-Dependents Anonymous. As I make an honest effort to work the Twelve Steps and follow the Twelve Traditions…

1. I know a new sense of belonging. The feeling of emptiness and loneliness will disappear.

2. I am no longer controlled by my fears. I overcome my fears and act with courage, integrity, and dignity.

3. I know a new freedom.

4. I release myself from worry, guilty, and regret about my past and present. I am aware enough not to repeat it.

5. I know a new love and acceptance of myself and others. I feel genuinely lovable, loving, and loved.

6. I learn to see myself as equal to others. My new and renewed relationships are all with equal partners.

7. I am capable of developing and maintaining healthy and loving relationships. The need to control and manipulate others will disappear as I learn to trust those who are trustworthy.

8. I learn that it is possible to mend – become more loving, intimate, and supportive. I have the choice of communicating with my family in a way which is safe for me and respectful of them.

9. I acknowledge that I am a unique and precious creation.

10. I no longer need to rely solely on others to provide my sense of worth.

11. I trust the guidance I receive from my higher power and come to believe in my own capabilities.

12. I gradually experience serenity, strength, and spiritual growth in my daily life.

ROAD TO RECOVERY

Eight Principles Based on the Beatitudes
By Pastor Rick Warren, Saddleback Church

1. Realize I'm not God. I admit that I am powerless to control my tendency to do the wrong thing and that my life is unmanageable.

   Happy are those who know they are spiritually poor.

2. Earnestly believe that God exists, that I matter to Him, and that He has the power to help me recover.

   Happy are those who mourn, for they shall be comforted.

3. Consciously choose to commit all my life and will to Christ's care and control.

   Happy are the meek.

4. Openly examine and confess my faults to myself, to God, and to someone I trust.

   Happy are the pure in heart.

5. Voluntarily submit to every change God wants to make in my life and humbly ask Him to remove my character defects.

   Happy are those whose greatest desire is to do what God requires.

6. Evaluate all my relationships. Offer forgiveness to those who have hurt me and make amends for harm I've done to others, except when to do so would harm them or others.

   Happy are the merciful. Happy are the peacemakers.

7. **R**eserve a daily time with God for self-examination, Bible reading, and prayer in order to know God and His will for my life and to gain the power to follow His will.

8. **Y**ield myself to God to be used to bring this Good News to others, both by my example and by my words.

Happy are those who are persecuted because they do what God requires.

BIBLE TRANSLATIONS

AMP   *The Amplified Bible*
Grand Rapids: Zondervan (1965)

CEV   *Contemporary English Version*
New York: American Bible Society (1995)

GNT   *Good News Translation*
New York: American Bible Society (1992)

GW   *God's Word Translation*
Grand Rapids: World Publishing Inc. (1995)

KJV   *King James Version*

MSG   *The Message*
Colorado Springs: Navpress (1993)

NAB   *New American Bible*
Chicago: Catholic Press (1970)

NASB   *New American Standard Bible*
Anaheim, CA: Foundation Press (1973)

NCV   *New Century Version*
Dallas: Word Bibles (1991)

NIV   *New International Version*
Colorado Springs: Biblica, Inc. (1978, 1984)

NJB   *New Jerusalem Bible*
Garden City, NY: Doubleday (1985)

NLT   *New Living Translation*
Wheaton, IL: Tyndale House Publishers (1996)
(Also called Life Recovery Bible)

NRSV   *New Revised Standard Version*
       Grand Rapids: Zondervan (1990)

PH   *New Testament in Modern English* by J. B. Phillips
       New York: Macmillan (1958)

TEV   *Today's English Version*

TLB   *The Living Bible*
       Wheaton, IL: Tyndale House Publishers (1979)

POETRY INDEX

REFERENCES

Anthony, St. of Padua (undated). *Be Satisfied With Me [Poem]*, retrieved November 15, 2015 from http://gnm.org/prayers-be-satisfied-with-me/

Arterburn, S. (2005). *Healing is A Choice,* Nashville, TN: Nelson Books

Baker, J. (1998). *Celebrate Recovery Participant's Guide,* Grand Rapids, MI: Zondervan Publishing House

Bass, E. & Davis, L. (1988). *The Courage to Heal,* New York, NY: Harper & Row

Bible (1965). *The Amplified Bible (AMP),* Grand Rapids, MI: Zondervan

Bible (1995). *Contemporary English Version (CEV),* New York, NY: American Bible Society

Bible (1992). *Holy Bible, Good News Translation (GNT),* New York: American Bible Society

Bible (1995) *God's Word Translation (GW),* Grand Rapids, MI: World Publishing, Inc.

Bible (1990, 1985, 1983). *King James Version (KJV),* Nashville, TN: Thomas Nelson Publishers

Bible (1979). *Living Bible (LB),* Wheaton, IL: Tyndale House Publishers

Bible (1993). *The Message (MSG),* Colorado Springs, CO: Navpress

Bible (1970). *New American Bible (NAB),* Chicago, IL: Catholic Press

Bible (1973). *New American Standard Bible (NASB),* Anaheim, CA: Foundation Press

Bible (1991). *New Century Version (NCV),* Dallas, TX: Word Bibles

Bible (1978, 1984). *New International Version (NIV),*Colorado Springs, CO: Biblica, Inc.

Bible (1985). *New Jerusalem Bible (NJB),* Garden City, NY: Doubleday

Bible (1996). *New Living Translation (NLT) – (also called Life Recovery Bible),* Wheaton, IL: Tyndale House Publishers

Bible (1990). *New Revised Standard Version (NRSV),* Grand Rapids, MI: Zondervan

Bible (1992). *Today's English Version (TEV),* New York, NY: American Bible Society

Blackaby, H., & King, C. (1990). *Experiencing God,* Nashville, TN: Lifeway Press

Bloch, D. (1991). *Listening to Your Inner Voice,* Center City, MN: Hazelden Foundation

Cloud, H., & Townsend, J. (1988). *Boundaries With Kids,* Grand Rapids, MI: Zondervan

CoDA (1986). *Co-Dependents Anonymous website,* retrieved November 15, 2015 from www.coda.org

Collins, M. (1911). *Light On the Path,* Chicago, IL: The Rajput Press

Falson, C. (1993). *I See the Lord [song],* Fredericksburg, VA: Maranatha! Music

Halliday, A., Halliday, J. (1994). *Silent Hunger,* Grand Rapids, MI: Baker Publishing Group

Hymnal (1989),*The Hymns of The United Methodist Hymnal,* Nashville, TN: Abingdon Press

Jakes, T.D. (2012). *Let it Go,* New York, NY: Atria Paperback Div. of Simon & Schuster, Inc.

Jakes, T.D. (2014). *Lost and Found: Finding Hope in the Detours of Life,* Bloomington, MN: Baker Publishing Group

Lucado, M. (2007). *Life Lessons with Max Lucado – Book of Philippines,* Nashville, TN: Thomas Nelson, Inc.

Model Mugging (2015). *Model Mugging Self Defense Training,* retrieved November 15, 2015, from http://modelmugging.org/self-defense-padded-assailant/

Mohr, B. (1997). *Living Life Inspirational Art* [from my living room wall decoration]. Can also be found at http://www.bonniemohr.com/store/genre/inspirational/living-life.html

Neal, M. (2012). *To Heaven and Back,* Colorado Springs, CO: Waterbrook Press

Phillips, J. (1958). *The New Testament in Modern English,* NewYork, NY: Macmillan

Riddle, J. (1999). *Revelation Song,* lyrics retrieved November 15, 2015 from http://www.azlyrics.com/lyrics/karijobe/revelationsong.html

Smalley, G. (2000). *Joy That Lasts,* Grand Rapids, MI: Zondervan

Songfacts.com (2015). *Allentown by Billy Joel,* retrieved November 15, 2015 from http://www.songfacts.com/detail.php?id=3161

Soper, S. (2006). Allentown history goes down in a pile of rubble, *The Morning Call, Collections, Public Housing,* retrieved November 15, 2015 from http://articles.mcall.com/2006-06-03/news/3666082_1_public-housing-housing-authority-new-homes

Stanley, C. (2011). Trials and joy, *In-Touch Magazine, 34,42*

Taylor, C. (undated). *Home Rules* [wall hanging]. Can also be found at
http://christianbook.com/home-rules-tapestry-
bannerette/pd/14427

Wardell-Halliday, J. & Imboden-Overstreet, J. (1975). *Thin Within
Workshops,* retrieved November 15, 2015 from
www.thinwith.com

Warren, R. (2002). *Purpose Driven Life Worksheet #1,* Grand Rapids,
MI: Zondervan

Wikipedia, (2015). *Carmen Miranda,* retrieved November 15, 2015
from https://en.wikipedia.org/wiki/Carmen_Miranda

Wikipedia, (2015). *Crocodile Tears,* retrieved November 15, 2015 from
https://en.wikipedia.org/wiki/Crocodile_tears

Wikipedia, (2015). *Jonestown Massacre,* retrieved November 15, 2015
from https://en.wikipedia.org/wiki/Jonestown#Mass_murder-
and-suicide

Wikipedia, (2015). *Lock Ridge Park,* retrieved November 15, 2015
from https://en.wikipedia.org/wiki/Lock_Ridge_Park

Wikipedia, (2015). *The Long Beach [Navy Ship],* retrieved November 15,
2015 from
https://en.wikipedia.org/wiki/USS_Long_Beach_(CGN-9)

Wikipedia, (2015). *Oak Glen, San Bernardino, CA,* retrieved November
15, 2015 from
https://en.wikipedia.org/wiki/Oak_Glen,_San_Bernardino_Co
unty,_California

Wikipedia, (2015). *The Wayfaring Stranger Song, by Tilman, C., 1891,*
retrieved November 15, 2015 from
https://en.wikipedia.org/wiki/The_Wayfaring_Stranger_(song)

ACKNOWLEDGEMENTS

"Life isn't about waiting for the showers to pass. It's about learning to dance in the rain" (Greene, as cited by Neal, 2012, p. 111).

"For when the disciple is ready the Master is ready also" (Collins, 1911, p. 34). I have had many masters *(teachers)* on my journey. Each teacher had an impact on my life and a progression in my recovery.

My children deserve special mention. All six have taught me some valuable lessons, as each and every one of them triggered my emotions. Those triggers turned into opportunities for me to reflect, journal, and provide more healing in my life. I have learned much about myself through them. I am glad I am able to leave these writings as a legacy for them and their children, for generations to come. Grandchildren and great grandchildren that I will never know will know me through what I have written here.

Carla, Lori, Brian, Matt, Jenny, and Becca: I love you all with all my heart.

I am so grateful that God gave me these six beautiful gifts. Brian, who took on the role of scapegoat in our dysfunctional family system, was the catalyst for the dramatic shift in my journey. His acting out caused me to look for help. To that end I was given the name of a therapist who had a noted reputation working with adolescents. Little did I know this would be the beginning of a seven-year relationship with that same therapist and me.

I thank the therapists who accepted me right where I was at the time, who listened with supportive ears, who modeled healthy behaviors, and showed me a different way to live: Bruce D. Webster, Alicia Megehee Lake, Gina Hernandez Tabrizy, Carol J. Ahrens, Barbara

Sager Siersma, and especially Vance B. Becker who changed my life by being the most loving male role model I've ever had. Other counselors who helped me are Casey L. Truffo Perriman, Janet Congo, Cheryl Graybill Dale and Patricia Lee. Mentors who I admire that I've had encounters with are Pastor Rick Warren, Pastor Tom Holliday, Pastor Rick Muchow, Pastor Tommy Hilliker, Pastor Brett Eastman, Lee Stroebel, Dr. John Townsend, Dr. Henry Cloud, Bill Butterworth, John Gray, Ph.D., and John Bradshaw. I've also learned and grown from the teachings of Pastor Greg Laurie, Dr. Charles F. Stanley, Joel Osteen, and Joyce Meyer.

I want to thank all the members of each and every therapy or support group in which I've participated. All were instrumental in my recovery process. I appreciate your love, support, and friendship. I especially want to thank two very important groups at Saddleback Church in Lake Forest, California: my ACA (Adult Children of Alcoholics) Celebrate Recovery Group, and my Single Parent's "Boundaries" Small Group. These two groups have not only impacted me profoundly, accepting and loving me for who I am, encouraging me to continue writing my poetry, but also they were the first ones to get excited and validated the need for these poems to be published. They made this book a reality for me. I love you, my very special friends.

A special "Thank You!" goes to the following supportive people for their encouragement and help with this manuscript: Amy Berry, my Graphic Designer/Artist who designed my front/back covers, Carol A. (Miller) Huss, my first editor/friend; Leanne Kaffler my accountability partner, friend, and proof-reader; Michelle Mastro for her contribution; Patricia Souza, my finishing editor, friend, and sister in Christ; my daughter, Lori Hall, who had a gift for arranging the flow of wording, so that it is more pleasing to the reader and editing throughout to make the book better; and my niece, Toni McGivern, who read many chapters and gave me countless hours of feedback.

I also want to acknowledge the members of my family of origin for special reasons. My mom, who introduced me to God and Jesus, bringing me up in the nurture and admonition of the Lord. I have much to say about her influences both positive and negative throughout the book. My dad, who when he was sober treated me like a princess. My older brother, Lamar, who was my knight in shining armor, and loved me unconditionally. My other brother Greg, who despite what happened in our childhood, gave me many gifts of learning about myself.

I also must add my two ex-husbands. Bill and I spent fifteen years together. He was my first love and holds a special place in my heart. He gave me four beautiful children of whom I'm proud to be their mother. Although we weathered many conflicts, I began a journey of recovery starting with the Naval Hospital Rehab Program in Long Beach, California, as a co-alcoholic *(co-dependent)*. My second husband Jeff and I spent ten years together. He gave me two beautiful *(unexpected)* daughters who I love dearly. Jeff and Bill both taught me many things about myself furthering me on my journey of discovery and recovery.

The last one I make mention of is my husband Glen, who God blessed me with for the last fifteen years. He showed me what I needed to learn by holding me accountable.

And finally, yet most importantly, I want to thank, praise, glorify, and honor the Trinity: Almighty God, the Father and Creator of the Universe, His Son, Jesus Christ, my Lord and Savior, and the Holy Spirit who continually leads and guides me in all wisdom.

> *For I know the plans I have for you, declares the Lord, plans to prosper you and not to harm you, plans to give you hope and a future. Then you will call upon Me and come and pray to Me, and I will listen to you. You will seek Me and find Me when you seek Me with all your heart. I will be found by you, declares the Lord (Jeremiah 29:11-14a).*